# PENGUINS

# PENGUINS

LLOYD S DAVIS
MARTIN RENNER

Illustrated with line drawings
by Sarah Wroot

Yale University Press
New Haven and London

To Frances

for being there through all of this

Published 2003 by T & A D Poyser, an imprint of A & C Black Publishers Ltd., and in the United States by Yale University Press.

ISBN 0-300-10277-1
Library of Congress Control Number: 113609
Printed and bound in the U.K. by St Edmondsbury Press

Typeset and designed by J&L Composition, Filey, North Yorkshire

A catalogue record for this book is available from the British Library.

Paper produced with elemental chlorine-free pulp, harvested from managed sustainable forests.

The paper in this book meets the guidelines for permanence and durability of the Committee on Production Guidelines for Book Longevity of the Council on Library Resources.

10 9 8 7 6 5 4 3 2 1

# Contents

# List of Figures

CHAPTER 7

CHAPTER 8

# List of Tables

# Preface

## WHAT MAKES A PENGUIN A PENGUIN?

This work does not pretend to be a complete summary of everything there is to know about penguins. Rather, it attempts to derive an understanding of the diversity of penguins by examining the most influential factors that affect their lives. In essence, this book has evolved from a thesis originally put forward by John Croxall and one of us (LSD) as part of the keynote address to the Third International Conference on Penguins, held in Cape Town, South Africa, in 1996 and subsequently published in Marine Ornithology. That thesis suggested that patterns and apparent paradoxes in penguin biology could be best explained by recognizing the importance of foraging distance on their lifestyles. Penguins must balance living in two worlds – water for feeding, land for breeding – and much of what they do is dictated by how far they must go when at sea: whether they are inshore foragers or offshore foragers.

# Acknowledgements

A book like this does not get written without leaving a debt to others that must be acknowledged. LSD wishes to thank his wife, Frances, especially, for her unstinting support; and his children, Daniel and Kelsey, for allowing him to steal time from the family to write this book that was above and beyond what any normal person might consider reasonable. MR thanks his parents, Klaus and Ruth, and his wife Heather for their enduring support. They let him pursue his dreams even when it took him to the other end of the globe. John Croxall's support in getting this project underway was invaluable. Andy Richford and, later, Nigel Redman of Poyser, displayed great patience, understanding and encouragement as this book was nursed through a relatively long gestation while other events competed for our time. Marianne Taylor was an especially good pilot as she steered the book through its production phases, aided and abetted by Sylvia Sullivan and J&L Composition. Dan Powell did the cover artwork and Sarah Wroot, illustrator extraordinaire and long-time friend of LSD, did an exceptional job of translating his sometimes crazy ideas into drawings that neatly complement the text.

Finally, a number of our colleagues read various parts of the book. Corey Bradshaw, John Darby, Dave Houston, Ian Jamieson, Melanie Massaro, Thomas Mattern, Rosana Paredes, Philip Seddon, Alvin Setiawan and Yolanda van Heezik managed to provide constructive criticism while remaining firm friends.

We thank you all.

CHAPTER 1

# Introduction

Imagine you are a bird wanting to become like a fish. You cannot shake off your past: those evolutionary events that have made you a bird. How, then, would you modify your body and lifestyle for a life in water? It is impossible to turn back the evolutionary clock, to have feet become fins again, to have ears become gills again. You are an air breather and must remain one.

This is precisely the sort of evolutionary dilemma faced by penguins. On the one hand there are advantages to be gained by exploiting the bountiful resources in the oceans; on the other, they cannot escape the constraints conferred by their past— they are birds from the tips of their feathers to the claws on their toes. And yet, the influence of the sea is stronger in penguins than for any other group of seabirds. Their aquatic lifestyle has determined their shape, their coloration, what they eat, when they eat, where they go on land, how they breed and, ultimately, their geographic range and distribution.

The streamlined spindle shape of penguins reduces drag when swimming in water; a shape also adopted by fish, seals and dolphins. This shape is extremely conservative between species, implying that there is a biomechanical constraint to penguin design, just as evolutionary constraints have also set boundaries to their design. All things are not possible. Any animal that must propel itself through water will move more efficiently if it is shaped like a spindle.

Heat loss is another design problem that must be solved for a warm-blooded animal to immerse itself in water below body temperature, because water acts as a heat sink. To insulate the core body temperature, other warm-blooded animals that have taken up an aquatic existence, such as seals and cetaceans, use a thick layer of blubber. In penguins, while there is a thin sub-dermal layer of fat, most insulation is provided by the feathers. The main feathers and even the downy feathers lock together, trapping a layer of air and insulating the body using much the same principle as that of a Thermos™ flask or double glazing.

As a consequence of their insulation for a life in water, penguins are able to withstand cold temperatures when on land and, therefore, go where other birds, if not angels, fear to tread: Antarctica. Their insulation pre-adapted them to move into colder climes or to remain in them in the face of environmental change. In the Antarctic and sub-Antarctic, penguins typically nest in the open. However, the efficiency of the penguins' feather survival suits means that in temperate and more tropical latitudes, overheating is a problem while on land. At lower latitudes, then, penguins must seek shelter when nesting—either under vegetation or in burrows and caves.

The ancestors of penguins could fly. By exchanging the ability to fly for short, powerful flippers that could propel them through the water, penguins gained access to huge food resources that most other seabirds could only scratch the surface of: schooling fish like sardines and anchovies, dense swarms of krill and cephalopods. But this increased underwater mobility came at a price: the loss of their aerial freedom and the ease with which they could move over large distances from their breeding areas. Penguins are limited in where they can breed by the proximity of a suitable food supply to a degree that their cousins, the albatrosses, are not.

Unlike whales and dolphins, penguins can never be emancipated from the land of their ancestors. Internal gestation of mammalian young meant that the potential was always there for a terrestrial mammal to evolve into an aquatic mammal that never need return to the land. But that is not a design option for penguins. As birds, they lay eggs that must be kept warm: a task they cannot accomplish in the sea. They are, therefore, consigned by their phylogenetic history always to be dependent upon land (or its icy projections) on which to breed.

Penguins are forced, then, to live their lives in two worlds (Chapter 4). As such, they must engage in a balancing act whereby the time in the water necessary for feeding is weighed against the time required on land to breed successfully. Unable to fly quickly to distant food sources, the further penguins must travel to their food supply, the longer they must typically be away from the nest. This sets up a different dynamic or range of consequences for those penguins that must travel a long way to feed (offshore foragers) compared with those that have a good food supply near to their breeding sites (inshore foragers).

Constrained as they are to breed on land, penguins must find a suitable terrestrial environment for breeding (Chapter 5): accessible from the ocean without wings, not too exposed to predators from which they cannot take flight, and protected from environmental factors, where appropriate, such as heat, insolation and rain. And all this must be within reasonable commuting distance of a good food supply.

Having established a place to breed, they must then find a suitable mate (Chapter 6). Because of the long incubation period associated with penguin eggs (over a month in all species), males must assist females to rear the young (i.e. the female could not lay the eggs, fast through incubation and rear the chicks by herself). Given that, like most seabirds, biparental care is a requisite for successful reproduction, it behoves a male to ensure that he is indeed the father of the offspring in which he will invest so heavily. The priority for a female is subtly different: she will benefit from choosing a partner most likely to result in the successful rearing of offspring, but the father of her chicks need not be the one who rears them for that to occur.

Once the eggs are laid (Chapter 7), parents must balance the time they spend foraging against the time that they and their partner must spend fasting at the nest. Get this wrong and it can result in desertions and starvations. Parents must ensure that once chicks hatch that they are able to feed them and, where there are two chicks, decide how to distribute the food resources to both of them.

Following breeding, penguins must weigh up any advantages of leaving to find food outside the breeding season against the costs of migration (Chapter 8). This is also a time for maintenance; a period when they must renew the feather survival suits that make their waterborne lives possible.

While in one sense the loss of flight liberated penguins, enabling them to become more fish-like and better adapted to an aquatic lifestyle, in another it also limited them, making them vulnerable—especially to us (Chapter 9).

Perhaps the most remarkable thing is that, given all these constraints, penguins are as successful and as diverse as they are. They are the world's only 100°C birds: breeding in climates from −60°C to +40°C. By examining how penguins balance the competing demands of their schizophrenic lifestyle within the limitations imposed through being flightless, we can distill patterns that explain the evolution (Chapter 2) and diversity (Chapter 3) of these remarkable birds.

CHAPTER 2

# Penguin evolution: an historical perspective

## THE LOSS OF FLIGHT

Penguins constitute a very distinct group of seabirds. Traditional systematics lumps them together into a single family (Spheniscidae), which is the sole representative of the order Sphenisciformes. Today there are 16 species[1] of extant penguins, divided into six genera.

No other group of birds has undergone such dramatic changes in adapting to an aquatic lifestyle. The most radical change of all was their loss of flight. Flightlessness is not something that is unique to penguins—it has evolved in just about every group of waterbirds (Table 2.1)—but in those other groups only a small proportion of their members became flightless while the rest retained their ability to fly. Penguins, together with ratites (kiwis, emus, and their kind), are the only systematic groups of birds in which *all* members are flightless; although, in the large, strictly terrestrial ratites the loss of flight had nothing to do with an aquatic lifestyle.

*Table 2.1 Distribution of flightless waterbirds other than penguins (see also McNab 1994) – as new species are continually being unearthed from subfossil deposits, this list is undoubtedly incomplete (N.B. The many flightless but largely terrestrial rails are not included here).*

| Species | Scientific name | Distribution | Status (Collar et al. 1994) |
|---|---|---|---|
| Galapagos Cormorant | *Nannopterum harrisi* | Galapagos | endangered |
| Atitlan Grebe | *Podilymbus gigas* | Guatemala | extinct |
| Puna Grebe | *Podiceps taczanowskii* | Peru | critically endangered |
| New Zealand Swan | *Cygnus sumnerensis* | New Zealand | extinct |
| New Zealand Goose | *Cnemiornis calcirans* | New Zealand | extinct |
| Giant Hawaiian Goose | *Branta hylobadistes* | Hawaii | extinct |
| Flightless Diving Goose | *Chendytes lawi* | North America | extinct |
| Flightless Steamerduck | *Tachyeres pteneres* | South America | not threatened |
| Falkland Steamerduck | *Tachyeres brachypterus* | Falkland Islands | not threatened |
| Moa-nalos | *Chelychelynechen quassus* | Hawaii | extinct |
| (giant Hawaiian ducks) | *Thambetochen xanion* | Hawaii | extinct |
| | *Thambetochen chauliodous* | Hawaii | extinct |
| | *Ptaiochen pau* | Hawaii | extinct |
| Amsterdam Island Teal | *Anas marecula* | Sub-antarctic | extinct |
| Campbell Island Teal | *Anas (aucklandica) nesiotis* | Sub-antarctic | critically endangered |
| Auckland Island Teal | *Anas (aucklandica) aucklandica* | Sub-antarctic | vulnerable |
| Finsch's Duck | *Chenonetta finschi* | New Zealand | extinct |
| New Zealand Coot | *Fulica prisca* | New Zealand | extinct |
| Chatham Island Coot | *Fulica chathamensis* | New Zealand | extinct |
| Great Auk | *Pinguinus impennis* | North Atlantic | extinct |

Why would penguins, then, need to become flightless to exploit the sea? Many seabirds are able to dive underwater without needing to become flightless. Inevitably, however, to get much below the surface must involve compromises for a bird that is required to fly both in air and underwater. Aerial flight calls for a light body, underwater diving for a heavy one.

There are two principal modes of diving in birds: wing-propelled diving, using the wings for propulsion underwater in a similar way to flying, and propulsion by

feet. Both modes are widespread and have evolved several times independently amongst birds. Foot-propelled divers have large webbed feet located near the rear of the body. They include loons (divers), grebes, cormorants, coots, and diving ducks. Wing-propelled divers, like penguins, auks and petrels, may also have webbed feet articulated at the rear, but they use them to paddle only when on the surface. When diving underwater, the feet are held backwards and help serve as a rudder.

A common pattern to flightless waterbirds suggests conditions under which the disadvantages of giving up flight can be counteracted. Firstly, most flightless birds are—or were—found on predator-free islands. This suggests that there would have been little selective pressure to retain flight as a means for escaping predators in the face of any advantages that accrued from becoming flightless. Secondly, all flightless waterbirds have a reliable food source near to their breeding grounds and, apart from some species of penguin, they are all non-migratory (Table 2.1). Giving up aerial flight inevitably means giving up an effective way to cover long distances quickly, and all flightless waterbirds, with the exception of some penguins, are inshore foragers. While some species of penguins undertake foraging trips over longer distances than those of many flying seabirds, and many penguins are migratory, the implication from the trends apparent in other flightless waterbirds is that inshore foraging is likely to have been the ancestral condition of penguins.

## WING-PROPELLED DIVING BIRDS: PENGUINS VS AUKS

With one small exception, penguins live and breed only in the Southern Hemisphere.[2] On the other hand, auks and their ilk (Alcidae) are found only in the Northern Hemisphere. Although living in opposite hemispheres, and only distantly related, auks and penguins show striking similarities. These result from convergent evolution: two groups come to resemble each other because by endeavouring to exploit similar ecological niches (in this case: 'flying' underwater), they become subject to similar selective pressures. The most apparent similarities between penguins and auks are their black-and-white plumage, upright stance, use of webbed feet for paddling on the surface, and short wings used for underwater flight.

However, only one member of the auk family, the extinct Great Auk *Pinguinus impennis*, was flightless. Somewhat surprisingly, given that they have retained an ability to fly, alcids can dive almost as well as penguins if maximum dive depth is corrected for body size (Burger 1991). But therein lies the rub: diving performance is related to body size. Bigger birds can dive deeper and for longer, meaning that more of the ocean becomes their oyster, so to speak. Large body size is not, however, conducive to efficient flight. The largest flying auks are only about the same size as the smallest penguin. This suggests that there are physical constraints that

limit the size of a bird that must achieve a compromise between flying and diving. To become bigger, so as to dive better, birds must forego flight altogether.

It is possible to construct a cline of flying ability/diving ability: albatross–petrel –auklet/diving petrel–guillemot–Little Penguin–Adelie Penguin–Emperor Penguin. That is, from large-bodied, large-winged species which were able to fly great distances but which could only scratch the surface of the sea, through small stocky species which could dive quite well but which were pretty inefficient flyers, and finally, to a range of flightless birds of increasing size and diving ability. It is not difficult to imagine that the ancestors of penguins went through similar stages during their evolution in the transition from flying to flightlessness.

## RECONSTRUCTING THE PAST OF PENGUINS: METHODOLOGIES

When studying evolution, scientists face a daunting problem: the processes that shaped today's fauna happened in the past. Because time-travel is still not practical, even for a scientist with above average amounts of funding, we can only study the traces that evolution has left behind. In that sense, it is much like detective work: reconstructing what has happened from evidence left at the scene of a crime. Except that, for the evolutionary biologist, there can be no eyewitness accounts to corroborate it. All the evidence must necessarily be circumstantial and the best we can hope for is persuasive evidence. Statistical 'proof', of the kind favoured by Karl Popper and those who espouse a scientific methodology based on manipulative experiments, is simply not possible. Nevertheless, not all methods of detective work are equal: some are better than others, depending upon the task at hand.

In the past, phylogenetic relationships were discerned on the basis of comparisons of morphology. However, classical comparative morphology is fraught with a major problem, which was alluded to above in the comparison of penguins and auks: convergent evolution can lead to superficial similarities, so that morphological similarity alone may be an unreliable guide to common ancestry.

Most evolutionary scientists today use cladistic analysis (Hennig 1950) to reconstruct phylogenies. The essence of cladistics is to look for *synapomorphies*, or 'shared derived characters', which provide evidence for monophyletic groups or clades (i.e. groups descended from a common ancestor). These contrast with *plesiomorphies*, or 'primitive characters'. For example, while feathers are an undeniable character of penguins, they can tell us little about the evolution of penguins from other birds because all birds possess feathers (i.e. feathers constitute a plesiomorphic character). On the other hand, non-pneumaticized bone is a feature of all penguins but not their nearest relatives. Hence, non-pneumaticized bone is a synapomorphic character that can be used to identify the members of the monophyletic group that we call penguins. The trick to cladistic analysis is being able to distinguish synapomorphic from plesiomorphic characters, and homologous (characters derived from a common ancestor) from convergent characters. The most common way to do this is by using an outgroup for comparison (Maddison *et al.* 1985). An outgroup is a closely related taxon that is known not to be a part of the monophyletic group being investigated.

Cladistic analysis usually involves analysing the data numerically using the principle of *parsimony* to find the shortest possible tree of evolutionary pathways. The logic here is that you minimize the number of times evolution should have to reinvent itself. For example, an evolutionary tree that lumped all the crested penguins together, so that a mutation or event resulting in the formation of crests would have to occur only once in a common ancestor, is arguably more believable than one that placed the various crested penguins on different branches and, therefore, required that crests evolved independently more than once. Different characters can be assigned different weights to account for their complexity and the likelihood of them developing several times independently during evolution. A penguin flipper, for example, is so complex that, using the language of the detective, it can be said to be beyond reasonable doubt that it evolved only once during the course of evolution.

This type of analysis, using parsimony, can be applied to all kinds of character-based datasets, be they morphological, molecular or behavioural data. Molecular datasets can also be analysed using *Maximum Likelihood*, which looks for the most likely tree overall. This requires making some *apriori* assumptions using a model for probabilities of nucleotide substitutions. In its favour, Maximum Likelihood is less susceptible to a problem known as long-branch attraction, which can give misleading results when parsimony analysis is used on molecular data (Felsenstein 1978).

Distance methods on the other hand, are rather complex mathematical techniques for calculating genetic distances between taxa based on how similar they are. They do not, however, distinguish synapomorphic characters from plesiomorphic ones but have to assume a constant rate of evolution (molecular clock). While distance methods have been used to reconstruct evolutionary trees for penguins from morphological data (Livezey 1989), the dependency on a molecular clock makes such evidence less reliable than evidence from cladistics (de Queiroz and Good 1997). By its very nature, some molecular data can only be analysed using distant methods (e.g. DNA–DNA hybridization (Sibley *et al.* 1988)).

## DATASETS

Several types of detective work have been used in attempting to shed light on the evolutionary history of penguins (Table 2.2). Each has its advantages and disadvantages. Fossils provide the only direct evidence of evolution and the only way of dating evolutionary events, but they are generally fragmented and difficult to relate to extant penguins.

Today, many people are putting an increasing amount of faith in molecular systematics, especially now that bootstrapping—a statistical method for obtaining an

*Table 2.2.   Approaches to phylogeny used on penguins*

| | Advantage | Disadvantage | Penguin example |
|---|---|---|---|
| **Fossil record** | only direct evidence | often only single bones, difficulty to link to extant genera | (Simpson 1975, Fordyce and Jones 1990) |
| **Extant morphology** | combines many genes, check for convergences (established criteria) | subjectivity, selection of characters, difficulty to find synapomorphies, convergent evolution | (Zusi 1975, Cracraft 1982, Livezey 1989, O'Hara 1989) |
| **Distance (molecular and morphology)** | easy to compute, DNA–DNA hybrid looks at whole genome, rel. cheap to obtain (protein distance) | theoretical issues: uses plesio and apomorphies, assumption of molecular clock is often invalid, problems of nuclear DNA | Molecular (Ho *et al.* 1976, Sibley *et al.* 1988)  Morphology (Livezey 1989) |
| **Molecular sequence** | sound theoretical basis (Hennig's cladistic), today large datasets with many characters, advantages of mitochondrial DNA (no recombination) | gene-trees ≠ organism trees, multispec. alignment, long-branch attraction, arbitrary weighting of codons, ML makes *apriori* model assumptions | (Grant *et al.* 1994, Hedges and Sibley 1994, Paterson *et al.* 1995, Edge 1996, Paterson *et al.* 1996, Cooper and Penny 1997, Nunn and Stanley 1998) |
| **Parasite data** | highly conserved (morphology), higher rate of evolution (DNA) | host switching | (Paterson *et al.* 2000) |
| **Behaviour characters** | can be analysed cladistically | too plastic? | (Jouventin 1982, Paterson *et al.* 1995) |

estimate of error (Felsenstein 1985)—provides a way to evaluate the reliability of molecular trees, but problems remain with these types of analyses (Felsenstein 1978, Weiler and Hoelzer 1997). Also, a gene tree need not necessarily be identical with the species tree (e.g. the path a cytochrome *b* gene took during evolution may not necessarily be the same as that of the species). This problem could be particularly relevant in events involving rapid radiation and large effective populations (Maddison 1997), as may have occurred during the evolution of penguins.

There has been debate about whether parasites can be used to investigate the evolutionary relationships of their hosts. Recent studies seem to confirm that some highly host-specific parasites, such as biting featherlice (Mallophaga), co-evolve with their penguin hosts and may be useful for phylogenetic reconstructions at both a morphological and molecular level (Paterson *et al.* 2000). However, even if host-switching is very rare, it could well occur over evolutionary time spans, and at this stage, evidence of penguin phylogenies based upon parasites should be treated with some caution.

# RELATIONSHIPS OF PENGUINS TO OTHER BIRDS

Penguins are such a highly distinct group that their monophyly, descent from a common ancestor, has never been questioned. For a while, however, there was debate about whether penguins were derived from flying ancestors or flightless birds such as ratites. This debate has long been settled in favour of flying ancestors.

All the evidence, morphological and molecular, agrees upon a range of candidates that are closely related to penguins. These include loons or divers (Gaviiformes), petrels and albatross (Procellariiformes), and at least some families, notably the frigatebirds (Fregatidae), of the order Pelecaniformes. These groups might have originated from a clade of waterbirds that lived in the late Jurassic–early Cretaceous (Cracraft 1982). However, as in any good 'whodunnit', the exact relationship between these various groupings remains a mystery.

## MORPHOLOGICAL EVIDENCE

The oldest penguin fossil has been dated to about 55 million years before present (MYBP) (Fordyce and Jones 1990), giving a minimum time scale for when penguins must have split from their ancestors. While there are no fossils linking penguins conclusively to other groups of birds, the fossilized remains of one early penguin, *Paraptenodytes*, reveals a pterygoid bone (a bone forming part of the palate) that is very similar to that found in petrels and quite different from that of present-day penguins; so much so, that if found alone, it would probably have been identified as a Procellariiformes (Simpson 1946, 1975). Although most systematists accept that there is a close relationship between penguins and procellariids (Sibley and Ahlquist 1990), the petrels may not be the closest of the penguins' living relatives.

Most of the early studies of penguin phylogeny were based on deriving relationships from overall similarity instead of synapomorphies. The first systematic studies using numerical cladistics of skeletal and behavioural characters concluded that penguins are a sister taxon to loons and grebes (Podicipediformes) (Cracraft 1982, 1985). This clade was placed beside a clade of Procellariiformes and Pelecaniformes and corroborated by high bootstrap values (Fig. 2.1) (Hedges and Sibley 1994).

This hypothesized relationship depends upon Procellariiformes (albatrosses, shearwaters, storm petrels and diving petrels) and Pelecaniformes (cormorants, anhingas, gannets and boobies, pelicans, tropicbirds, and frigatebirds) being monophyletic groups. The monophyly of Pelecaniformes, especially, is controversial.

*A penguin's closest living relative?: a Wandering Albatross chick (Photo: Lloyd Spencer Davis)*

There is no molecular study supporting this view (Sibley and Ahlquist 1990, Hedges and Sibley 1994, Cooper and Penny 1997, Siegel-Causey 1997) and a critical reanalysis of morphological and behavioural data does not sufficiently resolve the phylogeny to corroborate monophyly of the Pelecaniformes (Siegel-Causey 1997). Similarly, some molecular studies cast doubt on the monophyly of the Procellariiformes (Cooper and Penny 1997).

Cracraft's study did not include any fossil penguins. The close similarity of the pterygoid of *Paraptenodytes* to that of petrels, for example, might have changed the groupings. Clearly, the last word has not been heard on this issue and further research on morphology is required.

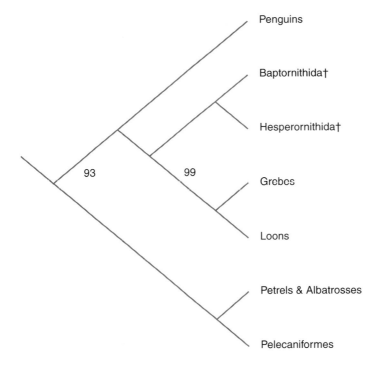

*Figure 2.1.   Cladogram based on morphological data including two extinct taxa from the Cretaceous (Cracraft 1982). Bootstrap values from Hedges and Sibley (1994).*

## MOLECULAR EVIDENCE

There have been a number of molecular studies that have tried to establish the large-scale relationships amongst birds. As with the morphological data, there is general agreement that penguins are related to other waterbirds including Gaviiformes, Procellariiformes and Pelecaniformes (Fig. 2.2). So far, however, the exact relationships between those groups (branching order) have not been resolved, with different studies reaching different conclusions.

### Distance

DNA–DNA hybridization is a technique that compares the overall similarity of nuclear DNA. By the nature of this technique, the data cannot be analysed cladistically. Nevertheless, according to the DNA–DNA hybridization data, penguins are a sister group to the loons (Gaviiformes) and petrels (Procellariiformes) (Sibley and Ahlquist 1990). Frigatebirds, herons (Ciconiiformes), and cormorants (Phalacrocoracidae) were amongst the groups basal to this assemblage. However, the branches separating different orders were very short, suggesting rapid radiation and poor phylogenetic resolution.

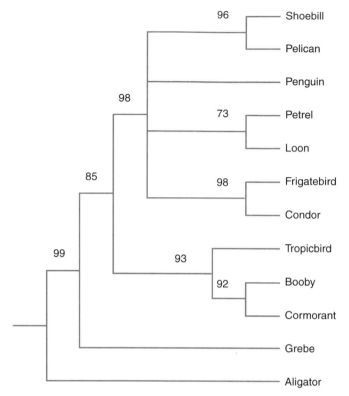

*Figure 2.2.    Most parsimonious tree inferred from DNA sequences of mitochondrial 12S and 16S rRNA genes (1.7 kb total). Numbers represent bootstrap values. Redrawn from Hedges and Sibley (1994).*

An older study (Ho *et al.* 1976) using immunological distance also found that penguins formed a clade with loons (Fig. 2.3).

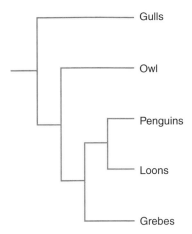

*Figure 2.3.   Phylogeny based on immunological distances (Ho et al. 1976).*

## Sequence studies

Molecular sequence data (12S and 16S rRNA) place penguins close to petrels, loons, pelicans (Pelecanidae) and frigatebirds, but have so far failed to resolve the exact positions (Hedges and Sibley 1994).

So where does that leave us? Both, the morphological and molecular evidence place penguins close to an assembly of loons, petrels, and at least some of the Pelecaniformes, in particular, frigatebirds. The latest molecular studies suggest that penguins are a sister group to a clade including petrels and loons (Fig. 2.4).

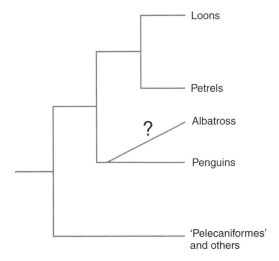

*Figure 2.4.   Nearest living relatives to penguins (according to or compatible with Sibley and Ahlquist 1990, Hedges and Sibley 1994, Cooper and Penny 1997).*

Interestingly, although today's loons (or divers as they are known in Europe) are foot-propelled divers, anatomical details suggest that they had wing-propelled ancestors.


# RELATIONSHIPS AMONGST LIVING PENGUINS


There are six clearly defined genera of extant penguins (*Aptenodytes*, *Eudyptes*, *Eudyptula*, *Megadyptes*, *Pygoscelis* and *Spheniscus*). Two questions that have preoccupied those working on penguin systematics are: how do the extant genera relate to each other and which is the most basal group?


## FOSSIL RECORD

Fossils provide the only direct evidence about what the ancestors of today's penguins looked like and where they lived. They also enable us to calibrate a time-scale for penguin evolution. By its nature the fossil record is fragmentary and rapid adaptive radiation often results in distinct genera appearing suddenly in the fossil record, making it difficult to discern relationships. Also, of course, it is mainly bones that are preserved and any differences that may have existed between species in attributes such as their plumage and behaviour are likely to go completely unnoticed. Many extant species, for example, would probably not be recognizable by their bones alone (Simpson 1975).


## DIVERSITY AND SIZE OF FOSSIL PENGUINS

Fortunately, penguins possess some very distinct bones. This often makes it possible to recognize a penguin from only a single fossil bone. This is just as well, because sometimes that is all we have. The tarsometatarsus and humerus are very dense and are the bones most likely to fossilize. Although a limited variety of bones greatly restricts the number of characters available for phylogenetic studies, it is clear that the level of diversity (based on comparisons of the tarsometatarsus and humerus) was greater in the past. That is, living penguins are much more similar to each other than penguins were in the past.

Some fossil penguins were as small as today's Little Penguin but many were very big, up to an estimated height of 1.7 m (Simpson 1976, Livezey 1989). The bias towards bigger species in the fossil record could be due to the fact that big bones are more likely to be preserved and are easier to find (Simpson 1975). While the transition to flightlessness probably occurred in birds about the size of the Little Penguin, rapid radiation with selection for larger size would have been possible once the birds were freed from the physical constraints required to get airborne.

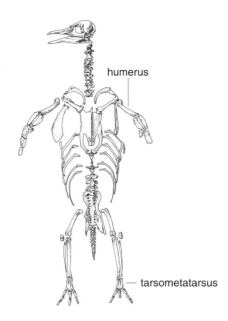

Certainly, most fossil penguins were already highly modified. None of the fossils is clearly ancestral to the penguins as we know them today and, therefore, they help little with respect to resolving questions about the relationships between living penguins.

## MONOPHYLY OF EXTANT PENGUINS

Compared with fossil penguins, the skeletal characters of recent forms appear rather uniform. Simpson lists seven synapomorphies (though not explicitly calling them such) that are shared only by recent genera and *Marpleornis* (Simpson 1975) (Table 2.3). The oldest fossils of the latter genus date back to the Miocene (up to 20 MYBP), but are mostly late Pliocene or Pleistocene. Recent genera are known only from fossil remains younger than about 3 million years (Simpson 1975).

## MORPHOLOGY

A skeletal study of penguins (Zusi 1975) provided good evidence for grouping *Megadyptes* and *Eudyptes*, *Spheniscus* and *Eudyptula*, and *Pygoscelis* and *Aptenodytes*, but did not include an outgroup comparison. Therefore, it is not possible to distinguish between ancestral and derived characters and the tree cannot be rooted (Fig. 2.5). Three possible scenarios for the evolution of extant penguins are shown in Figure 2.6. In many ways *Eudyptula* stands out from the rest of the penguins. It

*Table 2.3.    Synapomorphies of Marplesornis and all recent genera (Simpson, 1975)*

| Character | Description |
| --- | --- |
| humerus | slightly curved or nearly straight |
| humerus | narrower proximally |
| tricipital fossa | bipartite (usually somewhat weakly) |
| preaxial angle | present but variable from distinct to vague |
| tarsometatarsus | short |
| intermetatarsal foramina | two large |
| metatarsals | only weakly fused |

is smaller, nocturnal, has a more horizontal stance than other penguins, is unable to dive as deep, swims more slowly and does not porpoise: all characters that are thought to be 'primitive'. The best consensus of relationships between the genera based on morphology is given in Figure 2.7.

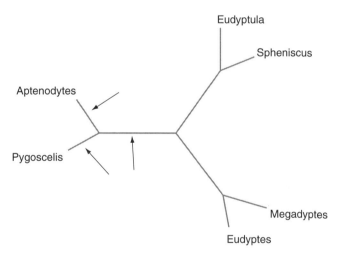

*Figure 2.5.    Topology of the penguin phylogeny. Likely places for the root are indicated by arrows. Based on Zusi 1989.*

## MOLECULAR STUDIES

There have been recent studies using protein data (Grant *et al.* 1994) and DNA–DNA hybridization (Sibley and Ahlquist 1990) all based on the nuclear genome, and sequence data from mitochondrial DNA (Paterson *et al.* 1995, Edge 1996, Paterson *et al.* 1996, Nunn and Stanley 1998, Paterson *et al.* 2000).

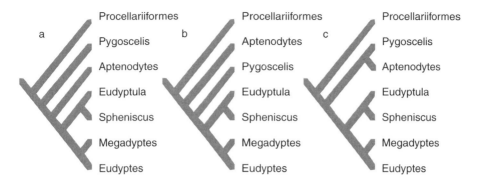

*Figure 2.6.   Three hypothesized penguin phylogenies depending upon where the root is attached in Fig. 2.5.*

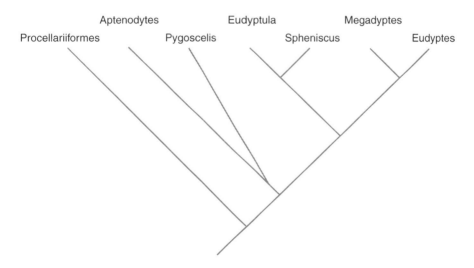

*Figure 2.7.   Phylogenetic relationships amongst extant penguin genera.*

Analysis of cytochrome *b* sequence data provides strong support for the grouping of *Megadyptes* with *Eudyptes* (Fig. 2.8). A clade of *Eudyptula* and *Spheniscus* is also evident, although the support for this is not as strong. Magellanic and African Penguins are sister taxa according to data from both cytochrome *b* (mtDNA) (Edge 1996) and isozymes (Grant *et al.* 1994), which is interesting considering that geographically the Humboldt Penguin is much closer to the Magellanic Penguin than is the African Penguin.

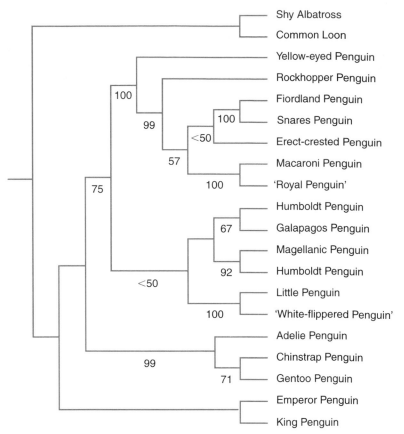

*Figure 2.8. Maximum likelihood tree redrawn from Edge (1996). Numbers represent bootstrap values from 100 replicates. The position of Erect-crested Penguins E. sclateri, Little and 'White-flippered' Penguins Ea. minor, and the root are not resolved. The same dataset analysed with parsimony yields an almost identical tree with very similar bootstrap values. The only difference is that parsimony places Pygoscelis at the base instead of Aptenodytes.*

## META-ANALYSIS AND CONCLUSIONS

We obtained and analysed mitochondrial cytochrome *b* sequences and sequences of mitochondrial 12 rRNA from GenBank (Cooper and Penny 1997, Nunn and Stanley 1998) and cytochrome *b* sequences from Kerry-Anne Edge's PhD thesis (Edge 1996) for all extant penguin species.[3]

A neighbour joining distance tree (Fig. 2.9), calculated from the cytochrome *b* sequence data in Edge's thesis (Edge 1996), can be used to visualize the distances between penguin taxa. These relate to divergence time and illustrate what has already been tentatively deduced from morphology. For example, *Spheniscus* penguins are all very closely related to each other and probably represent a very recent radiation.

Edge's data suggest that *Aptenodytes* is basal (Fig. 2.10). Analysing Nunn's complete sequence data on cytochrome *b* from *Aptenodytes*, *Eudyptes*, *Pygoscelis* and Procellariiformes, gives 100% bootstrap support for *Pygoscelis* being basal (rooted with *Hydrobates*) using both parsimony and Maximum Likelihood.

Based on a synthesis of all the information available, we have derived a tree of evolutionary relationships between living penguins (Fig. 2.11).

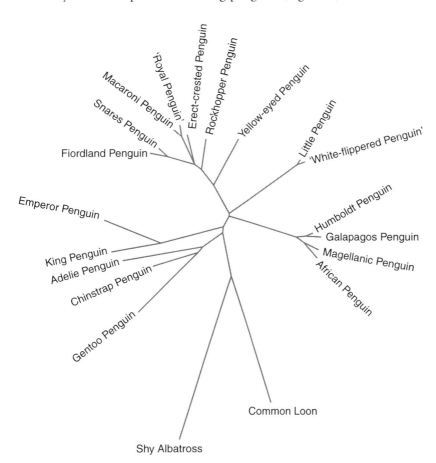

*Figure 2.9.* *Neighbour joining-tree to show branch lengths. Based on Kimura 2–P distance calculated from data in the appendix of Edge (1996).*

Whatever the genetic differences between penguins, there is no denying their outward similarities. These result mainly from becoming flightless divers: creatures of the water. By giving up their ability to fly they were no longer trapped by the trade-off between diving and flying and could evolve one of the most sophisticated

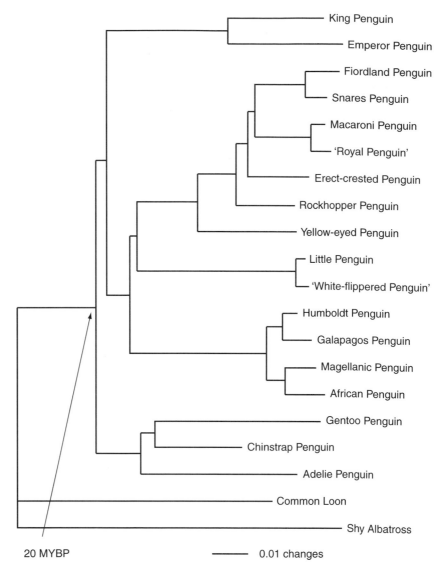

*Figure 2.10.   Neighbour joining-tree based on Kimura 2–parameter distance calculated from data in the appendix of Edge (1996). The arrow marks the appearance of the appearance of the first modern penguin (Marplesornis).*

bodies for underwater swimming found in the animal kingdom. Measurements of the hydrodynamic drag of penguins reveals lower drag coefficients than those previously known from any other shape used in engineering or nature (Bannasch

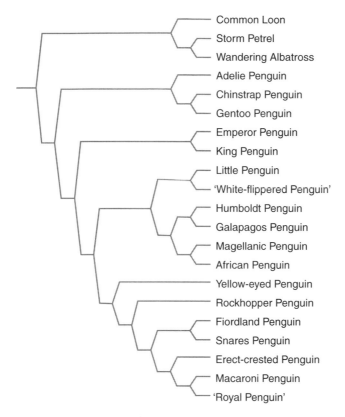

*Figure 2.11. Synthesis of penguin evolution. Based on Edge (1996), re-analysis of Nunn & Stanley (1998) (root), Grant's isosymes (1994) (support), and breeding biology (E. sclateri).*

1996). Likewise, the highly modified and stiffened flipper could evolve only after the ability for flight was lost (Raikow *et al.* 1988).

If no longer flying in air has made them different from other birds, living in the sea has made them similar to each other. The design of penguins has been constrained by the physical requirements of moving in water. In a sense they have swapped one compromise (flying/diving) for another (land/water). Much of the diversity that does exist between penguins can be explained by how they balance their lives between these two worlds.

CHAPTER 3

# Penguins today

## HOW MANY SPECIES OF PENGUINS ARE THERE?

The status of most penguin species is clearly defined and does not create much controversy. There are a few cases of allopatric populations, however, that might represent species in the making. Some authors regard these as subspecies, others as full species. Though these distinctions may often sound rather academic, they can be vitally important to the welfare of some populations: money for their conservation is far more likely to be forthcoming if species status is accepted. For the purposes of this book these disputes are largely irrelevant. The focus here is on understanding the behavioural, physiological and physical adaptations of penguins to their environment. A growing body of evidence suggests that penguins can show as much plasticity within populations as they can between species. Consequently, it is sufficient for our purposes to introduce the cast in this story, the species, with broad brushstrokes used mainly to characterize the different genera. Nevertheless, in the interests of addressing the issue of a common taxonomy we will briefly review the taxonomic evidence for the disputed taxa.

The status of the White-flippered Penguin and the Royal Penguin has been hotly debated. The former could be a subspecies of the Little Penguin, the latter a subspecies—or perhaps a colour morph only—of the Macaroni Penguin. Most of the recent ornithological handbooks treat White-flippered Penguins as a subspecies and Royal Penguins as a full species (Marchant and Higgins 1990, Sibley *et al.* 1990, del Hoyo *et al.* 1992, Williams 1995). Another potential species is the Northern Rockhopper Penguin. Depending upon the status accorded to each, this could mean that there are anything from 16 to 19 species of extant penguins. The status of these allopatric populations has been argued on the basis of their overall similarity, the occurrence of hybridization, and the distinctiveness of morphological measurements, behaviour, breeding phenology and vocalizations (Jouventin 1982, Woehler 1995). It has also been suggested that genetic distances, when compared to established species pairs, can provide evidence of whether two allopatric populations have diverged enough to be called separate species. The latter has been used especially to cast doubt on the status of some of the banded or *Spheniscus* penguins (Grant *et al.* 1994).

WHITE-FLIPPERED PENGUIN

White-flippered Penguins are distinguished from Little Penguins by the presence of a white margin on the leading and trailing edge of the flipper and paler plumage on their backs. White-flippered Penguins are restricted to Banks Peninsula and Motunau Island in New Zealand, but stragglers regularly occur in Otago and Cook Strait. Hybridization with Little Penguins is common where they meet in Cook Strait and Otago. On Motunau Island a hybrid population exists. In every area of contact, birds show a continuous range of White-flippered Penguin characters (Meredith and Sin 1988a, Renner unpubl. data, Hocken 1997).

Continuing gene flow is also indicated from studies of preen wax proteins and isozymes. Preen wax proteins of White-flippered Penguins are identical to those of Little Penguins but differ from those of other species (Jacob and Hoerschelmann 1981). A cline of isozyme frequencies was found from Banks Peninsula to Northland, New Zealand (Meredith and Sin 1988b). No fixed differences were detected, indicating continuing gene flow throughout that range. Genetic distances of cytochrome *b* sequences were small, being less than half the distance found between allopatric species that are regarded as good species and an order of magnitude smaller than well-differentiated species such as King and Emperor Penguins (Table 3.1). All this evidence suggests that White-flippered Penguins should be treated as a subspecies of Little Penguin. More comprehensive studies of their genetics, behaviour and vocalizations are needed to finally put this matter to rest: although a recent examination of DNA from Little Penguins throughout their range does not support separate species status for White-flippered Penguins (J. Banks, pers. comm.). Interestingly, this study provides evidence of two separate lineages, with the Australian (*E. minor novaehollandiae*) and Southland/Otago subspecies (*E. minor minor*) showing close affinities and all the rest, including *E. minor albosignata*, lumped together.

ROYAL PENGUIN

Royal Penguins differ from Macaroni Penguins by their white face and slightly larger size. Royal Penguins are restricted to Macquarie Island, but birds showing characteristics of Royal Penguins, as well as intermediate birds, are not uncommon at sites from Heard Island to Marion Island. Conversely, the amount of white in the face of Royal Penguins on Macquarie Island shows considerable variation, with some birds being indistinguishable from Macaroni Penguins.

Royal Penguins are on average larger and differ in their bill measurements, which has been used to argue they are distinct species (Woehler 1995). However, this paper analysed only means—without taking the variation of measurements into account—and, therefore, should not be used to argue for a split into two species. Genetic distances between Macaroni and Royal Penguins approach those found between other species (Table 3.1). However, the samples from which these distances were calculated originate from the extreme ends of the distribution of this group: South Georgia and Macquarie Island. Study of populations in-between might well reveal clinal variation.

The shape of feather crests differs amongst all crested penguin species, apart from the closely related Snares and Fiordland Penguins, and always differs between sympatrically occurring crested species. It seems likely that crest shape may be used for species recognition. The crests of Macaroni and Royal Penguins are identical. Closely related species of birds that are morphologically very similar often differ significantly in their vocalizations. The mating calls of Macaroni and Royal Penguins are identical, but differ from those of all other penguin species (Jouventin 1982). We feel compelled, on the basis of the current evidence, to regard Royal Penguins (*Eudyptes chrysolophus schlegeli*) as a subspecies of the Macaroni Penguin.

*Table 3.1.  Genetic distances log-determinant between closely related sister taxa, calculated from cytochrome b sequence data. DNA sequences from (Edge 1996). No sequence data are available for Northern Rockhopper Penguins*

| Taxa pair | Genetic Distance |
| --- | --- |
| Little – 'White-flippered' | 0.0069 |
| Macaroni – 'Royal' | 0.0110 |
| Humboldt – Galapagos | 0.0131 |
| Fiordland – Snares | 0.0192 |
| Magellanic – African | 0.0208 |
| Emperor – King | 0.0618 |
| Gentoo – Chinstrap | 0.0769 |

## NORTHERN ROCKHOPPER PENGUIN

The northern populations of Rockhopper Penguins in the Atlantic and Indian Oceans are described as Moseley's or Northern Rockhopper Penguins. They have longer crests and structurally different mating calls from those of other Rockhoppers. Southern Rockhopper Penguins as distant as Staten Island (at the southern tip of South America), Kerguelen and Macquarie Islands show only slight variation in their songs. Likewise, songs of Northern Rockhopper Penguins from Gough (in the Atlantic) and St. Pauls-Amsterdam Islands (in the Pacific) are very similar to each other, but differ substantially from the songs of the Southern Rockhopper Penguins (Jouventin 1982). Breeding in the southern populations is also two to three months later compared with the northern populations. Based mainly on the differences in their vocalizations, it has been argued that the northern populations should be treated as a separate species (*Eudyptes moseleyi*) (Jouventin 1982). In the absence of evidence to the contrary, it is a view for which we have a good deal of sympathy. There is a pressing need for more extensive genetic studies on Rockhopper Penguins to resolve the issue of their phylogenetic status.

## *SPHENISCUS* PENGUINS

The Humboldt, Magellanic and African Penguins are very similar morphologically and their status as separate species has at times been questioned (Clancey 1966, Grant *et al.* 1994). Humboldt and African Penguins readily interbreed in captivity and hybridization has been recorded in the wild between Humboldt and Magellanic Penguins where their ranges overlap in Chile. The extent of this hybridization is unknown. However, Magellanic Penguins are more genetically similar to African Penguins than to Humboldt Penguins (Grant *et al.* 1994, Edge 1996), which is not what might be expected if hybridizations between Magellanic and Humboldt were common. Consequently, Humboldt Penguins are deserving of species status. The Galapagos Penguin differs enough in external appearance from the Humboldt Penguin that its species status has never been questioned.

Morphologically the sister taxa of Magellanic and African Penguins are very close; the main difference being that the Magellanic Penguin has an extra breast band. However, in a few birds this is missing, just as a few African Penguins show a second breast band, although it is usually thinner than that in the Magellanic Penguin. There is no study comparing vocalizations or behaviour between these two taxa. Grant *et al.* (1994) found that the genetic distance between the two is more typical for subspecies than for species. Genetic distance based on cytochrome *b*, however, suggests that the two can be regarded as species, albeit very closely related (Table 3.1). Further studies, especially of their vocalizations, are desirable to clarify the specific status of Magellanic and African Penguins.


# THE PENGUIN GENERA

## *PYGOSCELIS*—GENTOO, CHINSTRAP AND ADELIE PENGUINS

These are the classic Antarctic penguins of cartoons. All three species are gregarious, breeding in colonies that sometimes can be huge. Colonies of Gentoo Penguins are generally the smallest, whereas the Chinstrap colony on Deception Island, South Shetland Islands, is the largest of all penguin colonies (an estimated five million pairs breed on the South Shetland Islands).

The plumage of all three species consists only of black and white. The bill is long, although feathers conceal the base of the Adelie Penguin's bill. *Pygoscelis* penguins moult once at the end of the breeding season (post-nuptial). The moult lasts between ten and twenty days depending on location and species.

### Gentoo Penguin (*Pygoscelis papua*) [Plate 1]                    *inshore forager*

This is the most northern penguin of this genus and also, in many other respects, the odd one out. In contrast to Chinstrap and Adelie Penguins, for example, some Gentoo Penguins can be found around their breeding colonies all year round and they forage much closer inshore than the other two *Pygoscelis* species.

*Identification:* 76 cm. Gentoo Penguins are characterized by a white patch around and behind the eye that joins on the crown. The orange-red lower mandible is also a distinct feature. Two subspecies are recognized (Stonehouse 1970a), a larger nominate form in the sub-Antarctic and a smaller, but otherwise similar, subspecies *(ellsworthii)* on the Antarctic Peninsula. Juveniles are very similar to adults, but the white eye-patch is not connected to their white eye-rings until they moult at an age of 14 months (Trivelpiece *et al.* 1985, Williams 1988).

*Distribution:* Mainly in the sub-Antarctic, but extending to the Antarctic Peninsula. Breeds on Staten, Falkland, South Georgia, South Sandwich, South Orkney, South Shetland, the Antarctic Peninsula, Marion, Prince Edward, Crozet, Kerguelen, Heard, and Macquarie Islands. There is some evidence that the size of colonies depends on the local width of the continental shelf, i.e. the available inshore foraging area (Robertson 1986, Adams and Wilson 1987, Bost and Jouventin 1990).

*Habitat:* Colonies are usually smaller than those of their congeners and are less densely packed. In the sub-Antarctic the nests are often found amongst tussocks, on the Antarctic Peninsula they nest on ice-free areas and beaches.

*Breeding:* At some colonies, birds are present year-round. Numbers in colonies increase prior to breeding. Birds go to sea daily before laying, albeit females may fast for about 5 days before laying the first egg. Clutch size is normally two with a laying interval of 3.4 days. Laying season is extended in northern breeding localities such as Marion and Crozet Islands (June to October/November)—where it is one of the few penguins to lay replacement clutches—compared with much more synchronous breeding at southern locations (October to November) such as South Georgia and the South Shetland Islands, where most nests are initiated within two weeks. Many females go to sea for 1–2 days between laying the two eggs. Incubation shifts are typically about 1 day at southern localities but may average 2–3 days at northern sites like Crozet. Incubation periods are 37 days for first eggs and 35 days for second eggs. Crèching occurs at 25–30 days of age. Fledging occurs at 80–105 days, but uniquely among penguins, fledged chicks return to the colony to be fed by parents for a further 5–50 days.

*Diet:* Dietary composition varies between season and locations but generally crustaceans, in particular krill (euphausiids), constitute the dominant prey item in the southern part of the range, whereas benthic fish are more commonly caught in lower latitudes. Cephalopods play only a minor role.

*Migration and vagrancy:* Gentoo Penguins can be found near their colonies all year round unless ice prevents access—as it can in the southern parts of their range. Nevertheless, vagrants have been found as far north as 43°S on the Argentinean coast as well as in Australia and New Zealand.

*Conservation and status:* IUCN category: Lower Risk[1]. Stable, not globally threatened. About 317,000 pairs.

## Chinstrap Penguin (*Pygoscelis antarctica*) [Plate 2]     *offshore forager*

This delicately coloured bird is arguably the most beautiful of penguins. In contrast to other adult penguins, apart from the Royal Penguin, this species has a white face. The face is separated from the white belly by a thin dark line running under the lower part of the chin—hence the name. The high concentration of this species in the western Antarctic might be due to a lack of islands at a suitable latitude in the eastern sector.

*Identification:* 77 cm. Chinstrap Penguins are medium-sized penguins, easily recognized by their white face and the fine black line across the cheeks. The demarcation between the black and white lies above the eye, isolating the dark eye in the white plumage. The bill is black. In contrast to most other penguins, juvenile Chinstraps closely resemble their parents. Until their first moult, juveniles can be recognized by dark spotting around the eyes and a slightly shorter bill (Trivelpiece *et al.* 1985).

*Distribution:* Intermediate between the Adelie Penguin in the south and the Gentoo Penguin in the north, breeding colonies are almost exclusively on the Scotia Arc. That is, around the Antarctic Peninsula on South Georgia, South Orkney, South Shetland, and South Sandwich Islands (vast numbers on the latter). Small numbers also breed on Bouvetøya, Peter First, Heard and Balleny Islands.

*Habitat:* Usually breeds on hillside slopes and rocky outcrops in colonies that sometimes can be enormous. At the South Shetlands, Chinstrap Penguins often breed amongst other *Pygoscelis* penguins, though usually on steeper slopes. Their marine distribution seems to be linked to the limits of the continental shelf and the confluence of the Antarctic circumpolar and Weddell Sea currents (Lishman 1985a).

*Breeding:* Arrives in colonies October/November with egg laying occurring November/December. Females may arrive on average 5 days later than their male partners. Both fast at the colony until egg laying. This can vary from about 2–3 weeks depending upon the location. Clutch size is usually two with a laying interval of 3.2 days. Females most often take the first incubation shifts, and the first four shifts average 5–10 days each. Incubation periods average 36 days for first eggs and 34 days for second eggs. Chicks crèche at 23–29 days and fledge at 52–60 days.

*Diet:* Chinstrap Penguins feed almost exclusively on krill (*Euphasia superba*). Other crustaceans and fish play a minor role.

*Migration and vagrancy:* Chinstrap Penguins leave their breeding colonies during winter, probably migrating north of the pack-ice and stay at sea until the next spring. Non-breeders have been recorded in Adelie Land, Antarctica (Thomas and Bretagnolle 1988) and stragglers have reached Australia and Tierra del Fuego.

*Conservation and status:* IUCN category: Lower Risk. Stable, not globally threatened. Total population estimated at 7,500,000 pairs.

## Adelie Penguin (*Pygoscelis adeliae*) [Plate 3]                              *offshore forager*

No penguin, indeed no other bird, breeds farther south than Adelie Penguins. Adelie Penguins show a number of specialized adaptations to restrict heat loss.

*Identification:* 71 cm. A medium-sized penguin recognized by its white eye-ring. Feathers on the back of the head are slightly elongated and can be raised to form a small crest. Flavistic (pale) birds not uncommon in some colonies. Immature birds up to 14 months of age differ from adults in having a white rather than black chin and they lack the white ring around their eyes.

*Distribution:* Breeds on shores around the Antarctic continent, South Shetland, South Orkney, South Sandwich, and Bouvetøya Islands. At sea Adelie Penguins are usually found from the edge of the shelf-ice to the northern extent of the pack-ice.

*Habitat:* Adelie Penguins breed in colonies from a few dozen to many thousands. Within the colonies, distinct sub-colonies can be recognized. The nests, depressions on the ground, are lined with small stones, which help to keep the eggs free of any meltwater from snow. Stones for building nests are often in demand. Adelies are highly gregarious on land and at sea. The availability of accessible ice-free nesting habitat limits the distribution of this species in the high Antarctic.

*Breeding:* Arrival is September/October and is latest at the southernmost breeding localities. Males tend to arrive slightly before females. Time from arrival to egg laying varies from three weeks at the northernmost parts of their distribution to about 12 days on Ross Island. A clutch of two eggs is laid, typically 3 days apart, from either late October or early November depending upon latitude. Laying is highly synchronous, with two-thirds of clutches initiated within a six-day period. The male takes the first incubation shift, which averages 11–17 days depending upon locality and year, and this is followed by a shift of similar length by the female of 11–13 days. The third shift, taken by the male, tends to be only about 5 days or less. The incubation period is 35 days for first eggs and 33–34 days for second eggs. Chicks are guarded for an average of 22 days, although this can vary from 17–30 days. Fledging occurs at 48–51 days on Ross Island, but at 60–61 days near the northern limits of their distribution.

*Diet:* Adelie Penguins are highly dependent on krill, usually *Euphausia superba*, although in some areas *E. crystallorophias* constitutes the dominant krill species. Fish and amphipods can be common in certain locations at certain seasons.

*Migration and vagrancy:* Adelie Penguins are migratory and after breeding do not return to their colonies until the next spring. Little is known about the non-breeding distribution of this species. There are only a few records of Adelie Penguins during the Antarctic winter. Recent work using satellite telemetry indicates that some Adelie Penguins from the Ross Sea leave this area in autumn and migrate about 600 km north of the Antarctic continent. Juveniles are suspected to travel even farther north than adults. Vagrant birds have been recorded as far north as South Georgia, Falkland Islands, Kerguelen, Macquarie Island, Tasmania, Heard Island, and the South Island of New Zealand.

*Conservation and status:* IUCN category: Lower Risk. Stable, not globally threatened. Population estimated at about 2,500,000 pairs.

## *APTENODYTES*—KING AND EMPEROR PENGUINS

The genus *Aptenodytes*, which consists of the King (*A. patagonicus*) and Emperor Penguins (*A. forsteri*), differs in many respects from the other living penguins. Apart from their outstanding size, their long slender bill and colourful plumage are their most apparent characteristics. No other birds can dive for as long or as deep as Emperor and King Penguins. In contrast to all other penguins, they lay only a single egg and build no nest at all, balancing their egg and, later, the chick, on their feet. The breeding biology of these two species is quite different from each other but both are extreme. They also have behavioural characteristics not found in other penguin species.

Moult can be pre-nuptial or post-nuptial in King Penguins; post-nuptial in Emperor Penguins. Emperor Penguins often moult away from the breeding colonies.

### King Penguin (*Aptenodytes patagonicus*) [Plate 4]                *offshore forager*

No other bird has a longer breeding cycle than King Penguins. They take 14 to 16 months to fledge a single chick. During the winter, chicks may be left to fast for one to five months (May to September/October). Adults can rear a maximum of only two chicks every three years.

*Identification:* 94 cm. The second-largest penguin species, similar in appearance to the Emperor Penguin but their ranges do not usually overlap. Cheeks are dark orange. The belly is white but the back is paler than other penguins, more of a grey than black. Immatures are similar to adults, but with duller facial plumage. Ear patches are pale yellow rather than orange and the throat is grey-white. Reaches adult plumage after two years (Stonehouse 1960).

*Distribution:* Restricted to the sub-Antarctic belt, well north of Emperor Penguins. Breeding colonies are found on the Falkland (re-colonized after extermination), South Georgia, Marion, Prince Edward, Crozet (over half of the world's population (Jouventin *et al.* 1984)), Kerguelen, Heard (re-colonized after extermination), and Macquarie Islands. At sea, King Penguins are usually found in ice-free waters. Telemetry studies have shown that they forage particularly along the Polar Front.

*Habitat:* The dense colonies, which can number several tens of thousand pairs, are located amongst tussocks, gently sloping beaches, and sometimes can be over a kilometre inland. No nest is built, but pairs still maintain breeding territories within pecking distance of each other.

*Breeding:* Arrives at colony September to November. Lays a single large egg (November–March) after a prenuptial moult and a pre-laying foraging trip of some 20 days. The breeding cycle is complicated as it takes 14–16 months to rear a chick from the time of egg laying. This means that adults can rear a maximum of two chicks every three years, and typically there are two cohorts present in the colony at any one time. The incubation period is 54 days with parents taking incubation shifts of 6–18 days. Chicks are guarded for 30–40 days. During winter chicks must undergo prolonged fasts, in some instances for up to 5.5 months, before fledging at 10–13 months of age.

*Diet:* King Penguins are specialized on pelagic fish, in particular lanternfish of the species *Electrona carlsbergi*, *Kreffichthys anderssoni* and *Protomyctophum tenisoni*, which can make up over 99% of the diet. Cephalopods play a minor role and, to an even lesser extent, so do crustaceans.

*Migration and vagrancy:* Owing to the extended breeding cycle some birds can be found in the colony at any time of the year. During winter, adults leave their chicks unattended and may travel extensively before returning. Stragglers have reached the Antarctic Peninsula, Mawson, Gough Island, South Africa, southern Australia (including Tasmania), the North and South Islands of New Zealand, as well as the New Zealand sub-Antarctic islands.

*Conservation and status:* IUCN category: Lower Risk. Stable, not globally threatened. Population estimated at over 1,600,000 pairs.

## Emperor Penguin (*Aptenodytes forsteri*) [Plate 5]    *offshore forager*

The Emperor Penguin is a bird of extremes in just about every way. It breeds during the Antarctic winter. Its morphology exhibits many adaptations to the extreme cold these birds experience when breeding.

*Identification:* 112 cm. The Emperor Penguin is bigger than any other living penguin. It is distinguished from the smaller King Penguin by its size, more robust stature, and a broad pale yellow connection between the orange-yellow ear patches and the pale yellow upper breast. Immature birds resemble adults but are smaller and have a white rather than black chin. Ear patches are whitish, becoming increasingly yellow with age.

*Distribution:* Breeds during the Antarctic winter in about 30 colonies around the southern parts of the Antarctic continent, usually on fast ice. Probably depends a lot upon polynias—areas of open water surrounded by sea-ice—during winter.

*Habitat:* Breeds during the Antarctic winter from March to December. Eggs and chicks are balanced on the feet to prevent them from coming into contact with the ice. No nests are built, which allows the colony to move around and huddle close together, providing some protection from the cold.

*Breeding:* Arrives March/April, with single egg laid May/June. Males may arrive a few days before females. Females fast for about 40 days from arrival till the end of laying. Males incubate the egg on their feet for the entire incubation period of 62–67 days; meaning that from the time of arrival to the end of incubation they must fast for about 115 days. Emperor Penguins are colonial but not territorial, huddling together to withstand the cold and winds of the Antarctic winter. Chicks are guarded for about 45 days and fledge when about five months old.

*Diet:* Fish, cephalopods and krill are taken to varying degrees, though cephalopods and fish probably represent the major components of the diet, especially in terms of mass.

***Migration and vagrancy:*** Little is known about post-breeding dispersal or migration. Adults stay close to the permanent ice for most of their lives. Juveniles equipped with satellite transmitters, however, migrated as far north as the Polar Front. Vagrants have turned up on the South Shetland Islands, Tierra del Fuego, the Falklands, South Sandwich Islands, Kerguelen Island, Heard Island, and New Zealand.

***Conservation and status:*** IUCN category: Lower Risk. Stable, not globally threatened. Population estimated to be about 218,000 pairs.

## *EUDYPTES*—ROCKHOPPER, MACARONI, FIORDLAND, SNARES, AND ERECT-CRESTED PENGUINS

With their yellow feather plumes and red bills, crested penguins are the most elaborately adorned of the penguins. Some species also have striking red eyes. Comprising five species, *Eudyptes* is more diverse than the other penguin genera. All crested penguins are offshore foragers and migratory, leaving the colonies deserted during the non-breeding season.

All species display obligate brood reduction. That is, they lay two eggs but raise only a single chick. Typically the surviving offspring is derived from the second egg, which, unlike those of other birds, is also much bigger than the first egg. In those species where two eggs hatch, hatching order is reversed from laying order: the chick from the second-laid egg hatches before the chick from the first egg.

Crested penguins are found throughout the sub-Antarctic, where they breed on just about any suitable island. The species seem to be stratified on a north-south axis. A concentration of species is found around New Zealand where four out of the five species breed, three of which are endemic.

All crested penguins are migratory and highly seasonal breeders. Adults return to the colony for a post-nuptial moult.

## Rockhopper Penguin (*Eudyptes chrysocome*) [Plate 6]     *offshore forager*

The Rockhopper Penguin breeds throughout the sub-Antarctic, sometimes in large colonies. It is smaller than its congeners, but no less aggressive. There is some evidence that the Northern Rockhopper or Moseley's Penguin *E. c. moseleyi* is deserving of separate species status. Whatever, the Northern Rockhopper and Southern Rockhopper are clearly closely related and much of what applies to one probably holds for the other, but actual data are still scarce.

***Identification:*** 61 cm. Rockhoppers are distinguished from other crested penguins by their smaller size and by having only a thin yellow supercilium. The feather plumes are yellow, not orange as in Macaroni Penguin, and thinner than in the remaining *Eudyptes* species. The red eye is distinctive. Southern Rockhopper Penguins differ from their Northern counterparts in having a narrower supercilium and shorter plumes, which reach just over the black throat. Their vocalizations are also different (Jouventin 1982). The Southern Rockhopper comprises two subspecies that have been described and can be identified in the field: the nominate form from South America and the Falkland Islands and the eastern subspecies *filholi* from the New Zealand sub-Antarctic islands. The eastern form mainly differs from the nominate subspecies in having a pink line of fleshy skin along the lower mandible, which is black in the nominate subspecies. Immature birds have only a narrow supercilium and a pale mottled grey chin. Identification of juveniles is difficult. Shape of the supercilium, bill shape, body size and underwing pattern can aid identification. Separation of juvenile Southern and Northern Rockhopper Penguins in the field is probably impossible.

***Distribution:*** The northern form of the Rockhopper Penguin breeds in cool temperate climates, generally north of the subtropical convergence, with breeding occurring on Tristan da Cunha and Gough Island in the Atlantic Ocean and St. Paul and Amsterdam Islands in the Indian Ocean. The breeding season starts three months earlier (July) than in the southern form. The latter is restricted to the northern sub-Antarctic and has a circumpolar distribution. Breeding colonies are around the Cape Horn area, Falklands, Prince Edward, Marion, Crozet, Kerguelen, Heard, Macquarie, Campbell, Auckland and Antipodes Islands. Campbell Island used to be the eastern stronghold of the species, but the population there has plummeted recently.

***Habitat:*** Breeding colonies are located on rocky slopes and amongst tussocks, sometimes in small caves and amongst crevices. A small nest is built from tussock, peat and pebbles.

***Breeding:*** Birds start arriving to breed in late July in the northern form, but in October/November in the southern form. Males arrive about a week before females. A clutch of two dimorphic eggs is laid 4.4 days apart. Male and female remain at the nest sharing incubation for the first 12 days or so; thereafter the male takes the first foraging trip and the female the next, both of which last nearly two weeks. In all, males fast for 33 days from arrival, whereas females fast for 39 days from arrival. Most of the first-laid eggs (A-eggs) are lost during incubation, which lasts for 34 days. The few chicks that hatch from A-eggs almost invariably die during the first few days of brooding. The guard stage lasts for 20–26 days. Fledging occurs at 66–73 days.

***Diet:*** Crustaceans, in particular euphausids, make up the bulk of food items consumed during most studies of this species. Fish and cephalopods play a minor role, though one study found 53% cephalopods (by mass). Over 90% of the diet of Northern Rockhopper Penguins breeding on Gough Island consists of crustaceans (mainly euphausids), with the remaining 10% being made up of fish and, to a very small extent, squid (Klages *et al.* 1988).

***Migration and vagrancy:*** The non-breeding pelagic range is poorly known. Moulting birds especially have been found in South Africa, Australia and New Zealand. The western subspecies (nominate form) has been recorded as far as the Snares Islands during moult (Tennyson and Miskelly 1989). Vagrants of the Northern Rockhopper have been recorded on the Chatham Islands (Moors and Merton 1984).

***Conservation and status:*** IUCN category: Vulnerable. This classification applies to all three subspecies. Total population estimated at about 2,000,000 pairs after substantial declines experienced over most of their range in recent years.

## Fiordland Penguin (*Eudyptes pachyrhynchus*) [Plate 7]                              *offshore forager*

Closely related to the Snares Penguin. Notable because it breeds during the winter.

***Identification:*** 67cm. Similar to Snares Penguin, with a thick yellow stripe running above the eye and ending in a drooping plume. Distinguished from Snares Penguin by its larger size, a series of white streaks on the cheeks and the lack of a fleshy margin at the base of the bill. Immature birds have a mottled white chin, thinner dull yellow supercilium and probably cannot be safely distinguished from Snares Penguin.

***Distribution:*** Endemic to New Zealand. Breeds in the cold temperate rainforest of the south-west coast of the South Island and Stewart Island.

***Habitat:*** Fiordland Penguins breed under high rainforest canopy, in dense shrub, under boulders and in caves. The nests are lined with twigs and grass. Colonies usually consist of loose groups; nests can be several metres apart. All breeding grounds are north of the subtropical convergence. However, this ocean front is close to most breeding sites and is likely to provide most of the food for breeding birds.

*Breeding:* The breeding season begins in June/July during the austral winter. Males arrive before females. Males fast for 40–45 days from arrival until their first foraging trip. A clutch of two dimorphic eggs is laid, with the larger second one being laid just over 4 days after the first. Both sexes share incubation for the first 5–10 days. Unlike other crested penguins it is typically the female that takes the first foraging trip of 13 days, with males being away for a similar period next. The incubation period for second eggs is 32 days, with the second-laid egg hatching several days before the first-laid egg. The smaller chick from the latter typically dies within a few days due to starvation. Chicks start to form crèches at 2–3 weeks of age and fledge at about 75 days.

*Diet:* From the limited information that is available it appears that the diet can vary considerably between locations. A study from Codfish Island (van Heezik 1990a) found that small pelagic fish larvae contributed over 80% of the food intake by mass, with the remaining portion made up by squid. On the west coast of the South Island, however, squid made up over 80% of the diet, crustaceans 13% and fish only 2% (van Heezik 1989). Both studies, nevertheless, indicate that Fiordland Penguins forage mainly in pelagic waters undertaking shallow dives.

*Migration and vagrancy:* Migrates into the Tasman Sea as indicated by at-sea observations and the occurrence of moulting birds in eastern Australia. Moulting birds regularly occur also on the Snares Islands. Vagrants have been recorded on the Chathams, Campbell and Macquarie Islands, and as far as Western Australia in Australia.

*Conservation and status:* IUCN category: Vulnerable. Population estimates put numbers between 2500–3000 nests, which may be used as a rough guide to the numbers of breeding pairs. Population appears to have declined over the last 100 years with recent declines apparent at localities studied.

## Snares Penguin (*Eudyptes robustus*) [Plate 8]       *offshore forager*

Similar in many respects to the Fiordland Penguin but endemic to the Snares Islands, which are about 100 km south of the nearest Fiordland Penguin breeding sites. With its breeding range confined to the just over 300 ha of the Snares group, it has the most restricted distribution of all penguins.

*Identification:* 65 cm. Similar to Fiordland Penguins (see above for differences). Differs from Erect-crested Penguin in having drooping feather plumes on the crest, the yellow facial stripe reaches further up the bill, and the bill is more conical. The underwing pattern is highly variable and of little use for identification in the field.

*Distribution:* Endemic to the Snares Islands south of New Zealand. Little is known about the non-breeding distribution.

*Habitat:* Breeds under the canopy of Olearia forests, as well as on coastal rock. The forest often dies as a result of penguin guano, creating clearings. The birds build a cup nest from peat, wood and pebbles and nest in dense colonies.

*Breeding:* Arrives August/September, with laying occurring in September/October. Males and females fast for 37 and 39 days, respectively, from arrival to their first foraging trip. Two dimorphic eggs laid 4.4 days apart. Nest relief pattern similar to that of Rockhopper Penguins. The incubation period is 33 days and like Fiordland Penguins, both chicks usually hatch, but only the first-hatched chick (from the B-egg) typically survives beyond the first few days. Chicks form crèches at about 33 days of age. Chicks fledge at about 3.5 months of age.

*Diet:* The little information that is available indicates that this species lives mainly on euphausiids, but also takes cephalopods and a few fish.

*Migration and vagrancy:* Thought to move westwards into the Tasman Sea. Vagrants have been recorded on Macquarie Island and on the Falklands (Lamey 1990b).

*Conservation and status:* IUCN category: Vulnerable. Population stable or increasing somewhat at about 26,000 pairs. Small breeding area makes it vulnerable to local perturbations.

## Macaroni Penguin (*Eudyptes chrysolophus*) [Plate 9]    *offshore forager*

This is probably the most abundant of all penguins in terms of total numbers. We include the Royal Penguin *Eudyptes chrysolophus schlegeli* as a subspecies of Macaroni Penguin.

*Identification:* 71 cm. In contrast to the other crested penguins, this species has orange, not yellow, feather plumes. They originate from a supercilium that meets at the front; i.e. higher up the head than in other species. Macaroni Penguins are also slightly larger than the other crested penguins. Most birds breeding on Macquarie Island have a white face and are referred to as Royal Penguins, sometimes being given species status ('*Eudyptes schlegeli*'). Immatures are similar to adults but lack the long feather crest. Instead only a short orange-yellow supercilium is present.

*Distribution:* The distribution of Macaroni Penguins extends from the sub-Antarctic to the Antarctic Peninsula, but overall they are found further south than the rest of the crested penguins. The range overlaps with that of the southern form of the Rockhopper Penguin. Breeding colonies are found on the Antarctic Peninsula, islands around Cape Horn, Falklands, South Georgia, South Sandwich, South Orkney, South Shetland, Bouvetøya, Prince Edward, Marion, Crozet, Kerguelen, Heard Island and Macquarie Island.

*Habitat:* Breeds on rocky slopes, beaches and amongst tussocks. Most birds build a small nest from pebbles and by scraping out some mud or sand, but many pairs are content with laying their two eggs on bare rock. Satellite telemetry studies indicate that Macaroni Penguins forage mainly along the Polar Front regularly travelling up to 400 km to reach a feeding site.

*Breeding:* Arrival of birds is highly synchronous within colonies, but varies between colonies (October/November). Males arrive 7–8 days before females. Interval from arrival to laying is about 19 days for males, but only about 11 days for females. From arrival until returning to sea, males fast for 35 days and females 40 days. Egg-size dimorphism of Macaromi Penguins (and Erect-crested Penguins) is amongst the largest known for any bird. The first-laid A-egg is about 61–64% smaller than the B-egg. In most cases the A-egg is lost before or on the day the B-egg is laid, and it almost never survives to fledging even though the embryo is viable. Laying interval is typically from 4.1–4.5 days. The male and female remain together on the nest for 9–12 days before the male goes to sea to forage for 12–14 days, followed by the female for 10–11 days. Incubation averages 35–36 days. Chicks form crèches when about 25 days old and fledge when 60–70 days old.

*Diet:* The diet is mainly composed of crustaceans. On Macquarie, euphausiids make up only half the diet by weight, with fish constituting the other half.

*Migration and vagrancy:* Macaroni Penguins are migratory and found only exceptionally near land during the non-breeding season. Vagrant dark-faced birds are known from South Africa, Antarctica, Campbell Island, and The Snares. Royal Penguins have been recorded, possibly breeding, on Heard, Kerguelen, Crozet Island, and Marion Island amongst dark-faced Macaroni Penguins and stragglers have been observed as far north as North Island, New Zealand.

*Conservation and status:* IUCN category: Near Threatened; Royal subspecies listed as Vulnerable. Total population about 10,000,000 pairs, of which nearly a million are the Royal subspecies that breeds on Macquarie Island. In parts of its range, such as South Georgia, there have been substantial reductions since the mid-1970s.

## Erect-crested Penguin (*Eudyptes sclateri*) [Plate 10] *offshore forager*

A little-known rather bizarre bird with a limited breeding distribution in a very isolated part the world.

*Identification:* 68 cm. Similar to other crested penguins, in particular Snares and Fiordland Penguins. When dry on land Erect-crested Penguins can be identified by the upright yellow feather plumes of their crests. Erect-crested Penguins have a distinct gular pouch, a more parallel bill, and the yellow supercilium attaches higher on the bill than in Snares and Fiordland Penguins. Identification at sea is extremely difficult because feather plumes droop down when wet. Immatures have a pale yellow supercilium without the long plumes and a mottled grey throat. They can be distinguished from other crested penguins by the lower supercilium, size and gular pouch.

*Distribution:* In an arc that characterizes the distribution of crested penguins, from the Antarctic Peninsula and South America through the sub-Antarctic islands in the Atlantic and Indian Oceans, Erect-crested Penguins form the terminal species in the east. They are now restricted to the Bounty and Antipodes Islands, with a few isolated pairs still breeding on the Auckland Islands. All these sites are south of the subtropical convergence but well north of the Polar Front. Until recently there were also some birds breeding on Campbell Island, but they seem to have disappeared from there now. Abundant sub-fossil material from the Chatham Islands has also been attributed to this species.

*Habitat:* Erect-crested Penguins breed on rocky slopes bordering the shore. A few pairs build nests but most lay their eggs onto the bare rock.

*Breeding:* Birds arrive at the colony in September. There is a long interval between arrival and laying: for males this appears to be about three weeks. After this long courtship period, two eggs are laid but the first, much smaller A-egg, is invariably lost—in most cases on the same day or before the B-egg has been laid. Egg-size dimorphism is extreme. Laying interval is 5 days, with incubation lasting about 35 days. Age of crèching and fledging are not known accurately, but the former occurs at about 21 days and the latter seems to be similar to Macaroni Penguins.

*Diet:* Diet has never been studied in this species, but judging from its long foraging trips, like other crested penguins it probably lives mainly on pelagic crustaceans and fish.

*Migration and vagrancy:* Erect-crested Penguins do not come to land after their post-breeding moult and their winter distribution at sea is unknown. Some birds moult regularly on other sub-Antarctic islands south of New Zealand and, less commonly, on the South Island of New Zealand. Vagrants have been recorded from Northland (North Island of New Zealand), Tasmania, southern Australia, Heard Island (Speedie 1992) and the Falkland Islands (Napier 1968).

*Conservation and status:* IUCN category: Endangered. While available estimates put the total population at 165,000–175,000 pairs, this is likely to be an overestimate, with recent spot sampling at selected colonies suggesting continued declines in line with substantial reductions observed at the Antipodes and a former breeding site, Campbell Island, over the last three decades.

## MEGADYPTES—YELLOW-EYED PENGUIN

The genus *Megadyptes* contains only a single species, the Yellow-eyed Penguin, which is endemic to southern New Zealand. Recent phylogenetic studies have shown *Megadyptes* to be the sister taxon of the crested penguins, *Eudyptes*. Yellow-eyed Penguins share the strong reddish bill and yellow feathers on the head with the crested penguins, but differ distinctively in many other respects.

### Yellow-eyed Penguin (*Megadyptes antipodes*) [Plate 11]                *inshore forager*

Generally Yellow-eyed Penguins rear two chicks, forage close inshore and do not migrate. In contrast to most other penguins, Yellow-eyed Penguins do not breed in dense colonies, but in loose groups with nests out of sight of each other. Yellow-eyed Penguins have a very long chick-rearing period (typically more than 100 days). Consequently, breeding takes from September to February. Moult occurs at the end of the breeding period.

*Identification:* 76 cm. Adults are unmistakable with their yellow eyes and yellow eye-stripes that join on the back of the head. Moulting birds and birds at sea can be confused with crested penguins. Immature birds are similar to adults but have a pale yellow chin and a less vivid yellow eye-stripe.

*Distribution:* Endemic to New Zealand, Yellow-eyed Penguins breed on the east and south coast of the South Island, on and around Stewart Island, the Auckland Islands, and Campbell Islands.

*Habitat:* They nest in dense vegetation in dunes and coastal forest, with nests typically being isolated from each other. At sea, Yellow-eyed Penguins forage in pairs or alone.

*Breeding:* Adults resident at breeding grounds year-round. Two similar sized eggs laid in September-October. Both parents alternate nest attendance every day or two during incubation, which is remarkably variable, lasting from 39–51 days. Chicks are guarded for 40–50 days; rarely form crèches. Hatching is synchronous within a brood, with chicks in nearly two-thirds of nests hatching on the same day as their sibling. Chicks do not fledge until about 106 days old.

*Diet:* Yellow-eyed Penguins feed mainly on fish. Both pelagic and demersal species are taken. Cephalopods are taken to a lesser extent, but may be more important for immatures and for adults in years when available fish stocks are limited.

*Migration and vagrancy:* Resident. Adults can be found near the breeding colonies throughout the year. Juveniles disperse as far north as East Cape, North Island, but none have been recorded in Australia.

*Conservation and status:* IUCN category: Vulnerable. Population estimates put the total at 5000–7000 birds, including approximately 2000 breeding pairs. Large-scale fluctuations in numbers reported on the Otago Peninsula over more than half a century: illustrates the vulnerability of inshore foragers to variations in local conditions.

## EUDYPTULA—LITTLE PENGUIN

*Eudyptula* is a 'monotypic' genus. It comprises only a single species, the Little Penguin *Eudyptula minor*. The Little Penguin is different in many ways from all other penguins. It is the smallest of all penguins and the only nocturnal species. Its more horizontal posture gives it a different silhouette compared with the upright stance of other species.

In many respects, however, *Eudyptula* is an Antipodean version of *Spheniscus*. Just as with *Spheniscus*, *Eudyptula* breeds in burrows and generally forages close inshore. Even more striking is the close resemblance of juvenile *Spheniscus* with Little Penguins.

## Little Penguin (*Eudyptula minor*) [Plate 12]        *inshore forager*

The Little Penguin is the world's smallest penguin and, at about 1 kg, is thought to be about the size of the first penguins that evolved from flying ancestors. Six subspecies are recognized. The breeding season can be extremely variable. Little Penguins moult once at the end of the breeding season.

*Identification:* 40 cm. The Little Penguin closely resembles juveniles of the genus *Spheniscus*, but their ranges do not overlap. Upper parts are pale blue to a dark grey-blue depending upon age, season and subspecies. The transition from the dark upper parts to the white plumage of the lower body is not as well defined as in other penguins, going through shades of grey and brown, especially on the face.

*Distribution:* Little Penguins are widely distributed in Australia (from Western Australia along the southern coast of Australia up to New South Wales) and in New Zealand (from Northland to Stewart Island and the Chatham Islands). The White-flippered Penguin *E. m. albosignata* is an endangered subspecies, restricted to Banks Peninsula and Motunau Island (South Island, New Zealand) that has often been treated as a full species. Geographic variation of size, extent of white on the tail and flipper, and colour tone of the back is considerable. Six subspecies have been described: *novaehollandia* in Australia, *iredaei* in northern New Zealand, *variabilis* from Cook Strait, New Zealand, *albosignata* on Banks Peninsula, *minor* in the lower part of the South Island, New Zealand, and *chathamensis* from the Chatham Islands.

*Habitat:* In contrast to the other species, Little Penguins are nocturnal. That means they generally do not enter the shore before dusk and leave it before dawn. They forage during the day and often will sleep beside the nest at night after they have fed chicks. This species nests in burrows, under trees, in rock crevices, and sometimes in caves. Usually nests are clustered to form colonies, but single breeding pairs are not uncommon. At sea Little Penguins are often found alone or in small groups of up to ten birds, but sometimes these groups can be much larger. Although foraging trip durations can be highly variable, Little Penguins tend to stay close to the coast.

*Breeding:* The breeding season of Little Penguins is highly variable from place to place and in some areas from year to year. It usually begins somewhere from late June to September, although there is no clearly defined period of arrival, with penguins continuing to visit the colony outside of the breeding season. In Western Australia, egg laying may begin as early as April. Typically, a clutch of two eggs is laid an average of 2.8 days apart. In many areas there are second or, sometimes even, third clutches laid, either in response to breeding failure (replacement clutches) or after successfully fledging chicks (double brooding). Incubation tends to last for 33–37 days, depending upon locality. Most foraging trips of breeders during both incubation and chick rearing tend to last less than a day. However, especially during incubation, trips of a week or more are not uncommon at some localities. Chicks are guarded for 20–30 days, but in some situations this can be as low as 8 days. Chicks of cave-dwelling Little Penguins may form small crèches. Fledging varies between 48–63 days.

*Diet:* Little Penguins feed mainly on fish, especially sardines and anchovies, but also cephalopods and to a very small degree crustaceans.

***Migration and vagrancy:*** Juveniles disperse widely after fledging. Adults sometimes undertake long trips at sea during the non-breeding season, but return regularly to the colony throughout the year.

***Conservation and status:*** IUCN category: Lower Risk. Not globally threatened. Total population estimated at about 1,000,000 birds of which about half may be breeders, giving something in the order of 250,000 pairs. The population of the White-flippered subspecies, *E. m. albosignata*, consists of about 2,200 pairs and is listed as Endangered.

## *SPHENISCUS*—AFRICAN, MAGELLANIC, HUMBOLDT, AND GALAPAGOS PENGUINS

The black-and-white head pattern, a black stripe running down the flanks and naked skin exposed on the head are distinctive features of this genus. The hooked beak is deep and strong. *Spheniscus* penguins must have radiated fairly recently as indicated by the close morphological similarity amongst these species. All *Spheniscus* penguins are for the most part allopatric, however, so that most birds can be safely identified by their location.

Young and immature birds lack the distinct black and white plumage of the adults. Chicks, especially, closely resemble Little Penguins. Definitive means of identification of immature birds have yet to be determined.

The most tropical of the penguin genera, they constitute the northern end of penguin distribution. While *Spheniscus* penguins breed in much warmer climates than other penguins, their breeding areas are associated with cold, nutrient-rich currents.

Timing of the breeding season is far more flexible in *Spheniscus* than in other penguins, with some populations breeding throughout the year. The moult is much more variable within *Spheniscus* than within other penguin genera. Magellanic Penguins moult after the breeding season, whereas Humboldt and Galapagos Penguins moult one to four weeks before breeding and African Penguins can moult either before or after breeding.

## African Penguin (*Spheniscus demersus*) [Plate 13]                    *inshore forager*

This is the only penguin breeding in Africa and it was probably the first penguin encountered by Europeans. Numbers declined significantly during the Twentieth century and their future has been jeopardized recently by major oil spills.

***Identification:*** 68 cm. The only penguin occurring regularly in southern Africa, African Penguins (like Humboldt Penguins) differ from Magellanic Penguins in that they lack a second dark breast band (although some African Penguins do have an additional breast band). The area of naked skin reaches all around the eye and is more extensive than that in Humboldt Penguins. Immature African Penguins have a grey face and lack the pied pattern of adults. Adult plumage occurs after 14 months.

***Distribution:*** As the name suggests, the African Penguin is endemic to southern Africa with the largest concentrations along the Benguela Current, which brings nutrient-rich water to the west coast of South Africa and Namibia.

*Habitat:* African Penguins breed in burrows, rock crevices and under shrubs, often forming large colonies. Breeding is poorly synchronized. Their loud braying voice led to them also being called Jackass Penguins. Birds forage close inshore, especially during the breeding season.

*Breeding:* No well defined period of re-occupation occurs. Birds may be present at colonies year-round. Courtship is said to take 25 days. Peaks in egg laying can occur in June and November/December. The breeding interval for successful breeders is 10.5 months and failed breeders relay after 4 months. Two eggs are laid, 3 days apart. The incubation period is 38 days for first eggs, 37 days for second eggs. Incubation shifts average 1.1 days for successful breeders. Hatching is typically asynchronous. Chicks may be guarded from 25–40 days, with crèches occurring where birds nest on the surface. Fledging occurs when chicks are 73–81 days old. Moult is usually post-nuptial, but may sometimes precede breeding.

*Diet:* Mainly fish (over 80%), in particular anchovy. Cephalopods and crustaceans are taken as well, but to a much lesser extent.

*Migration and vagrancy:* Non-migratory. Vagrants have been found as far north as Setta Cama, Gabon, and Inhaca Island, Mozambique.

*Conservation and status:* IUCN category: Vulnerable. Total population estimated at 56,000 pairs. Huge decline in numbers over the last 100 years, with numbers now less than a quarter of what they were.

## Magellanic Penguin (*Spheniscus magellanicus*) [Plate 14]     *offshore forager*

Magellanic Penguins are similar to African Penguins — to which they are very closely related — but they breed on the opposite side of the Atlantic. The Magellanic Penguin is also the only migratory, offshore-foraging species in this genus.

*Identification:* 71 cm. It is the only *Spheniscus* Penguin found over most of its range, but overlaps the distribution of Humboldt Penguins around Puerto Montt, Chile. Humboldt Penguins lack the second dark breast band found in Magellanic Penguin and have more extensive areas of bare facial skin. However, as both of these characters are subject to individual variation and hybrids do occur, not every bird might be identifiable. Some immature birds undergo partial head moult during winter and gain the pied head pattern of adults.

*Distribution:* Breeds around the southern tip of South America from 40°S in Argentina to 37°S in Chile, as well as on the Falkland Islands. The largest colonies are found on the Atlantic side of South America.

*Habitat:* Breeds in burrows where digging is possible, otherwise on the surface or under bushes. Colonies form in a variety of habitats from low forests to grassland to bare rocks, often on islands or headlands. Some colonies on the Argentinean side number several hundreds of thousands of pairs.

*Breeding:* Arrival occurs in September/October, with males arriving more than two weeks before females: males arrive 24 days before egg-laying compared to only 8 for females. A clutch of two eggs is laid nearly 4 days apart. Males take the first foraging trip (i.e. females take the first incubation spell) of about 15 days, with females going to sea for around 17 days on the next trip. The incubation period is 40 days for first eggs and 39 for second eggs. Chicks are guarded for 29 days, during which time they are fed every 1–2 days. Fledging usually occurs at about 60 days, but can go as high as 120 days. Moult is post-nuptial.

*Diet:* Fish, mainly anchovies and sardines, are supplemented by cephalopods. Considerable variation between sites and years has been recorded, however, and one study found a small crustacean to be the main prey item.

*Migration and vagrancy:* Magellanic Penguins are migratory, some birds moving as far north as Peru and Brazil in winter. Vagrants have been recorded in South Georgia, on the Antarctic Peninsula, Australia, and New Zealand.

*Conservation and status:* IUCN category: Lower Risk. Not globally threatened. Population estimated at 1,300,000 pairs.

## Humboldt Penguin (*Spheniscus humboldti*) [Plate 15]          *inshore forager*

Endemic to the cold nutrient-rich waters of the Humboldt Current, the Humboldt Penguin breeds in a hot Mediterranean-like to desert climate. Populations fluctuate under the influence of El Niño events, which can cause significant breeding failure and adult starvation.

*Identification:* 70 cm. Similar to Magellanic Penguins, Humboldt Penguins lack the second dark breast band and have a wider white band around the head. Humboldt Penguins also have more extensive areas of bare skin than Magellanic Penguins, including a pink fleshy patch at the base of the lower mandible. Immature birds are very similar to those of Magellanic Penguins but are generally darker on the head.

*Distribution:* Endemic to the Humboldt Current, breeding range of Humboldt Penguins extends from 5°S in Peru to 37°S in Chile, with isolated colonies existing as far as 42°S near Puerto Montt.

*Habitat:* Humboldt Penguins nest in burrows—often dug into thick guano deposits, among boulders, in sea caves and sometimes in the open. Most birds depart the colony after sunrise and forage in close proximity to the colony. Foraging distances vary with location but Humboldt Penguins are typically inshore foragers. They are gregarious in the breeding colonies but are less so at sea. Captive birds moult once a year.

*Breeding:* While Humboldt Penguins can potentially breed year-round, there are often two distinct peaks in laying, similar to African Penguins. At Punta San Juan in Peru, laying extends from March to December with peaks in April and August/September (Paredes *et al.* 2002). About 50% of females lay two clutches per year, with most of those being double broods (i.e. successful breeders re-laying). A clutch of two eggs is laid 3.3 days apart. The incubation period lasts 41 days. Chicks hatch asynchronously: on average 2.6 days apart. Moult is pre-nuptial in captive birds.

*Diet:* Small schooling fish like anchovies and sardines are the staple diet of Humboldt Penguins, supplemented with the odd squid.

*Migration and vagrancy:* Probably sedentary. No vagrants have been reported. However, recent satellite telemetry studies have revealed that, especially in years of poor food supply, these penguins will travel large distances (Culik *et al.* 2000).

*Conservation and status:* IUCN category: Vulnerable. Total population of 13,000 birds. Population trend continues the decline evident over the last 100 years. Vulnerable to El Niño events.

## Galapagos Penguin (*Spheniscus mendiculus*) [Plate 16]          *inshore forager*

The northernmost of all penguins, Galapagos Penguins breed right on the equator. Populations fluctuate greatly in response to the influence of El Niño to a degree that the future survival of the species is endangered.

*Identification:* 48 cm. They are the smallest of the *Spheniscus* penguins. Distinguished by their relatively large bill and narrow white line around the face.

*Distribution:* The Galapagos Penguin is endemic to the Galapagos Islands, where it breeds on Isabela, Fernandina and possibly Bartholomew. Distribution seems to be correlated with the Cromwell Current, which provides cold nutrient-rich surface water.

*Habitat:* They breed mainly in caves or crevices of old lava flows and in burrows.

*Breeding:* Birds present at colony year-round. Generally two peaks in egg laying: June–September and December–March. Two eggs are laid, 3–4 days apart. Mean incubation shifts are 1.1 days for males and 2.0 days for females, suggesting that males forage for longer. The incubation period is 38–42 days. Hatching is asynchronous; usually 2–4 days apart. Fledging takes place when chicks are about 60 days old. Moult is pre-nuptial, occurring 1–4 weeks before the onset of breeding.

*Diet:* The main prey items taken by Galapagos Penguin are small fish like mullet and sardine.

*Migration and vagrancy:* Galapagos Penguins remain close to their breeding islands throughout the year. A record from the Pacific coast of Panama might well have been ship-assisted.

*Conservation and status:* IUCN category: Endangered. Total population estimated at 1500–4000 pairs, although this is suspected to be an overestimate. Population vulnerable, and fluctuates in response, to ENSO events.

# THE REMAINING CAST

There is little doubt that the penguins today represent but a small remaining part of the cast of an evolutionary drama that has been played out since their flying progenitors opted for a flightless aquatic existence. All modern-day penguins, like their ancestors, are confined to the Southern Hemisphere, but they occur over an exceptionally wide range of latitudes, from the equator to 78°S (Fig. 3.1). It is difficult to reconstruct the conditions under which penguins evolved (Fordyce and Jones 1990). Stonehouse (1969) estimated that during the Tertiary period (3–64 million years ago) penguins around New Zealand inhabited waters with sea surface temperatures of 18–20°C, while Jenkins (1974) put sea surface temperatures of waters around Australia inhabited by penguins during the Eocene (40 million years ago) at 12–16°C. These conditions broadly overlap those experienced by *Spheniscus* and *Eudyptula* penguins today, which tend to be non-migratory, inshore-feeding species that nest in burrows (Croxall and Davis 1999) in climates that vary from tropical to warm temperate, with surface water temperatures ranging from 23°C down to 10°C (Stonehouse 1970b). The biogeography of penguins also suggests that they arose first as subtropical/temperate inshore feeders confined to the coast (Cracraft 1973).

The formation of the circumpolar Southern Ocean about 25 million years ago, when Australia and South America separated from Antarctica, was associated with extensive cooling from the late Eocene/Oligocene (Berkman 1992), ice formation on land and sea surface temperatures of around 10°C (Williams 1995). In essence, the insulation required by homeotherms such as penguins for a water-borne

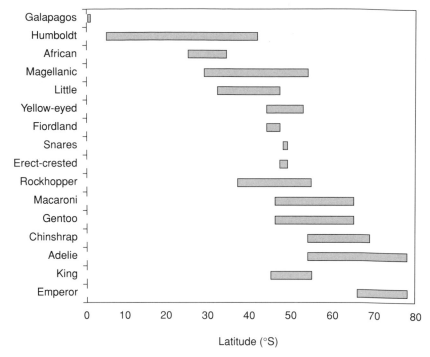

*Figure 3.1.   The range of latitudes in which extant species of penguins breed.*

existence (water conducts heat away from the body 25 times faster than air), pre-adapted penguins to go where other birds could not. Their feather survival suits that insulated them for life in water, meant that they could survive the worst winds and weather that the sub-Antarctic and Antarctic could throw at them.

The latitudes at which extant penguins breed relate pretty much to their phylogenetic groupings (Fig. 3.1). Although penguins are popularly presented as creatures of the ice and snow of Antarctica, this is true for only two of the genera, *Aptenodytes* and *Pygoscelis*. However, while the fossil record, biogeographical and paleoclimatological evidence, and cladistic analyses of morphology (O'Hara 1989), suggest that penguins evolved in subtropical/temperate environments and only later exploited the more extreme climatic conditions associated with the high latitudes of a cooler Earth, cladistic analyses of mDNA and behavioural characteristics of penguins suggest that *Aptenodytes* and *Pygoscelis* are the most basal (i.e. most closely related to the ancestral penguins) of the extant groups of penguins (Chapter 2).

These two positions need not be as contradictory as they might appear. Modern *Aptenodytes* and *Pygoscelis* representatives might still be derived from inshore-feeding, non-migratory ancestral stock that inhabited subtropical to temperate environments prior to the 'sudden' cooling of the Antarctic continent associated with the formation of the circumpolar current during the late Eocene/Oligocene. If, as seems likely, penguins were evolving during the late Palaeocene/early Eocene, then Antarctica (as part of Gondwanaland) at that time was covered with a temperate forest and surrounding water temperatures were around 15°C or more (Berkman 1992). A paucity of fossilized penguin material from the Antarctic continent may simply reflect a lack of appropriate ice-free sampling sites rather than being indicative of an absence of penguins in that area during the early stages of their evolution.

The two modern representatives of *Aptenodytes*, King and Emperor Penguins, are distinguished by their large body size and the fact that they are the only living penguins that are restricted to laying a single-egg clutch. Yet there would be few who would argue that either of these two characters necessarily represents the ancestral condition: flying and wing-swimming are incompatible at body weights in excess of about 1 kg and, therefore, flightlessness must have arisen in proto-penguins that were no larger than today's Little Penguin (Stonehouse 1975). Further, scenarios for the evolution of brood reduction in penguins suggest that the proto-penguins laid two-egg clutches (Edge 1996) and, hence, the single-egg clutches of King and Emperor Penguins represent a derived trait associated with abandoning nest-sites and carrying the egg atop their feet.

Even if, as seems probable, penguins evolved as birds of about 1 kg in predator-free, subtropical/temperate environments with a persistent food supply close to shore, from that point on they were free to radiate into whatever forms successfully balanced their lives in two worlds.

CHAPTER 4

# Living in two worlds

Penguins are commonly associated with snow and ice—in cartoons, in storybooks, in our imaginations. In reality, however, it is a different story. Certainly, Emperor Penguins breed in Antarctica in the heart of winter (Stonehouse 1953) when air temperatures can reach a bill-chattering −60°C (Le Maho *et al.* 1976, Le Maho 1977). But as we have seen in the previous chapter, penguins can also be found breeding right on the equator, where Galapagos Penguins lay their eggs in temperatures that can exceed 40°C and any exposed eggs can literally be fried by the sun (Boersma 1975).

We tend to associate penguins with uniformity. Indeed, most cartoons rely for their humour on the notion of penguins being anonymous conformists. How often do we give penguins credit for their versatility? Yet there is no other group of birds that can claim the title of '100 degree birds', breeding from −60 to +40°C as they do.

What we perceive as uniformity—a morphological similarity—results from physical constraints imposed by living and moving in an aquatic environment; an environment more resistant to movement of objects through it than is air. Square fish don't move so well. Similarly, a square penguin would require much more

*The world's only 100 degree birds: Adelie Penguins in a snow storm (Photo: Lloyd Spencer Davis)*

energy to move as fast as a streamlined one and, in the biased lottery that is Natural Selection, it was always on the cards that those penguins with the most streamlined tickets would win out (Plate 3).

So what we have is a superficial uniformity imposed by one environment that masks a versatility in another. Or perhaps that is not quite the right perspective? Perhaps it is the morphological adaptations of penguins for life in water that empowers them with an ability to breed virtually wherever they want to? After all, it was the insulation necessary for an aquatic life that enabled penguins to go where other land animals cannot. Antarctica in winter is no place for sissies.

But if it were as simple as that, then why don't we find penguins in the Northern Hemisphere? Why are there no penguins in Tahiti? Why are there no inland penguins? The fact of the matter is that the distribution of penguins is the result of a fine and complex balance of living a life in two worlds. They must balance the requirements for living on land, where they breed, against the requirements for living in the sea, where they feed.

## ACHIEVING A BALANCE—PATTERNS

In a sense the situation is not unlike someone managing a bank account. Such persons are free to determine their spending pattern within constraints imposed by the costs of their purchases and the amount of their income. The constraints imposed upon penguins are ecological ones. The 'money' (energy) they spend needs to be balanced against their 'income' (food). While there are countless possible permutations for producing a balanced budget, there are some patterns that will be more advantageous, some patterns that will generally do better than others.

In contrast to morphological constraints imposed by the hydrodynamics of water, ecological conditions, which affect the boundaries within which energetic balance must be achieved, can be highly variable. Hence, the behavioural responses of penguins to ecological constraints are considerably more flexible. Even so, patterns are evident.

## INSHORE VERSUS OFFSHORE FORAGERS

As a generalization, penguins can be placed into two broad categories based upon their foraging distance—how far they travel to get food: *inshore foragers* and *offshore foragers* (Croxall and Davis 1999).

Inshore foragers tend to feed close to the breeding colony (<50 km during the incubation period). They are characterized by having short fasts and are often residential, staying at the colony year-round or at least being able to stay there for periods that extend beyond those associated with breeding.

Offshore foragers feed at considerable distances from the colony, necessitating long fasts during incubation. These species are typically migrants, returning to the breeding colony only for the discretely timed events associated with breeding and, sometimes, moulting.

These two patterns are consistent across neither genera nor localities. For example, Gentoo Penguins are inshore foragers while the congeneric Adelie and Chinstrap Penguins are offshore foragers. Magellanic Penguins forage offshore, while the rest of the *Spheniscus* species tend to be inshore foragers. Sympatric populations of Gentoo Penguins and crested penguins adopt different strategies, with the latter all being offshore foragers.

To the extent that penguins have abandoned flight and taken to the water, it follows that the availability of suitable prey in an area around a breeding colony will influence whether the penguin has to travel a short or long distance to get sufficient to eat. All other things being equal, this will mean that offshore foragers need to be away from the nest for longer periods than inshore foraging birds. The persistence of prey within an area is also a prerequisite for birds to remain resident year-round. What is perhaps less intuitively obvious, is that such foraging patterns can have major impacts upon the life history parameters of penguins (Table 4.1).

Table 4.1. Species of Living Penguins

| Species | Scientific Name | Principal Location | Latitude (°S) | Body Mass (Kg) | Foraging Type | Migratory | Nest Type | Diet | Porpoising |
|---|---|---|---|---|---|---|---|---|---|
| **Inshore** | | | | | | | | | |
| Galapagos | *Spheniscus mendiculus* | Galapagos | 0 | 2.1 (M), 1.7 (F) | □ | □ | □ | □ | □ |
| Humboldt | *Spheniscus humboldti* | Peru, Chile | 5–42 | 4.9 (M), 4.5 (F) | □ | □ | □ | □ | ◧ |
| African | *Spheniscus demersus* | South Africa | 24–35 | 3.3 (M), 3.0 (F) | □ | □ | □ | □ | ◧ |
| Little | *Eudyptula minor* | Australia, New Zealand | 32–47 | 1.2 (M), 1.0 (F) | ◧ | ◧ | □ | □ | □ |
| Yellow-eyed | *Megadyptes antipodes* | New Zealand, Auckland Is. | 46–53 | 5.5 (M), 5.1 (F) | □ | □ | ◧ | ◧ | ◧ |
| Gentoo | *Pygoscelis papua* | sub-Antarctic, Antarctic | 46–65 | 5.6 (M), 5.1 (F) | □ | ◧ | ■ | ■ | ■ |
| **Offshore** | | | | | | | | | |
| Magellanic | *Spheniscus magellanicus* | Argentina, Chile, Falklands Is. | 29–54 | 4.9 (M), 4.6 (F) | ■ | ■ | □ | □ | ◧ |
| Fiordland | *Eudyptes pachyrhynchus* | New Zealand | 44–47 | 4.1 (M), 3.7 (F) | ■ | ■ | ◧ | ◧ | ■ |
| Snares | *Eudyptes robustus* | Snares Islands | 48 | 3.3 (M), 2.8 (F) | ■ | ■ | ■ | ◧ | ■ |
| Erect-crested | *Eudyptes sclateri* | Antipodes Is., Bounty Is. | 47–49 | 6.4 (M), 5.4 (F) | ■ | ■ | ■ | ◧ | ■ |
| Rockhopper | *Eudyptes chrysocome* | sub-Antarctic | 37–53 | 2.5 (M), 2.3 (F) | ■ | ■ | ■ | ◧ | ■ |

| Species | Scientific Name | Principal Location | Latitude (°S) | Body Mass (Kg) | Foraging Type | Migratory | Nest Type | Diet | Porpoising |
|---|---|---|---|---|---|---|---|---|---|
| Macaroni/'Royal' | *Eudyptes chrysolophus* | sub-Antarctic | 46–65 | 5.2 (M), 5.3 (F) | ■ | ■ | ■ | ◨ | ■ |
| Chinstrap | *Pygoscelis antarctica* | Antarctic | 54–69 | 5.0 (M), 4.8 (F) | ■ | ■ | ■ | ■ | ■ |
| Adelie | *Pygoscelis adeliae* | Antarctic | 54–77 | 5.4 (M), 4.8 (F) | ■ | ■ | ■ | ■ | ■ |
| King | *Aptenodytes patagonicus* | sub-Antarctic | 45–55 | 16.0 (M), 14.3 (F) | ■ | ■ | ■ | □ | ◨ |
| Emperor | *Aptenodytes forsteri* | Antarctic | 66–78 | 36.7 (M), 28.4 (F) | ■ | ■ | ■ | ◨ | □ |

**Key**

| Symbol | Foraging Type | Migratory | Nest Type | Diet | Porpoising |
|---|---|---|---|---|---|
| □ | Inshore | resident | burrow | fish | never or very seldom |
| ◨ | Either | either | forest | fish, cephalopods, crustaceans | occasionally |
| ■ | Offshore | migratory | open | crustaceans | routinely |

*Plate 1*

Adelie Penguin (*Pygoscelis adeliae*)
(Photo: Lloyd Spencer Davis)

Gentoo Penguin (*Pygoscelis papua*)
(Photo: Lloyd Spencer Davis)

Chinstrap Penguins (*Pygoscelis antarctica*) (Photo: Martin Renner)

*Plate 2*

Yellow-eyed Penguin (*Megadyptes antipodes*)
(Photo: Melanie Massaro)

King Penguins (*Aptenodytes patagonicus*)
(Photo: Lloyd Spencer Davis)

Emperor Penguin (*Aptenodytes forsteri*) (Photo: Lloyd Spencer Davis)

Plate 3

Fiordland Penguin (*Eudyptes pachyrhynchus*) (Photo: Lloyd Spencer Davis)

Snares Penguins (*Eudyptes robustus*) (Photo: Martin Renner)

*Plate 4*

Macaroni Penguins: the Royal subspecies (*Eudyptes chrysolophus*) (Photo: Corey Bradshaw)

Erect-crested Penguin (*Eudyptes sclateri*) (Photo: Martin Renner)

*Plate 5*

Rockhopper Penguin (*Eudyptes chrysocome*) (Photo: Lloyd Spencer Davis)

Little Penguin (*Eudyptula minor*) (Photo: Martin Renner)

*Plate 6*

African Penguins (*Spheniscus demersus*) (Photo: Lloyd Spencer Davis)

Magellanic Penguins (*Spheniscus magellanicus*) (Photo: Lloyd Spencer Davis)

*Plate 7*

Humboldt Penguin (*Spheniscus humboldti*)
(Photo: Lloyd Spencer Davis)

Galapagos Penguin (*Spheniscus mendiculus*)
(Photo: Lloyd Spencer Davis)

Humboldt Penguins in northern Chile gather together in large rafts before returning to the
land in the evening (Photo: Lloyd Spencer Davis)

*Plate 8*

A pair of Brown Skuas work in tandem to steal an egg from a Rockhopper Penguin nesting in the Falkland Islands (Photo: Lloyd Spencer Davis)

Egg dimorphism in Erect-crested Penguins breeding on the Antipodes Islands: the small, slightly greenish first-laid egg is on the right, the larger white second-laid egg on the left (NB photo is of abandoned eggs) (Photo: Lloyd Spencer Davis)

## TECHNIQUES FOR MONITORING AT SEA MOVEMENTS AND BEHAVIOUR

The penguins we see are the penguins of the land. Breeding. It has been the same for the scientist as it has for the lay-person. For most of the 20th century, the biology of the penguin was the biology of the terrestrial breeder. Penguins were leading a Jekyll and Hyde existence, but as biologists we saw only Dr Jekyll.

Thus, much of what is known of penguins has been predicated on the assumption that what we saw on the land was the most important component of their biology. What happened at sea was a mystery. It is only during the last 25 years that technological innovations have allowed us to glimpse the other half of the lives of penguins.

Over the last couple of decades or so, various devices have been fitted to penguins to monitor their at-sea behaviour. Generally these fall into two categories: *transmitters* that emit a signal, used primarily to monitor the location of foraging penguins, and *data loggers* that store information in an onboard microchip from one or more transducers that measure parameters such as pressure (depth), temperature, speed, light and whether it is wet or dry (in or out of water).

Transmitters initially involved radio telemetry and, more recently, satellite telemetry. Traditional radio telemetry is limited by the need for 'line of sight' between the transmitter and receiver, and the need to take bearings from two or more receivers simultaneously so as to be able to compute locations from triangulation (e.g. Davis *et al.* 1988, Sadleir and Lay 1990, Mattern 2001). This is labour intensive, requires receiving antennae to be as high as possible to maximize the radio horizon (when often there may not be suitable vantage points located along the coastline), and penguins cannot be tracked when they go beyond that horizon. An alternative means of using radio telemetry is to attach the receiving antenna to an aircraft, such as a small plane or helicopter (Weavers 1992), but this is expensive and typically provides relatively few data points for the money and effort expended.

Satellite telemetry involves the signal from the transmitter being detected by receivers on orbiting satellites. The French-based Argos system, consisting of three polar-orbiting satellites, is by far the most common system used for satellite telemetry of wildlife. The satellites are able to compute the location of a detected transmitter using the Doppler effect. The accuracy of this depends upon the number of signals the satellite receives from the transmitter while it passes over it. The most accurate classes of locations, Classes 2 and 3, are usually within $\pm$ 500 m (Kerry *et al.* 1995). The disadvantage of satellite telemetry is that it is expensive, both to buy the transmitters and to access the information, and, even with advances in miniaturization, the transmitters can still be relatively large attachments that undoubtedly affect the swimming of penguins in some way.

In contrast, data loggers tend to be smaller, cheaper and do not require large sums of money to access their data. The disadvantage of them is that to retrieve the information you must recapture the bird to download the information to a computer. If the bird fails to return or the logger falls off before the bird returns, all data are lost along with the logger. Also, if locations of the animal are required, there has been until recently no way, within the size constraints of a package small enough for penguins, to compute geographic locations accurately. By using the changing light intensities associated with sunrise and sunset, coupled with an accurate clock, locations can be determined using data loggers, albeit rather crudely at the moment (Wilson 2001). The most promising development of late has been the miniaturization of GPS loggers so that they are small enough to put on penguins. And, on the satellite side, within limits it is possible to transmit other data, as well as location data, via satellites. Nevertheless, the two vexing problems remain of cost versus information retrieval.

## DIVING PATTERNS

As with any emerging technology, the initial stages involve mainly description. Hence, the 'diving patterns' of penguins have been described in elaborate detail (Wilson 1995). There are some notable theoretical issues associated with how penguins dive as deep as they do (Kooyman *et al.* 1971, Kooyman *et al.* 1972, Kooyman 1975, Kooyman and Ponganis 1990, 1994), but for the most part, descriptions of diving patterns in penguins are not too instructive in terms of providing insight into their varied lifestyles.

In brief, all penguins are capable of diving to great depth. As would be expected from physiological principles, larger penguins can dive somewhat deeper and for longer than smaller ones (Wilson 1995).

However, penguins spend most of their time diving to depths considerably less than they are capable of: most penguins feed in the top 70 m of the sea (Kooyman and Ponganis 1990) where, being visual feeders, there is sufficient light for them to be able to see their prey. Until such time as theoretical questions are developed based upon the human-derived categorization of diving patterns (e.g. V-dive, U-dive, flat-bottomed dive) these detailed descriptions have little more than curiosity value.

## SWIMMING SPEED AND PORPOISING

One parameter that data loggers are capable of measuring is speed, which is essentially a measure of how fast the water flows across a penguin. These devices need to be calibrated (Gales *et al.* 1990b) to allow for the "bending" of water flowing around the penguin's body, which increases the apparent speed somewhat (Bannasch *et al.* 1994). It turns out that all penguins travel at a similar speed when swimming underwater, which is about 2 m/s (Culik *et al.* 1994). Little Penguins tend to go a bit slower than this and the large Emperor Penguins, a bit faster (Wilson 1995). When travelling like this, the penguins tend to remain close to the surface and maintain a constant bearing.

Penguins are also capable of 'porpoising': a mode of very fast travel where they propel themselves out of the water, allowing them to catch a breath (Plate 3) as they 'fly through the air' without slowing down. The effect is not unlike a porpoise or dolphin surfacing and, hence, the name. When porpoising, penguins increase their speed to about 3 m/s (Wilson 1995). The interesting thing is that only some penguins porpoise regularly (Table 4.1). The traditional explanation for these differences in behaviour is that those penguins that porpoise regularly when leaving their colony sites are subject to predation and that they porpoise as a means of quickly moving through the danger zone near the edges of the colonies (Wilson 1995, Yoda *et al.* 1999). It is certainly true that penguins of virtually all species, when panicked at sea, will porpoise; so there is no doubt that it does have an escape function when faced with the immediate threat of a predator. However, to put all porpoising down to predator avoidance is to miss an important point about the routine use of porpoising in some species: they are those species that typically forage a long way offshore. It doesn't take a rocket scientist to work out that a penguin that can travel 50% faster, will get to a feeding area more quickly. Of course, just like using gasoline in a car, the faster you go the less energy efficient it is (or, to put it another way, the more gas it takes to travel the requisite distance).

Surface swimming is energetically very costly due to the associated drag and this surface drag increases exponentially with increased speed (Kooyman and Davis 1987). At a certain speed it will become energetically less expensive for penguins to leap clear of the water when breathing, much as dolphins and porpoises do (Au and Weihs 1980). Kooyman (1987) calculated theoretical swimming velocities at which different species of penguins should porpoise. This theoretical speed depends upon the size of the penguin, with Little Penguins predicted to porpoise at 2.6 m/s, medium-sized penguins like Macaroni and Gentoo Penguins at 3.2–3.4 m/s, King Penguins at 3.9 m/s and Emperor Penguins at 4.4 m/s (Kooyman and Davis 1987). This might explain why the large offshore foragers, the King and Emperor Penguins, either seldom or never porpoise, respectively: it is just too costly for them to maintain such high velocities

Blake and Smith (1988) recalculated the theoretical crossover speeds for the medium-sized Humboldt Penguin, and Emperor Penguins, on the basis that previous models had overestimated the correction factor needed for different masses. These predicted even lower speeds at which it should pay penguins to porpoise (about 1.5 m/s for Humboldt Penguins and 3.1 m/s for Emperor). However, Humboldt Penguins in a captive environment did not porpoise below 3.0 m/s and the average speed of porpoising in this species was 3.7 m/s (Hui 1987). It seems that the time needed to breathe (about 0.3 seconds) may place a lower limit on the speed of porpoising (Hui 1987, Blake and Smith 1988). More recently, Yoda *et al.* (1999) used data loggers that monitor acceleration to show that Adelie Penguins do not porpoise until at speeds considerably in excess of predicted threshold levels. They argued that as leaps represented only 3.8% of the distance travelled while porpoising, that it is likely to provide only marginal energy savings and, therefore, be unimportant for travel to and from foraging sites. But from a foraging penguin's perspective: time savings could potentially be as important as energy savings.

Culik *et al.* (1994) have shown that the 2 m/s speed of travelling dives is the most energetically efficient and there has been an assumption that selection will result in penguins travelling to their foraging grounds at this optimal speed (Wilson 1991). However, just as there are times when it might pay you to travel more quickly in your car, other factors may favour expediency over efficiency. For offshore foragers, they need to balance the time they are away from the colony against the bounty they can obtain at large distances from the colony. To use the analogy again: if the aim is to go and replenish your gasoline supplies and gasoline is cheaper and readily available by travelling a long way versus the more meagre supplies closer to home, *but there is a limit to how long you can be away from home*, it may pay you to travel using the faster less fuel-efficient mode so as to avoid the negative consequences of taking too long. More work needs to be done on this to quantify the relative costs and benefits. However, we propose that porpoising could well be used at times by offshore foragers as a quick means of travelling to feeding sites. If the increased costs of travel associated with going faster can be offset by increased prey captured (by, say, getting to a more productive area) and/or increased time available for foraging, then optimal travel speeds may be higher than simply the most energy-efficient travel speeds (Norberg 1981). In support of this, Adelie Penguins have been observed porpoising in open water many kilometres from any land (Davis unpubl. obs.). Even an inshore species like the African Penguin, which is said not to porpoise routinely (Wilson 1995), has been observed porpoising at 5.3 m/s for 6.3 km to get to a feeding area (Heath and Randall 1989).

Much of the pioneering research and innovative developments regarding the at-sea behaviour of penguins can be attributed to Rory Wilson. Yet in his excellent review of the foraging ecology of penguins, Wilson (1995) treats foraging distance from the colony as just another descriptive element of the foraging trip, like dive pattern, dive depth and swimming speed. This misses the crucial role that foraging distance plays in affecting the breeding biology of penguins (Croxall and Davis 1999). How far a bird has to travel to get its food will affect how long it will be away from the nest and how much energy it uses. Macaroni Penguins, which forage offshore, have metabolic rates when foraging that are 25% higher than those of inshore Gentoo or African Penguins (Croxall and Davis 1990). Even within a species, individuals that travel further for food do so by upping the energetic ante: African Penguins that travel further increase their swimming speed and decrease their resting time (Wilson and Wilson 1990). These considerations, in turn, have ramifications for the mating system, patterns of parental care and the prospects of rearing one or two chicks.

## INSHORE VERSUS OFFSHORE—PHYLOGENETIC CONSTRAINT OR ECOLOGICAL COMPROMISE

Penguins lead a life in two worlds, breeding on land but feeding at sea. Both the male and female within a pair must contribute to the care of their offspring. Throughout incubation and until such time as the chicks no longer require protection, this means that one parent should always be in attendance at the nest. Incubation periods in penguins can range from 32 days (St. Clair 1990) to 64 days (Prevost 1961), with the majority being around 33–34 days for second eggs (Williams 1995). The guard stage can vary from 8 days (Numata 2000) to 80 days (du Plessis *et al.* 1994), with most guarding lasting for two to four weeks. Consequently, each time a penguin goes to sea from the completion of laying until the end of the guard stage, it must essentially solve the behavioural equivalent of an algebraic equation whereby the time it spends away feeding ($x$) must be balanced against the time it will next spend on the nest fasting ($y$) in such as way that $y$ will be a function of $x$:

$$y = f(x)$$

While feeding, a penguin must acquire enough energy to (i) replenish its fat reserves to a level sufficient to sustain its next fast, (ii) cover the elevated costs associated with foraging, and (iii) after hatching, bring back enough food to sustain the growth and development of the chicks.

Net energy gained from foraging per day (G) can be represented as:

$$G = I - (RMR + F)$$

where I is the daily energy intake from food that is consumed, RMR is the resting metabolic rate of an inactive penguin (i.e., the metabolic rate as measured in the field of an inactive penguin, equivalent to incubating or brooding costs) and F is the excess energy required for foraging over and above RMR)[1].

To be able to withstand the next fast:

$$R_{t=0} + G^*x > K + RMR^*y$$

where $R_{t=0}$ is the energy stored in the body's fat reserves at the start of the foraging trip and K is the minimum threshold of fat reserves which triggers abandonment of the nest.

Solving this for *x*, the minimum foraging trip will need to be:

$$x > (RMR^*y + K - R_{t=0})/G$$

However, a foraging bird must also get back before its partner deserts the nest (i.e., before its partner's reserves reach the critical threshold). Therefore:

$$RMR'^*x < R'_{t=0} - K$$

where $R'_{t=0}$ is the fat reserves of the partner at the start of the foraging trip and RMR' is the partner's resting metabolic rate (i.e., energy per day used while incubating)[2]. And so the maximum foraging trip length must be:

$$x < (R'_{t=0} - K)/RMR'$$

Within these minima and maxima, there is no one unique solution and interspecific comparisons reveal a variety of patterns of fasting and foraging (Fig. 4.1 shows fasting foraging patterns for different species). These patterns suggest a trend: as foraging distances increase, so too do periods of fasting and foraging and, consequently, the number of foraging trips is reduced. That is, although multiple solutions are available to penguins, when given a close food supply, inshore foragers tend to make many short foraging trips even though, being comparable in size to offshore foragers, they could potentially fast for much longer. Part of this must reflect the economics of foraging costs. If travelling costs are relatively high, then foraging trips of offshore foragers will be predictably longer, not so much due to the longer travelling time taken to get to the food but because of the economic advantages that will accrue from making fewer trips (if F increases, then G must decrease—unless I is increased to compensate—so that the minimum trip length must increase).

*Living in two worlds: Adelie Penguins going to sea must essentially solve the behavioural equivalent of an algebraic equation (Photo: Lloyd Spencer Davis)*

## EXAMPLES OF INSHORE FORAGERS

### YELLOW-EYED PENGUINS

The Yellow-eyed Penguin is endemic to the New Zealand region. Its breeding range encompasses the south-east coast of the South Island and Stewart, Auckland and Campbell Islands (Moore 1992). Adults are resident on or near the breeding grounds throughout the year (Darby and Seddon 1990). During a long 'pre-egg' phase, equivalent to courtship, adults may be present at the nest for periods that exceed one day but, nevertheless, during this time they have access to the sea and feed regularly. During incubation, incubation spells can range from 1–7 days, which according to Seddon (1989) average 2.0 days for males and 1.8 days for females, suggesting that females may forage for slightly longer (leaving their

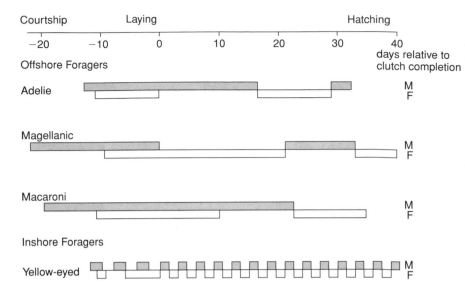

*Figure 4.1.  Attendance patterns: bars indicate periods when at the nest. Grey bars = males;*
*White bars = females*

partners to incubate for slightly longer), albeit Seddon and van Heezik (1990) found that incubating males and females both took mean spells of 1.4 days. Foraging trip durations for parents with chicks average 10–15 hours, and while the time away from the nest does not increase between the guard and post-guard phases, the proportion of that time they spend at sea does (Edge 1996). Radio telemetry revealed that the median maximum foraging distance from the colony (Moore 1999), even during incubation, was only 15.7 km, and no penguin was recorded more than 57 km from the colony. Yellow-eyed Penguins feed primarily on demersal species of fish (van Heezik 1990b), and the mean maximum dive depth of 34 m recorded during incubation foraging trips is consistent with them foraging over the shallow inshore shelf (Seddon and van Heezik 1990).

## AFRICAN PENGUINS

The African Penguin is confined to the coastal waters of southern Africa and breeds on 18 low-lying offshore islands, concentrated mainly on the west coast within the region of the cold, nutrient-rich Benguella current (Frost *et al.* 1976b). While there are winter and summer peaks in breeding, African Penguins breed at all times throughout the year (Cooper 1980). During incubation, mean incubation spell length is 1.1 days (Cooper 1980) to 1.9 days (range 1–11) (Seddon and van Heezik 1991c), albeit, for pairs where the eggs are deserted, the last shift before desertion averages 5.4–6.6 days (Cooper 1980, Seddon and van Heezik 1991c). Observations from surveys at sea reveal that African Penguins are spread along the coast, with 79% of penguins being within 12 km of the shore (Siegfried *et al.* 1975). However, while they stay inshore, many range quite widely from their breeding colonies (up to 75 km or more), with only 8% of birds seen at sea being within 12 km of a breeding island (Siegfried *et al.* 1975). During chick rearing, parents are away at sea for almost exactly 24 hours (mean = 0.98 days) and, from St Croix Island, they travel on average a maximum distance of 33.4–44.0 km from the colony, depending upon the season (Heath and Randall 1989). Parents with larger chicks travel further and swim faster (Wilson and Wilson 1990). Despite swimming faster, for trips up to 30 hours duration, the further they swim, the longer the duration of the trips.[3] More than 95% of the diet of African Penguins, by mass, consists of pelagic schooling fish, especially Anchovy *Eugraulis capensis* (Wilson 1985b). Mean maximum dive depths range between 46.5–62.4 m, depending upon locality and season (Wilson and Wilson 1990). However, most prey items are caught within 20 m of the surface (Wilson and Wilson 1995).

# EXAMPLES OF OFFSHORE FORAGERS

## MACARONI PENGUINS

Macaroni Penguins breed on islands of the sub-Antarctic, with some breeding as far south as the Antarctic Peninsula. Like all crested penguins, following a lengthy period of fasting during courtship and for a time post-laying, when partners attend the nest together, the initial foraging trips taken by males and females during the incubation period are long. At South Georgia mean foraging trip durations of 8 males and females were 14.5 days and the mean maximum distance from the colony, as determined by satellite telemetry, was 454 km (Barlow and Croxall 2002, Barlow *et al.* 2002).

Satellite telemetry of the Royal subspecies of Macaroni Penguins, which breed on Macquarie Island (54°30'S, 158°57'E), found that during all stages of the breeding season they foraged offshore in deep water (greater than 2000 m) associated with the polar frontal zone (Hull *et al.* 1997). The greater the time spent away from the nest, the greater was the distance travelled by the penguins and the greater the area over which they foraged. During incubation, male Royal Penguins took average foraging trips of 22 days and travelled up to a maximum distance of 660 km from the colony, while females travelled as far as 415 km on trips that averaged 14 days (Kooyman *et al.* 1999). Even during chick rearing, they foraged as far as 116 km from the colony during the guard stage and 201 km when the chicks were crèching. Royal Penguins tend to dive during daylight hours (4:00–21:00) and dive less on the first day of a foraging trip, consistent with travelling to an offshore foraging zone before getting down to the business of feeding seriously (Hull 2000). Although capable of diving to more than 100 m, they rarely did so and 79% of dives were less than 60 m.

## KING PENGUINS

King Penguins have a circumpolar distribution, breeding on sub-Antarctic islands. They are unusual in taking over a year to rear their chicks. This means that at any time during the year some parents will have chicks that require feeding and that within the colony there will often be chicks of widely different ages. During the late summer months at Possession Island (46°25′S, 51°40′E) in the Crozet Archipelago, parents go away on foraging trips that average 6–9 days, travelling to feeding areas associated with the Antarctic Polar Front about 300 km south of the colony (Putz *et al.* 1999). Travelling speeds are fastest on the first and last days of foraging trips, indicating that birds travel purposefully to the feeding area. Foraging trips of those incubating eggs, however, are significantly longer (about 16 days) and they do not work as hard as parents brooding chicks: tending not to dive as deep. Average maximum depths reached by King Penguins foraging during the incubation period compared with those with young chicks were 205 m versus 280 m in 1993, and 283 m versus 299 m in 1995 (Charrassin *et al.* 1999). Those with large chicks forage even deeper. Movements to greater depths are likely to result in more encounters with their main prey, myctophid fish, which increase in density below 200 m during the day. Also, birds with chicks spend twice as long diving at night as incubating parents (Charrassin *et al.* 1998).

King Penguins breeding on Macquarie Island were tracked during foraging trips lasting 12–21 days: maximum distances from the colony ranged from 312–623 km (Wienecke and Robertson 2000). Dive depths rarely exceeded 200 m.

In contrast to the summer foraging trips, two birds tracked from Possession Island during winter foraging trips that lasted 53 and 59 days, travelled 1600 and 1800 km from the colony, respectively (Putz *et al.* 1999). Winter foraging trips for King Penguins on the Falkland Islands average only 19.8 days (4–48) with mean maximum distances from the colony of 664 km (Putz in litt.).

## INTRASPECIFIC COMPARISONS

To determine whether these inshore/offshore foraging patterns apparent from interspecific comparisons are responses to different ecological constraints (i.e. how far penguins need to travel to get to their food source and how it is distributed) or whether they are phylogenetically fixed solutions to the fasting/foraging problem, we need to examine intraspecific differences in nest attendance patterns to see whether they also correlate with ecological conditions.

### LITTLE PENGUINS

Little Penguins are generally regarded as inshore foragers (Croxall and Davis 1999). However, their pattern of breeding varies throughout their range. At the western limits of their range, on Penguin Island, Western Australia, where abundant food supply is available throughout winter via the Leeuwin Current (Wienecke *et al.* 1995), egg-laying can occur from May until November (Klomp *et al.* 1988) and they can often fledge two broods per year (Wienecke 1993). This is not too dissimilar to the inshore-feeding African Penguins on Dassen Island, South Africa (Cooper 1980), or Galapagos Penguins (Boersma 1976). At Phillip Island, Victoria, Australia, while nearly half of Little Penguin pairs will re-lay if they lose their eggs or chicks, only 16% of successful breeders lay a second clutch (Reilly and Cullen 1981). Even more extreme, Little Penguins breeding in Wellington Harbour (Kinsky 1960, Bull 2000) and Motuara Island in the Malborough Sounds, New Zealand (Renner 1998) may very occasionally re-lay if their breeding attempt fails, but successful breeders never lay a second clutch and they are absent from the colony for part of the year. This is more reminiscent of offshore foragers.

There is no obvious latitudinal gradient associated with either the length of the breeding season or the prevalence of double clutches. Little Penguins breeding in New Zealand at Oamaru and on the Otago Peninsula, near the southern limit of their range, have much longer breeding seasons than those further north in Marlborough and Wellington, with nearly half (48%) of the successful breeders at one site on the Otago Peninsula laying a second clutch (Perriman and Steen 2000).

This suggests that the pattern of breeding may be dictated by local ecological conditions, especially those associated with food supply.

At Oamaru (45°0'S, 170°58'E) on the south-east coast of New Zealand's South Island (Fig. 4.2) the breeding season can extend for up to nine months depending upon the year. The earliest date on which eggs have been laid is 6 May, and the latest, 5 October. All chicks have usually fledged by some time in January, although this can vary by a month either side. In the best year recorded so far (1995), 40.6% of pairs laid two clutches (D. Houston, pers. comm.). In contrast, on Motuara Island (41°05'S, 174°15'E) in the Marlborough Sounds, New Zealand (Fig. 4.2), breeding is much more synchronized, with most chicks hatching within two weeks of each other in one year and, even in the most variable season, within about three months (Renner 1998). There have been no known examples of successful breeders re-laying during four seasons at Motuara (M. Renner, M. Numata, T. Mattern and L. Davis, unpubl. data).

At Motuara, Little Penguins took foraging trips during the incubation period that averaged 6.1 days over three seasons (range = 4.7–7.2) (Renner 1998, Numata 2000). In contrast, at Oamaru 47% of the foraging trips taken during the incubation period were of only one day in duration and the mean trip length was only 3.1 days (Numata 2000) (Fig. 4.3). Given that repeated studies have shown in penguins that duration of absence correlates with distance travelled from the colony, it is reasonable to assume that Little Penguins breeding on Motuara Island travel further to get their food during the incubation period than do those breeding at Oamaru. There are several lines of evidence that are consistent with this.

Radio telemetry of Little Penguins on single day foraging trips at Oamaru, during both incubation and chick rearing, showed they foraged within a mean maximum distance of 19.2 km from the colony. Those taking longer trips typically moved northwards along the coast, staying in waters less than 20 m deep and within 10 km of the shore (Mattern 2001). In contrast, Little Penguins at Motuara Island, when taking foraging trips of more than one day, travelled out of Queen Charlotte Sound and headed into Cook Strait, travelling in water 50–100 m deep before going beyond the receiving range (Mattern 2001).

Penguins at Motuara were in significantly poorer body condition than those at Oamaru (Numata *et al.* 2000). The duration of the foraging trip at both Oamaru and Motuara was negatively related to the condition of the bird at the start of the foraging trip, with parents in poorer condition staying away longer, and this was true for both males and females. Also, the proportion of body mass gained was significantly correlated with how long the foraging bird spent away from the nest (Numata *et al.* 2000).

At Motuara, parents were more likely to fail to co-ordinate nest relief during incubation. Birds that failed to return in time from foraging to relieve their incubating partners had gained less mass on their foraging trip (i.e., they had been less successful feeding) than did birds that successfully co-ordinated nest relief. As for the incubating birds, male penguins that abandoned their nests at Motuara had been fasting for a longer period than normal and were in significantly poorer con-

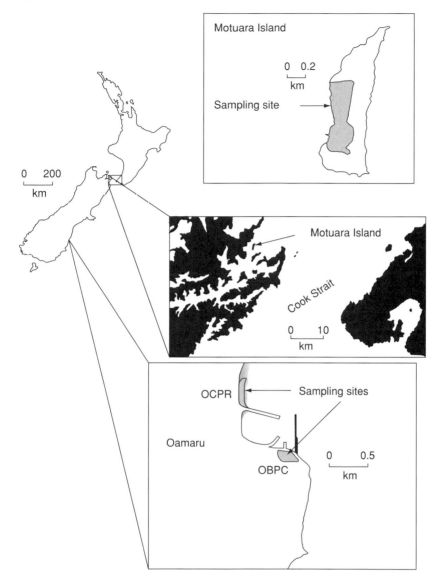

*Figure 4.2.   Location map of the sampling sites. The Oamaru study consisted of two sampling sites: the Oamaru Blue Penguin Colony (OBPC) and Oamaru Creek Penguin Refuge (OCPR).*

dition than males that were relieved, even though there had been no difference in their condition at the beginning of the fast (sample sizes of incubating females that abandoned the nest were too small to analyse adequately). The mean time birds had been incubating before abandoning the nest was longer than for other spells (Numata 2000). In all, during Numata's (2000) study, 24% of clutches at Motuara

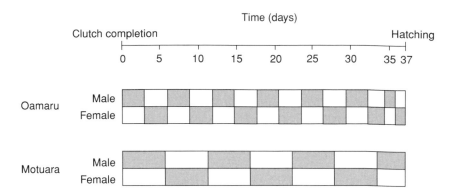

*Figure 4.3.  The mean pattern of nest attendance in Little Penguins breeding at Oamaru and on Motuara Island during the incubation period in the 1998–99 breeding season. Shaded areas show periods of attendance.*

were deserted because of failed nest relief (compared to only 9% at Oamaru); a result reinforced by Mattern (2001), who found that desertions accounted for 46% of all egg losses on Motuara but only 7% at Oamaru. The nett effect of this was that only 33% of clutches hatched at least one chick at Motuara compared to nearly twice that (65%) at Oamaru (Numata 2000). Renner (1998) demonstrated that at Motuara the probability of a nest producing any chicks was inversely related to the mean foraging trip length of the parents: as foraging trip duration increases during incubation, the probability of hatching decreases.

At Motuara Island, the highest cause of chick mortality is from starvation, with Renner (1998) finding that 38% of all chicks died of starvation over two seasons. Numata (2000) found similarly that 33% of chicks at Motuara died because of desertion or starvation, while none were lost to starvation at Oamaru. Chicks start to die within three days of hatching if they are not fed (Renner 1998) and at Motuara one-third of *all* chick deaths were because the adult at sea foraging did not return to the nest in time to feed the chicks. Whereas 80% of Oamaru nests are relieved on the day the first chick hatches, 70% of Motuara nests are *not* relieved at hatching and, as the sitting bird has been incubating for an average of five days in these cases, there is little likelihood of the chick being fed until the foraging bird returns.

Once hatching has occurred, parents alternate nest attendance every day at both Motuara and Oamaru, with the mean foraging trip during the guard stage being 1.1 days at both. Parents at both locations lose body mass during this period and body condition tended to be greater in parents of one-chick broods compared with two-chick broods, indicating that parents are having to work hard to feed chicks at both Oamaru and Motuara. Nevertheless, the condition of Motuara birds was significantly lower than that of Oamaru penguins during the guard stage. The duration of the guard stage was also significantly shorter at Motuara (15 days,) than at Oamaru (20 days) (Numata 2000), suggesting that both parents were required to forage to satisfy the needs of their growing chicks at an earlier stage. The brood size affected the guard stage duration at both colonies, with the guard stage being significantly prolonged by the parents of single chicks (Motuara: 19 days; Oamaru: 26 days) compared to that exhibited by the parents of twins (Motuara: 13 days; Oamaru: 18 days) (Numata 2000). The probability of a chick fledging at Oamrau (77%) is nearly twice that of chicks at Motuara (42% over three seasons) (Renner 1998, Numata 2000).

All the evidence suggests that food supply is poorer at Motuara than Oamaru and is consistent with the penguins needing to travel further offshore during incubation. The significant thing is that the penguins are able to respond to the conditions and alter their behaviour accordingly.

## MAGELLANIC PENGUINS

Magellanic Penguins, unlike the other members of their genus, are offshore foragers (Croxall and Davis 1999). Males arrive at the colony some 17 days before the females (Scolaro 1987) and another eight days of courtship elapses until the eggs are laid. Consequently, in this species it is the males that take the first foraging trip after the eggs are laid, as by then they have been fasting for nearly a month (there is some suggestion that females may go to sea briefly between laying the first and second egg (Williams 1995). Males are at sea on the first foraging trip for about two weeks, although in some years at Punta Tombo, Argentina (44°02'S 65°11'W), this can be longer (Yorio and Boersma 1994a). Satellite telemetry of a single male from Punta Tombo showed that during this period it travelled north 521 km from the colony and 152 km from the Argentinean coast (Stokes and Boersma 1999). Although that male was at sea for 26 days, this was close to the average first foraging trip of 24 days taken by males that particular season. Further north at Estancia San Lorenzo, Peninsula Valdes, Argentina (42°04'S, 63°37'E), a sample of mainly females taking their first incubation period foraging trips found that they did not exceed 303 km from the colony and the most frequented area was 120 km east of the colony in water 80 m deep, which coincided with a frontal system with enhanced productivity (Wilson *et al.* 1995).

Satellite telemetry of Magellanic Penguins breeding at Seal Bay (51°23'S, 58°02'W) in the Falkland Islands, observed that birds that foraged at sea for from 20–31 days travelled 396–689 km from the colony (Putz *et al.* 2002). This study did not monitor the breeding status of individuals being tracked, so that the exact stage of breeding or even whether they were breeders or failed breeders is unknown. At another location in the Falkland Islands, New Island South (51°42'S, 61°17'W), Magellanic Penguins foraged at maximum distances of only 48–87 km during late incubation (Boersma *et al.* 2002). Much, if not all that difference, is likely to be accounted for by foraging trips late in incubation being shorter than the initial foraging trips at the start of incubation(Scolaro 1987); however, the duration of trips was not given in Boersma *et al.*'s (2002) study.

Nevertheless, evidence is accumulating that Magellanic Penguins can behave quite differently even in colonies that are reasonably close to each other. Radl and Culik (1999, in litt.) studied the foraging trip durations during chick rearing of Magellanic Penguins breeding at two colonies in southern Chile: Magdalena Island (52°55′S, 70°34′W) and Otway Sound (52°58′S, 71°12′W) over three successive breeding seasons. Birds at Magdalena foraged further from the colony (maximum distances of 55 km versus 20 km), fed at greater depths (averages of 28.6–46.4 m at Magdalena compared with 24.8–28.2 m at Otway) and took longer to return to the colony and their chicks (trips averaging 17.7–38.2 hours at Magdalena over the three seasons compared to 8.8–12.0 hours at Otway).

## HUMBOLDT PENGUINS

Flexibility in response to different ecological constraints on foraging is not just evident between different locations: in some areas conditions may also vary markedly between years. Nowhere is this more apparent than with the effects of El Niño on Humboldt Penguins. Breeding within the confines of the nutrient-rich cold current that sweeps up the western side of South America, and with which it shares its name, the Humboldt Penguin breeds on the coast and offshore islands of Chile and Peru.

Under normal circumstances, the birds are inshore foragers with 90% of all locations from birds tracked at sea occurring within 20 km of the colony during late incubation and early chick rearing (Culik *et al.* 1998). Incubation spells average two days. Satellite telemetry of foraging Humboldt Penguins from Pan de Azúcar Island (26°09′S, 70°40′W) during the 1994–95 and 1995–96 austral summers revealed that 90% of locations were within 35 km, although one bird did reach a mean maximum distance of 92 km from the colony (Culik and Luna-Jorquera 1997b). However, in response to a strong El Niño Southern Oscillation (ENSO) event in 1997–98, which increased sea surface temperatures, penguins from Pan de Azúcar travelled up to 895 km as marine productivity decreased (Culik *et al.* 2000).

Parents of chicks at Pan de Azúcar spent more than twice as long on foraging trips (36 hours) compared with parents at Puñihuil, 1500 km south (17 hours). While the latter caught mainly fish (95.5% of the diet), crustaceans made up most of the diet of penguins at Pan de Azúcar when fish stocks were reduced due to El Niño. Crustaceans provide less energy, and reproductive success at Pan de Azúcar was only 0.25 fledglings/nest compared with 1.6 fledglings/nest at Puñihuil (Hennicke and Culik 2000).

# DIET

Penguins need prey in high densities and/or very close by to compensate for the high costs of getting to the food (swimming is more expensive and slower than flying), as well as to catch enough food to be able to feed chicks frequently (usually every day or two). This is probably one of the main reasons that penguins are restricted to the Southern Hemisphere. Tropical waters are, for the most part, not very productive. The penguins that occur at low latitudes, such as Galapagos, Humboldt and African, do so in areas where there is upwelling of cold currents bringing nutrient-rich waters from further south. The intervening areas are quite barren by comparison and would seem to act as a barrier to penguin dispersal into the Northern Hemisphere (Davis 2001b).

In juggling their lives between two worlds, it might seem intuitively obvious that the availability of prey should be one factor that will influence how long penguins spend at sea. But just what constitutes the potential prey of penguins and how can it be measured?

Determining exactly what penguins eat used to rely on the collection of vomits or partial vomits that were occasionally spilled on the ground when parents fed their chicks (provides only a qualitative description of food items delivered to chicks) or what was euphemistically described as 'sacrificing' birds to collect their stomach contents (much more quantitative, but ethically questionable). During the last 20 years, scientists have relied on the water-offloading technique to sample the diet of penguins (Wilson 1984). This involves pumping water into their stomachs down a tube inserted through their bills, causing them to vomit up the contents of their stomachs. To reliably collect all the stomach contents, this procedure needs to be repeated several times on the same individual (Gales 1987). While this technique is not without its own problems, it is safe to use with penguins. Collecting the stomach contents of parents during chick rearing will deprive their chicks of a meal, but as Robertson *et al.* (1994a) demonstrated in a study of Adelie Penguins, the loss of a single meal had no measurable effect on the survival or growth of chicks. The chief problem to overcome is that of the effects of digestion on the stomach contents. Fortunately the otoliths of fish and the beaks of squid tend to be more persistent than other body parts and can be used to calculate the size of the original prey items (van Heezik 1988), although even these are subject to digestive erosion (van Heezik and Seddon 1989), and corrective factors may need to be applied (Gales 1988).

Penguins tend to feed on schooling fish, krill (euphausiids) and, to a lesser extent, squid. While for some species at certain localities or seasons the diet may consist largely of a single species, the reality is that most penguins, within limits, eat what is available.

Penguins breeding at relatively low latitudes, such as the *Spheniscus* penguins and Little Penguins, are predominantly fish-eaters; targeting schools of small fish such as anchovy and sprat.[4] The bills of predominantly fish-eating penguins like this are often hooked at the end of the top mandible, a feature which aids the holding of prey (see Plate 12). Even so, their diet is largely dictated by what fish are there. The diets of Magellanic Penguins studied simultaneously at two colonies only 60 km apart were significantly different and, even within a single colony, the diet varied considerably between seasons and years (Thompson 1993). The size distribution of anchovy eaten by African Penguins reflects seasonal changes in fish migration (Laugksch and Adams 1993). Fish species taken by Little Penguins breeding in Victoria, Australia, also vary between sites and years (Cullen *et al.* 1992) and a study in Western Australia concluded that the penguins were largely opportunistic, with their diet being similar to catches of commercial bait fishermen (Klomp and Wooller 1988).

The temperate inshore-feeding Yellow-eyed Penguin feeds mainly on fish too, with fish making up about 87% of the diet by mass (van Heezik 1990b). Most are pelagic species (van Heezik 1990b), although demersal fish can form a significant part of the diet (van Heezik 1990a). Faced with reduced availability of fish in some years, Yellow-eyed Penguins will switch to taking squid in large quantities but, because their chicks fare less well on such a diet, growth rates are depressed even though meal sizes may actually be larger (van Heezik and Davis 1990).

Crested penguins are another group that will take squid in large quantities depending upon the circumstances. Squid constituted 53% by mass of the stomach contents of Rockhopper Penguins in the Falkland Islands (Croxall *et al.* 1985) but only 5% at Marion Island (Cooper *et al.* 1990). Similarly, cephalopods made up 85% of the diet by mass of Fiordland penguins during the post-guard stage of chick rearing at Jackson's and Martin's Bays, Fiordland (van Heezik 1989) but only 16% on Codfish Island (van Heezik 1990a). Otherwise, Rockhopper and Macaroni Penguins feed mainly on crustaceans (includes krill) with some fish thrown in (Cooper *et al.* 1990).

King Penguins feed predominantly on myctophid fish, which live in dense schools and perform daily vertical migrations (Hindell 1988a, Cherel and Ridoux 1992, Olsson and North 1997). However, in winter they take a greater diversity of prey, suggesting that when faced with a change in prey availability they adopt a more opportunistic feeding behaviour (Cherel *et al.* 1996). Again, squid appear to be utilized primarily in response to reduced supplies of fish, with King Penguins breeding on Heard Island taking squid only during the winter months from April to August (Moore *et al.* 1998). King Penguins are unable to utilize squid as efficiently as they are fish (Adams 1984).

The diet of Emperor Penguins varies considerably from place to place. Fish makes up about 90% by mass of the diet of Emperor Penguins breeding in the western Ross Sea region of Antarctica with a single species, Antarctic Silverfish *Pleuragramma antarcticum*, making up nearly 90% of that (Cherel and Kooyman 1998). These results echoed those of Gales *et al.* (1990a) from Princess Elizabeth Land in Antarctica, but in the eastern Weddell Sea, 90% of the prey caught by Emperor Penguins is krill (*Euphausia superba*) (Klages 1989). In the same area, squid beaks are found in nearly all stomach samples but, as squid beaks tend to be persistent and accumulate, if only fresh beaks are considered then it is apparent that squid constitute only a minor part of the diet (Piatkowski and Putz 1994). However, food delivered to Emperor Penguin chicks at the Taylor Glacier Colony on the Mawson Coast of Antarctica was made up of 69% by mass of squid (Robertson *et al.* 1994b).

The Pygoscelid penguins are often portrayed as feeding almost exclusively on krill. And to a certain extent, that is true. In the area of the Antarctic Peninsula, such as Signy Island, the krill species *E. superba* makes up 98.3–99.1% of the diet of Adelie Penguins by mass and more than 99.8–99.9 % of the diet of Chinstrap Penguins (Lishman 1985b). This result is echoed at other sites around the Antarctic Peninsula (Croxall and Furse 1980, Coria *et al.* 1995). However, at places away from the Peninsula—such as Adelie Land (Ridoux and Offredo 1989, Wienecke *et al.* 2000) and the Vestfold Hills of East Antarctica (Puddicombe and Johnstone 1988, Whitehead *et al.* 1988)—*E. superba* is not so dominant and another krill species (*E. crystallorophias*) and fish play important roles in the diet. For Adelie Penguins provisioning chicks in the Ross Sea, the Antarctic Silverfish *P. antarcticum* may even be the most important prey item (Ainley *et al.* 1998), just as it is for Emperor Penguins breeding in the area.

Gentoo Penguins rely more on fish than do their two Pygoscelid cousins, especially at the northern limits of their distribution such as sub-Antarctic Marion Island and Macquarie Island, where fish constitute 53% by mass of the diet (Adams and Klages 1989) and 59% (Hindell 1989), respectively. At the Kerguelen Islands, the proportion of krill *E. vallentini* in the diet of Gentoo Penguins closely matched that from net hauls in a year of high plankton availability (Bost *et al.* 1994). Gentoo Penguins breeding sympatrically with Macaroni Penguins on South Georgia, while feeding on the *E. superba* that formed virtually the sole constituent of the Macaroni diet, also dove deeper, preying on benthic-demersal fish (Croxall *et al.* 1988a). Ironically, then, when krill biomass around South Georgia was drastically reduced in 1994, it was the Gentoo Penguins which suffered most, their breeding success being reduced by 90% from average values compared with virtually no reduction in Macaroni breeding success (Croxall *et al.* 1999). Although Gentoo Penguins switched almost entirely to fish (86% of the diet compared with an average of just over one-third of the diet in other years), meal sizes delivered to chicks were drastically reduced (meal mass being only 15% of that delivered in the six other years from 1989–1995). By comparison, Macaroni Penguins switched from their almost total reliance on krill (90% of the diet in other years) to a diet that consisted two-thirds of amphipods (*Themisto gaudichaudii*). While meal sizes brought to chicks were somewhat reduced (85% of that delivered in the six other years from 1989–1995), breeding success (46%) was very close to average (46.8%), albeit fledglings were about 10% lighter than normal (Croxall *et al.* 1999).

What becomes apparent from reviewing the literature on diet in penguins, is that even though the diets of penguins may be dominated by single species of prey in given localities or seasons, the penguins themselves are quite capable of shifting to different prey depending upon the circumstances. Indeed, excavation of abandoned

Adelie Penguin colonies on the Antarctic Peninsula (the oldest nearly 650 years old) suggests that over time the penguins have changed their diets probably in response to changes in prey availability associated with periods of global cooling and warming (Emslie *et al.* 1998).

Given the apparent feeding flexibility of penguins, together with the ecological mantra that two species cannot occupy the same niche simultaneously, there has been considerable interest paid to the diet of sympatrically-breeding species of penguins. The expectation has been that competition will ensure their diets are different. In fact, for the most part, it has not turned out that way. Where different species of penguins breed sympatrically, they typically feed on whatever is locally abundant and, consequently, have similar diets. Macaroni and Rockhopper Penguins on Marion Island have broadly similar diets and any dietary segregation, as such, is the result of differences in the timing of breeding, with Macaronis beginning 3–4 weeks earlier than the Rockhoppers (Brown and Klages 1987). This presumably means that the peak demands made by the two penguin species on the food source are different. This seems to be true of sympatrically breeding crested penguins, generally, with diets tending to largely overlap and differences in timing of breeding and foraging ranges being suggested as important ecological segregating mechanisms (Cooper *et al.* 1990).

An exception to this apparently occurs on Codfish Island (46°45′S, 167°40′E), a tiny island situated below New Zealand's South Island, where penguins from three different genera breed: Yellow-eyed, Fiordland and Little Penguins. Yellow-eyed Penguins preyed largely on the demersal Blue Cod *Parapercis colias* (77% by mass); and while both the Fiordland and Little Penguins ate juvenile forms of fish and squid that formed part of the pelagic macro-zooplankton, Fiordland Penguins consumed mainly Ahuru *Auchenoceros punctatus* (63%), while Little Penguins took mainly squid (*Nototodarus sloanii* and *Moroteuthopsis ingens*) (58%) (van Heezik 1990a). Croxall *et al.* (1999) suggest that dietary segregation could result from inter-species competition when food supplies are low.

FORAGING DIFFERENCES BETWEEN MALES AND FEMALES

Competition has also been suggested to result in intra-specific sex differences in diet. It has been proposed that dietary segregation of males and females will reduce competition for food, leading to selection for differences in attributes such as bill and body size between males and females (Warham 1975, Agnew and Kerry 1995). However, such a proposition confuses cause and effect. Firstly, there is little evidence that males and females have different diets (e.g. Cherel and Ridoux 1992). Secondly, even if they did, it is not at all clear that it should be an adaptation to reduce competition between males and females, but is more likely to be a by-product of other selective forces that create differences between males and females, such as sexual selection (Davis 1991). Natural selection operates most strongly at the level of the individual and not for the good of the group. When invoking selective arguments, one should nearly always look for individual advantage.

None of that is to say that there will never be differences in male and female foraging or provisioning behaviour. Clarke *et al.* (1998) found that female Adelie Penguins at Bechervaise Island (67°35′S, 62°49′E) in the Eastern Antarctic and at Edmonson Point (74°21′S, 165°10′E) in the Ross Sea consistently took longer foraging trips and ranged over greater distances than did males, especially during the guard stage of chick rearing. Ninety percent of males at Bechervaise foraged within 20 km of the colony when their chicks were less than three weeks old, whereas the majority of females travelled 80–120 km to the edge of the continental shelf to feed. Ainley *et al.* (1998) found that for parents engaged in long foraging trips, more of the food gathered was used for self-maintenance. This fits with findings for flying seabirds, which show that when the fat reserves of parents provisioning chicks go below a certain threshold, they undergo longer foraging trips primarily for self-maintenance (Davis and Cuthbert 2001). Female penguins are generally somewhat smaller than males and, consequently, have smaller reserves (Chappell *et al.* 1993a). This suggests that males should more readily be able to sustain foraging for their chicks, thereby tending to stay closer to the colony so as to deliver food frequently to the chicks. Additionally, a study of Chinstrap Penguins found that body size was the best predictor of meal size delivered to chicks (De Leon *et al.* 1998). Hence, we might expect to find that males tend to deliver more food to their chicks (frequency and meal size) and forage in somewhat different places to females as a consequence of differences in body size. However, any such separation in feeding niches is likely to be a consequence of whatever selection leads to sexual dimorphism in body size and not caused by selection for intersexual dietary segregation.

Emperor Penguins are the most sexually dimorphic of all penguins for body size (Davis and Speirs 1990), and while females and males consume similar prey at Auster Colony (67°23′S, 64°02′E), they differ in the relative proportions of those prey in the diet. The diet of females consists of 72% fish (by mass), 16% squid and 12% krill, whereas males take 53% fish, 2% squid and 43% krill (Wienecke and Robertson 1997). Partly this could result from differences in foraging ability: nearly one in five dives by males exceeded 300 m in depth, whereas only one in one thousand dives by females went below 300 m (Wienecke and Robertson 1997). Diving capability tends to be correlated with body size (Wilson 1995).

Even for males, should food supply be low, then it should pay them to look after themselves in the first instance and their chicks second. Gentoo and Macaroni Penguins at South Georgia responded to the collapse of krill stocks in 1994 by maintaining feeding frequency to their chicks but decreasing the meal size that was delivered (Croxall et al. 1999). In most other instances, it seems, parents react to food shortages by increasing foraging trip durations and, thereby, reducing feeding frequency. During the 1998/99 breeding season at Bechervaise Island, a season of apparently reduced food supply, both male and female Adelies foraged further off-shore and spent longer at sea. Meal masses brought to chicks were maintained, but the longer foraging trip durations reduced feeding frequency, with a consequent reduction in breeding success (Irvine *et al.* 2000). However, should food supply fall drastically, as it did during the 1994/95 season when all chicks at Bechervaise died of starvation, meal sizes are reduced as the birds forage even further afield (Irvine *et al.* 2000). King Penguins also take longer to obtain food in the face of decreasing marine resources, with breeders accumulating their own body fuel reserves and reducing feeding frequency to chicks (Le Maho *et al.* 1993).

This has led authors to suggest that monitoring the foraging trip durations of penguins may provide a cheap and effective biological monitor of marine resources (Croxall *et al.* 1988b, Davis and Miller 1990, Le Maho *et al.* 1993, Miller and Davis 1993, Davis 1997).

Foraging Trip Durations and Sea-Ice

Foraging trip durations will be influenced, then, by the distance needed to be travelled to get to the food (see Table 7.3) and the distribution of the food.

Another factor that affects foraging trip times in the Antarctic is the presence of sea-ice. Swimming through water is a lot faster for penguins than walking across frozen water. In some years the sea-ice that forms around colonies over winter can be late breaking out. For example, in the calm conditions of the 1968/69 breeding season at the Cape Crozier colony of Adelie Penguins, Ross Island, the ice did not break out until late December (i.e., after hatching). In that season, exhausted by their travels across the ice, fewer birds attempted to breed and, of those that did, they were much more likely to desert their eggs. Desertions result mainly from the incubating bird being unrelieved before its fat reserves have become depleted. But worse was in store for the penguins breeding on Ross Island.

In March 2000, the largest iceberg ever recorded (named B-15), broke off the Ross Ice Shelf. A large piece of it (B-15A), 160 km long by nearly 40 km wide, floated towards Ross Island. As it did so, it rammed into the Ross Ice Shelf, breaking off a second large berg (C-16), over 50 km long by nearly 20 km wide. C-16 ran aground north of Ross Island in November 2000, and B-15A grounded itself alongside C-16 two months later. The bergs are so massive that they block currents

moving into McMurdo Sound. As a consequence, the sea-ice that formed there during the winter was thicker than normal and, coupled with calm conditions, failed to break out during the summer. For the penguins breeding on Ross Island it has been a disaster. The colony of about 1200 Emperor Penguins at Cape Crozier failed to raise a single chick in 2001. Only about 30% of the normal number of pairs laid eggs at the large Adelie Penguin colony at Cape Crozier. At Cape Bird, another large Adelie colony, so many eggs were deserted that hundreds lay scattered about the colony, the skuas too satiated to eat them (M. Potter, in litt.). There was total reproductive failure at the small colony at Cape Royds, the southernmost penguin colony in the world, where the birds had to walk about 130 km from the colony to reach the ice edge (H. Mayell, National Geographic News, 17 January 2002).

## THE DANGER OF CATEGORIES

In our efforts to understand a complicated world we inevitably categorize and in doing so, simplify. While that may help us discern the big picture, the truth can often be in the detail; detail that is lost in this process of categorization. While the label of inshore or offshore forager is useful, when applied to a species it can give the impression that the associated characteristics are somehow genetically fixed, specific to that species. As scientists we love to deal in means, in average descriptions. But to do so can miss the importance of the inherent variability in behaviour. Animals, we are learning, are more plastic than we thought, more flexible in their behaviour. Everything need not be programmed by the genes: there is advantage to be gained from being able to respond to available conditions. If animals have become adapted to particular environments and seek out similar environments and conditions, then it is likely that they will have the appearance of behaving similarly. But put animals in different conditions and they may well respond differently. Such differences are most likely to be seen at the extremes of their ranges where conditions are likely to be more different. Similarly, ecological conditions change through time or may fluctuate in a given area. Hence, it is advantageous for animals to have flexible responses.

Nevertheless, however flexible penguins may be, their flightlessness and need for an adequate food supply places strict limits on where they can breed. The first thing a penguin must do is find a suitable place to nest where it can balance its life in two worlds.

CHAPTER 5

# A place to breed

Had penguins been mammals, they could have, potentially at least, forsaken the land for ever. Internal gestation is the key to the totally aquatic existence of cetaceans and dugongs. But penguins are birds and, as such, they must lay eggs. The development of young in self-contained capsules outside of the mother's body has some definite advantages for birds. Levels of parental investment can be readily adjusted early in the development of the young and, for those that fly, it beats flying about with a belly full of babies. A consequence of their legacy as birds is that penguins are tied to the land. Unlike the eggs of sea turtles or those of other aquatic reptiles, penguin eggs cannot just be dumped in sand on some isolated shore, requiring little more terrestrial time than a stroll up the beach on a moonlit night.

No, birds are homeotherms and their eggs must be kept warm for development to take place. Consequently, parents must incubate their eggs to ensure the survival of their offspring. But to be on land for breeding (courting, incubating or brooding) is to be on a diet: the source of their sustenance being separate from the site of procreation. While ostensibly this is the same for all seabirds, for one that cannot fly the importance of the proximate food supply is magnified. Albatross and petrels can cover hundreds of kilometres, thousands even (Weimerskirch *et al*. 1993, Waugh *et al*. 2002). They have to balance the same equation of fasting and foraging (Chapter 4), but the leeway they have is greater, opening up a much greater potential range of breeding sites (Davis and Cuthbert 2001).

# FOOD SUPPLY

Penguins have less choice: they can only breed in places that are within easy reach of food; food both for the parents and for the chicks. Given that all penguins are capable of withstanding relatively long fasts (Croxall and Davis 1999), whereas chicks need to be fed frequently to survive and grow quickly, it is much more crucial that food be near to the breeding place during chick rearing rather than during courtship or incubation.

Indeed, the timing of breeding of seabirds is typically synchronized to the pattern of availability of food such that the peak availability of food near to the breeding site occurs during chick rearing (Davis and Cuthbert 2001). Because of this, and because the peak load on parents in terms of energy demands can be demonstrated to occur during chick rearing (Chappell *et al.* 1993a, Chappell *et al.* 1993b), authors have assumed that food availability during chick rearing is limiting (Mock and Schwagmeyer 1990, Clarke 2001). However, it is possible that food availability during either courtship or incubation could be limiting even though the energetic demands at that time may be lower. Ainley *et al.* (1995) tested the hypothesis that competition for food during the chick-provisioning stage of reproduction limited the number of conspecific Pygoscelid penguins within a region. Contrary to the hypothesis, they did not find a negative relationship between colony population size and the total number of breeding pairs from other colonies within parental foraging range. However, they did observe significant negative correlations at 150 and 200 km, "well beyond foraging range". But in fact, 200 km is not beyond the foraging range of Adelie Penguins, at least, during the incubation period (Davis and Miller 1992, Kerry *et al.* 1995), and may well be within the foraging range of all three Pygoscelid species just prior to the courtship period. Food limitations during courtship have been demonstrated experimentally to limit the breeding effort of shearwaters (Cuthbert 1999).

Generally, the length of the breeding season correlates negatively with latitude. The higher the latitude, the greater is the seasonal variation in food supply and the shorter the window of opportunity for breeding (Croxall and Gaston 1988, Costa 1991). Exceptions help to prove the rule: double brooding and an extended breeding season are characteristic of Little Penguins at the northern limit of their range, such as Penguin Island, Western Australia (32°17′S) (Klomp *et al.* 1988) and Bowen Island, Jervis Bay (35°07′S) (Fortescue 1995) but are also found near the southern limit of their range at Oamaru (45°06′S) and Taiaroa Head (45°46′S) Otago, New Zealand (Perriman *et al.* 2000, Perriman and Steen 2000). However, double brooding is absent at some places in the middle of their range such as Tasmania (43°S) (Hodgson 1975, Gales 1985) and Motuara Island, New Zealand (41°06′S) (Renner 1998). It seems likely that such variation reflects local differences in food supply as a result of specific currents (Reilly and Cullen 1981, Wienecke *et al.* 1995). These can mask the general latitudinal trend in seasonality of food supply, which tends to correspond to sea-surface temperatures (Warham

1975). Little Penguins at Oamaru forage for shorter periods, travel less distance, are heavier, their chicks gain weight faster and they have higher breeding success than those breeding on Motuara Island (Chapter 4, Numata *et al.* 2000, Mattern 2001).

Similarly, Magellanic Penguins breeding in southern Chile foraged for a significantly shorter duration during chick provisioning at Otway Sound (9 hours) than at Magdalena Island (18 hours) (Radl and Culik 1999). The authors concluded that "short foraging trips like the ones at Otway are only possible when prey availability near the feeding grounds is sufficiently high and travel distances therefore small" (Radl and Culik 1999).

While access to a suitable food supply must be the primary determinant of potential breeding sites, a number of secondary factors play a role in determining whether such sites are suitable for breeding.

## PROTECTION FROM INSOLATION

The feathers of penguins constitute their survival suits. Penguin feathers are short (30–40 mm), stiff and lance-shaped, with insulation being provided by a relatively long afterfeather (downy filaments) which traps air (Dawson *et al.* 1999). Unlike flying birds, the feathers of penguins are evenly and densely packed (three to four times the density of flying birds) (Stahel and Gales 1987) over the surface of the body rather than being arranged in tracts (Dawson *et al.* 1999). The latter would be impractical for penguins because water could seep through to the skin (Stahel and Gales 1987). The tips of the feathers are stiff and coarse, interlocking with each other to provide a waterproof seal to the plumage. Hence, the rigid feather suit is able to resist compression when the penguin dives, preventing much of the trapped air from being forced out and thereby insulating the penguin's skin from the heat-stealing waters. Waterproofing is also enhanced by preening the feathers with oily secretions from the uropygeal gland at the base of the tail (Stahel and Gales 1987).

10µm

*Magellanic Penguins nesting in burrows at Punta Tombo, Argentina (Photo: Lloyd Spencer Davis)*

As effective as this survival suit has been in allowing a homeotherm to inhabit the underwater world, it can create problems of overheating when upon land (Davis 1993). While heat stress can occur even in Antarctic penguins while on land (Chappell and Souza 1988), the problem is most pronounced for those breeding at lower latitudes. This applies especially to the *Spheniscus* penguins and Little Penguin. To the extent that they can, these penguins avoid the worst of the heat by going to sea during the day and returning to the colony in the evening (Frost *et al.* 1976a), with Little Penguins usually being nocturnal (coming ashore after sunset and departing before sunrise) (Klomp and Woller 1991). However, the need to incubate eggs and brood chicks dictates that one or other of the parents must spend the days ashore in attendance at the nest. Exposure to the sun is most likely to threaten them with heat stress. They avoid it principally by nesting underground in a burrow (Frost *et al.* 1976a). Temperatures in burrows of African (Frost *et al.* 1976a, La Cock 1988) and Magellanic Penguins (Frere *et al.* 1992) remain more constant than those of surface breeding birds. The parents also avoid overheating by confining display activities to the early morning or late evening (Frost *et al.* 1976a). In addition, all penguins can rid themselves of excess heat through postural thermoregulation (Frost *et al.* 1976a), panting (Boersma 1975, Chappell and Souza 1988) and, in the case of the *Spheniscus* penguins, through evaporative heat loss from patches of bare skin on the face (Frost *et al.* 1976a). Most heat, however, is dissipated through the feet and flippers (Boersma 1975, Wilson *et al.* 1998), which are infused with blood vessels that act as an arterio-venous heat exchange system (Frost *et al.* 1975). Even so, the capacity of penguins to rid themselves of excess heat

*Bare patches of skin on the face of Sphensicid penguins, like this Humbodlt Penguin, assist with evaporative heat loss (Photo: Lloyd Spencer Davis)*

is limited (Baudinette *et al.* 1986) and penguins, despite being homeotherms, do not maintain a constant body temperature. Body temperatures of Galapagos Penguins on land range from 38°C to 42°C and these are on average 2°C warmer than their body temperature when in the water (Boersma 1975). Similarly, in the African Penguin, body temperature varies according to whether the bird is in or out of the water and the level of activity (Wilson and Gremillet 1996), with muscle-generated heat during swimming able to elevate the body temperature when in water.

Given the potential effect of the sun on the comfort of their insulated insides (and they have dark backs as well), it is a wonder that a penguin breeding from the equator to about 45°S would consider breeding anywhere other than underground. But certainly, while all the penguins breeding at latitudes lower than 45°S can be classified as burrow breeders, in all species some individuals nest above ground, usually under bushes, but sometimes in the open (Plate 15). In the case of Magellanic Penguins, breeding success may not be poorer for those under bushes (Frere *et al.* 1992); and, as burrows can be prone to flooding in areas exposed to rain, such as those of African Penguins (La Cock 1988, Seddon and van Heezik 1991a) or Little Penguins breeding on Motuara Island (Renner and Davis 2001), breeders may at times actually be worse off in burrows.

## Site Selection

To demonstrate that penguins are actively choosing certain characteristics in their breeding sites, it is not enough to simply catalogue the characteristics of penguin nests. It must be shown that these characteristics differ from the surrounding available sites, otherwise the birds could be just setting up home randomly for all we know. The nest site characteristics of Yellow-eyed Penguins have been measured in detail and compared with randomly selected sites nearby (Seddon and Davis 1989). Yellow-eyed Penguins nest from 44°S on New Zealand's South Island to 53°S on the sub-Antarctic Auckland Islands. They typically nest in forest or dense vegetation and their nests are distinguished by having much greater overhead cover in the first one metre above ground than the surrounding areas (Seddon and Davis 1989). This is consistent with this species, too, seeking shelter from the sun. Numbers of Yellow-eyed Penguins breeding on New Zealand's Otago Peninsula declined during the latter half of the 20th century, coincident with the removal of coastal forests that provided their nesting habitat (Darby and Seddon 1990). Analysis of the population from 1981 to 1992 shows that there is a positive relationship between the number of fledglings produced in a given year and the rainfall two years earlier (Peacock *et al.* 2000): while such a relationship could well be spurious, it is tantalizing to speculate that increased rainfall would have promoted growth of vegetative cover, which provided benefits in terms of shading once the plants had developed to a suitable size two years later.

## Effect of nest site selection on coloniality

One consequence for Yellow-eyed Penguins of needing to find nest sites suitably enclosed by vegetation is that their nests tend to be quite dispersed, with distances between nests being up to 150 m (Darby and Seddon 1990). Though it has been maintained that Yellow-eyed Penguins need to have nests that are visually isolated from each other to breed successfully (Darby, pers comm.), it remains unclear whether this is so or whether the isolation is simply an outcome of a preference for densely-covered nest sites, which will tend to be dispersed and hidden from neighbours. In that sense, Yellow-eyed Penguin nests may be thought of as the equivalent of those of burrow-dwellers, which are also visually isolated from those of their neighbours.

However, it would be wrong to dismiss the notion that nest site selection can have a strong influence on sociality in penguins. Little Penguins are amongst the most heterogenous of penguins in terms of their breeding sites. They nest in burrows or under bushes or rocks, as solitary pairs or in loose aggregations; but they are also found nesting in caves in tight colonial aggregations. Cave-dwelling Little Penguins interact more and exhibit a much more varied behavioural repertoire than do their burrow-dwelling brethren (Waas 1990). It is possible, then, that the social system of the very loosely colonial Yellow-eyed Penguins will be affected by their

*Adelie Penguins normally nest in colonies, but occasionally individual pairs will nest by themselves (Photo: Lloyd Spencer Davis)*

proclivity for isolated nest sites. Although not aurally isolated from each other, the physical separation of nests may reduce the likelihood of cuckoldry that is a feature of colonial breeding in penguins (see Chapter 6).

At latitudes above 45°S, ambient air temperatures are such that penguins are usually able to breed in the open. Fiordland Penguins breed in the coastal rain-forests of south-west New Zealand (McLean and Russ 1991, McLean *et al.* 1993) in caves or under dense vegetation, but as they breed during the winter (Warham 1974) in an area of high rainfall, it is likely that any shelter they seek is from the rain (to protect their downy chicks from hypothermia) rather than the sun. Penguins that inhabit the sub-Antarctic and Antarctic typically nest in the cheek-by-jowl dense colonies characteristic of seabirds, but often within a particular area they aggregate into smaller sub-colonies.

Some penguins that breed in the sub-Antarctic, such as the Snares Penguin and the northern subspecies of the Gentoo Penguin, use vegetation to line their nests and, as this becomes fouled with guano, the whole sub-colony may shift to an adjacent site the following year. In contrast, Rockhopper, Macaroni and Erect-crested Penguins tend to nest on rocks and so are much more persistent in their use of nest sites from year to year. Similarly for the Antarctic-breeding Pygoscelid penguins: they line depressions in the ground with stones and exhibit high levels of nest fidelity from year to year. In contrast, the *Aptenodytes* species, the King and Emperor, do not make a nest but carry the single egg on their feet. King Penguins still defend a nesting territory, but Emperors breed on sea-ice during the heart of

*Gentoo Penguins in the southern part of their range line their nests with stones, as do the other Pygoscelid penguins (Photo: Martin Renner)*

the Antarctic winter and move around within the colony, huddling with the other parents, as one means of staying warm.

Overall, it is the feather survival suit of the penguins that enables them to breed in cold climates. Penguins evolved in temperate climates (Stonehouse 1967) but their adaptations for a life in water meant that they were able to move into cooler climes or to remain in an area in the face of environmental change.

## PROTECTION FROM PREDATORS

### ADULTS

'Flight' has two meanings and for birds they are linked: flight is in one sense an ability to move through air; it is, in another, to flee from danger. For birds, the ability to fly provides a safety net against predators in particular. To give up flight, then, would seem to be either foolhardy or an indication that it was not needed for escape. Indeed, flightlessness is a characteristic of many New Zealand native birds, which evolved in the absence of any mammalian predators. Flightlessness in waterbirds has evolved where the birds are on isolated islands free from terrestrial predators (Chapter 2). An absence of mammalian predators was probably a prerequisite for the precursor penguins to be able to abandon flight (and a reason why the ecologically similar auks of the Northern Hemisphere have, for the most part, been unable to do so in the face of the threat of predation from mammalian carnivores).

Today, areas of penguin habitat are being exposed to mammalian predators introduced by humans (e.g. Berruti 1981, Apps 1983, Alterio and Moller 1997, Alterio *et al.* 1998), but for the most part these do not seriously affect the adults; albeit Little Penguins, because of their diminutive size, are vulnerable (Harrigan 1992, D'Amore and Jessop 1995, Hocken 2000).

For adult penguins, the greatest risk of predation comes from marine predators in the form of seals (Penney and Lowry 1967, Conway 1971, Boswall 1972, Hofman 1973, Dawson 1974, DeLaca et al. 1975, Dawson 1984, Todd 1988, Moore and Moffat 1992, Hofmeyr and Bester 1993, Rogers and Bryden 1995, Schweigman and Darby 1997), sharks (Brooke and Waller 1976, Hocken 2000), and killer whales (Randall and Randall 1990, Williams *et al.* 1990, Guinet 1992). The risk of seal predation, in particular, can be high when penguins enter or exit the water at their colonies, although this is not true across all species. Leopard Seals *Hydrurga leptonyx* often patrol the margins of Pygoscelid penguin colonies, where penguins are most vulnerable getting in or out of the water. Leopard Seals in Prdyz Bay, Antarctica distribute themselves along the fast-ice edge in locations where departing penguins congregate and are estimated to take 2.7% of the adult Adelie Penguins over the course of a breeding season (Rogers and Bryden 1995). In contrast to the apparent haste Adelie Penguins exhibit getting out of the water, Humboldt Penguins at Chile's Algarobbo Island will congregate in large rafts on the surface prior to exiting the water, seemingly untroubled by marine predators (Plate 17).

*For adult penguins, the greatest risk of predation comes from marine predators in the form of seals: a Leopard Seal kills an Adelie Penguin (Photo: Lloyd Spencer Davis)*

Seals may sometimes prey upon penguins on land: fur seals have been observed killing Erect-crested Penguins within a colony and then eating them (Davis 2001c).

There has been speculation that Yellow-eyed Penguins may have been preyed upon by a huge extinct eagle (Holdaway 1991), but there is no real evidence for this and it seems rather fanciful given the dense forests Yellow-eyed Penguins would have inhabited on mainland New Zealand during the time when they were co-existing with the eagles. However, birds of prey can be a problem for penguins in more open habitats such as the Falkland Islands, where Striated Caracaras *Phalcoboemus australis* may attack Rockhopper colonies.

## EGGS AND CHICKS

If the adults are not especially vulnerable to predation when on land for breeding, the same cannot be said for their progeny. Predation of eggs and chicks by other birds, such as skuas (Plate 18), giant petrels and gulls, can be high (Muller-Schwarze and Muller-Schwarze 1973, Trivelpiece and Volkman 1982, Brooke 1985b, Davis and McCaffrey 1986, Hunter 1991, St. Clair and St. Clair 1992, Young 1994, Emslie *et al.* 1995). Introduced mammals, such as cats (Berruti 1981) and mustelids (Ratz 1997, Ratz 2000) may also target the eggs and chicks. Predation by reptiles is also a possibility, with King Skinks *Egernia kingii* taking Little Penguin eggs on Penguin Island, Western Australia (Meathrel and Klomp 1990).

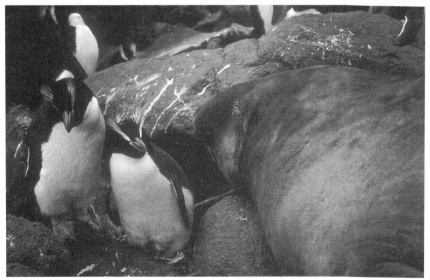

*While not preying directly on eggs or chicks, large phocid seals can cause death and destruction when they lumber into a penguin colony: an Elephant Seal in a colony of Erect-crested Penguins (Photo: Lloyd Spencer Davis)*

Ironically, the most voracious predators are other seabirds: birds adapted to live off the fruits of the sea, as are the penguins, but which are not averse to the opportunistic pickings available within penguin colonies. Southern Giant Petrels *Macronectes giganteus* kill an estimated 11.2% of Marion Island's King Penguin chicks (Hunter 1991). Most South Polar Skuas *Catharacta maccormicki* feed on fish (Young 1963), but some set up territories within Adelie Penguin colonies during the breeding season and supplement their diet with penguin eggs and chicks (Young 1994). While the level of predation by skuas can vary from year to year and from one site to another, in one study, skuas took 18.3% of eggs and 23.2% of chicks (Davis and McCaffrey 1986). It is easiest for skuas and the like to attack penguin nests that are on the edges of colonies and, strikingly, the susceptibility to predation of eggs and chicks in peripheral nests is much greater than those in central nests within colonies: 27.1% of eggs in peripheral nests were taken compared with only 5.9% in central nests, and 30% of chicks in peripheral nests fell prey to skuas, whereas only 10% of those in central nests did so (Davis and McCaffrey 1986). Nests in the centre of a Magellanic Penguin colony lost only 6.3% of eggs to predators compared to 23.1% of those in a peripheral area (Frere *et al.* 1992).

The question arises then: if being in a central nest can offer such profound protection from predators, why do some penguins nest in smaller sub-colonies rather than one large colony which would reduce the proportion of nests exposed to the periphery (Davis 2001a)? This may be because for a bird that cannot fly, access to nests at the centres of large colonies becomes increasingly difficult as they must run a gauntlet of pecks from their colonial neighbours, and there has been a suggestion that there is an optimum size for Adelie Penguin colonies (Oelke 1975). Ainley (1983) found that older breeders, while avoiding the periphery of a sub-colony, also avoided the deep centres, with no breeders older than 8 years breeding more than 5 nests in from the sub-colony periphery and nearly half (47.1%) of all breeders 8 years and over nesting within one or two sites of the periphery. However, on Deception Island, where Chinstrap Penguin colonies are estimated to contain up to 150,000 adults (Shuford and Spear 1988), colony size is a much better predictor of breeding success than is nest position, with parents in large colonies enjoying greater success irrespective of their nest location (Barbosa *et al.* 1997). King Penguins and Macaroni Penguins may also be found nesting in massive colonies.

Formation of sub-colonies could be dictated by topography with not all areas within a colony area being equally preferred. Ridges are favoured by Adelie Penguins breeding in the Antarctic because they are more likely to remain free of snow and meltwater (Moczydlowski 1989), although at lower latitudes snowdrifts are not a problem and the Adelies do not exhibit a preference for ridges (Volkman and Trivelpiece 1981). Avoiding snowmelt cannot be the whole answer, even in the high latitudes, because monitoring of Adelie Penguin sub-colonies in the Northern Colony at Cape Bird, Ross Island, has shown that these sub-colonies expand and retract, new ones form and others disappear; indicating that the intervening ground between sub-colonies may be suitable for breeding after all.

A place protected from predators and the elements cannot be the sole determinants of nest site selection. Philopatry (returning to the natal area) and nest fidelity (returning to a previously used nest site) are characteristic of penguins to varying degrees. It turns out that choice of nest site is governed also by the influence it can have on getting a mate.

## CHAPTER 6

# Mate selection and courtship

To breed, penguins must come ashore. Penguins lay large eggs (albeit, relative to their body size, their eggs are proportionately smaller than those of other birds (Lack 1968)) and, as incubation time is typically a function of egg size (Rahn and Ar 1974, Boersma 1982), penguins have long incubation periods.[1] All penguins have incubation periods in excess of one month (Williams 1995). As well as the need for the eggs to be incubated, chicks hatch in a semi-precocial state (Furness and Monaghan 1987) and for the first two-three weeks must be brooded to protect them from predators and temperature changes. As penguins are unable to feed when ashore, what this all means is that to breed successfully, penguins are obligatory biparental carers (Davis 1991).

While differential investment in the size of the gametes of males and females in a sexually reproducing species should incline males to maximize their reproductive success by seeking further matings (Trivers 1972), they are constrained from doing so because the cost of abandoning females is too high: that is, to ensure their reproductive success, males must contribute to the care and survival of their offspring. As a consequence, monogamy is the norm for penguins, as it is for other seabirds

(Rowley 1983, Black 1996). There is a popular misconception, however, that monogamy means that penguins 'mate for life' and that sexual selection will be weak (Davis 1991)

Sexual selection is the selection of attributes in one sex that increase mating opportunities. Such selection can come about in two ways. There can be selection for attributes that give members of one sex an advantage when competing with other members of the same sex for mating opportunities (intrasexual selection). This usually, but not always, involves competition between males. Alternatively, selection can occur through attributes in one sex being favoured by members of the opposite sex (intersexual selection or mate choice). This usually, but not always, involves choice by females. Largely, these differences are a consequence of the differential investment by the sexes in their gametes. Females produce relatively few eggs and these are costly; hence, they tend to be more discriminating because the costs of a failed mating opportunity are high. On the other hand, males produce millions of sperm; and, as sperm are comparatively inexpensive to produce, they can afford to make more mistakes and so they lose nothing by trying to compete with other males for as many mating opportunities as they can. This means that sexual selection often results in sexual dimorphism, with characteristics being selected in males, especially, that enhance their ability to compete against one another and/or that are favoured by females (N.B. these processes are not mutually exclusive). Classical sexually-selected traits include the peacock's tail and the antlers of deer.

The intensity of sexual selection is strongest in polygamous species. This is because the variation in reproductive success is greatest. Think of it this way: if there are equal numbers of males and females and one male gets to sire the offspring of many females, then he will enjoy great reproductive success (as measured by the offspring produced), whereas many other males must miss out altogether. This variability accounts for the intensity of selection on those attributes—such as large body size, bright colouration or whatever—that influence mating success. In contrast, in monogamous species, sexual selection is said to be less intense because nearly all individuals get to breed and to breed only once, irrespective of their attributes. However, sexual selection can be relevant in monogamous species where favoured traits allow individuals to breed early and either (i) there is an advantage to breeding early so that they have greater reproductive success, (ii) they are able to secure more extra-pair copulations, or (iii) they have the opportunity for additional breeding attempts within a season (Davis and Speirs 1990).

Such selection is capable of producing sexual dimorphisms in monogamous species (Møller 1988). However, a lack of morphological secondary sexual characteristics, by definition, provides no evidence for sexual selection (Davis 1991). Penguins are typically described as monomorphic and, while there may be slight differences, they are to all intents and purposes, sexually indistinguishable (Burley 1981). Yet sexual selection need not proliferate sexually dimorphic traits if the traits being selected are conditional (i.e. the perceived value of the trait varies according to the relationship between the individuals involved) (Davis 1991) or there are mutual mating preferences for the same trait by both sexes (Jones and Hunter 1998).

## SEXUAL DIMORPHISM AND PENGUINS

*Sexual differences?: a pair of Magellanic Penguins sit outside their nest burrow in the Falkland Islands (Photo: Lloyd Spencer Davis)*

Penguins are the fodder for thousands of cartoons because they look like clones of each other. However, slight morphological differences do occur between the sexes, principally in body, bill and flipper size, with males tending to be larger (Table 6.1).

It has been suggested that the sexual dimorphism in bill sizes is driven by selection for separation in feeding niches between males and females to reduce competition in the face of limited food supplies (Agnew and Kerry 1995, Chapter 4). However, this illustrates a common misconception about how natural selection operates. Natural selection does not act for 'the good of the species' but for the individual (Trivers 1985). While one can conjure up benefits that could accrue to a species as a whole if males were to forage differently from females, such a scenario is unlikely ever to be an evolutionary stable strategy as it would always be open to 'cheating'. If, for example, males could garner more resources by feeding on the same prey as females, it would always pay those that did so (in terms of their reproductive output and evolutionary fitness), rather than those that behaved selflessly for the good of the group and fed elsewhere. Consequently, those that forage in less endowed areas or on less profitable prey would leave fewer offspring and whatever

Table 6.1. *Levels of sexual dimorphism (DI) for bill length, bill depth, flipper length and body mass. DI = male value/female value.*
Data from Agnew and Kerry (1995) and Williams (1995)

| Species | Location | Bill length Male (mm) | Bill length Female (mm) | Bill length DI | Bill depth Male (mm) | Bill depth Female (mm) | Bill depth DI | Flipper length Male (mm) | Flipper length Female (mm) | Flipper length DI | Body mass Male (kg) | Body mass Female (kg) | Body mass DI |
|---|---|---|---|---|---|---|---|---|---|---|---|---|---|
| **Offshore** | | | | | | | | | | | | | |
| Emperor | Terre Adelie | 81.5 | 80.4 | 1.01 | | | | 362 | 347 | 1.04 | 38.2 | 29.5 | 1.29 |
| King | Heard Is. | 95.6 | 87.4 | 1.09 | 18.8 | 17.9 | 1.05 | 273 | 261 | 1.05 | 11.9 | 10.5 | 1.13 |
| Adelie | Mawson | 40.4 | 37.0 | 1.09 | 19.6 | 18.2 | 1.08 | 194 | 189 | 1.02 | 4.8 | 4.0 | 1.20 |
| Chinstrap | Deception Is. | 49.0 | 46.2 | 1.06 | 20.5 | 18.6 | 1.10 | 193 | 187 | 1.03 | 3.9 | 3.7 | 1.05 |
| Macaroni | Macquarie Is. | 68.9 | 61.3 | 1.12 | 30.5 | 26.7 | 1.14 | 215 | 205 | 1.05 | 5.9 | 4.0 | 1.48 |
| Rockhopper | Falkland Is. | 44.8 | 40.0 | 1.12 | 20.6 | 17.6 | 1.17 | 176 | 168 | 1.05 | 4.3 | 3.7 | 1.16 |
| Fiordland | South Is. | 51.3 | 44.0 | 1.17 | 25.8 | 21.9 | 1.18 | 185 | 176 | 1.05 | 4.9 | 4.8 | 1.02 |
| Snares | Snares Is. | 58.7 | 52.0 | 1.13 | 27.7 | 24.3 | 1.14 | 183 | 177 | 1.03 | 2.6 | 2.5 | 1.04 |
| Erect-crested | Antipodes Is. | 58.5 | 52.5 | 1.11 | 26.0 | 22.6 | 1.15 | 212 | 204 | 1.04 | 6.4 | 5.4 | 1.19 |
| Magellanic | Punta Tombo | 58.8 | 54.5 | 1.08 | 25.0 | 21.6 | 1.16 | 195 | 186 | 1.05 | 4.5 | 3.8 | 1.18 |
| **Inshore** | | | | | | | | | | | | | |
| Gentoo | South Georgia | 55.5 | 50.4 | 1.10 | 17.3 | 15.4 | 1.12 | 241 | 231 | 1.04 | 6.7 | 6.4 | 1.05 |
| Galapagos | Galapagos Is. | 58.2 | 53.9 | 1.08 | | | | 119 | 114 | 1.04 | 2.1 | 1.9 | 1.11 |
| African | Dassen Is. | 60.5 | 55.5 | 1.09 | 23.0 | 21.0 | 1.10 | | | | 4.0 | 3.5 | 1.14 |
| Little | Bass Strait | 39.1 | 36.8 | 1.06 | 14.3 | 12.4 | 1.15 | 121 | 118 | 1.03 | 1.2 | 1.1 | 1.09 |
| Yellow-eyed | Otago Peninsula | 54.4 | 52.8 | 1.03 | 20.7 | 19.4 | 1.07 | 209 | 204 | 1.02 | 5.5 | 5.1 | 1.08 |
| Humboldt | Various | 65.0 | 60.0 | 1.08 | | | | 174 | 165 | 1.05 | 4.9 | 4.5 | 1.09 |

genes influenced their foraging would diminish in the population relative to those of penguins that behave selfishly. That is not to say that there cannot be feeding differences between males and females, but these are likely to be *consequences* of any differences in morphology, not a *cause* of them. To date there is not much evidence of differences in diet between male and female penguins (Croxall and Lishman 1987), although there may be behavioural differences in foraging that could contribute to such differences (Clarke *et al.* 1998).

To the extent that the body shape and design of penguins is tightly constrained by the hydrodynamics of moving through water (Bannasch 1995), it is unlikely that flipper size and body size could vary much independently of each other. Indeed, they covary, with 93% of the variation in flipper length between species being able to be explained by differences in the cube root of their body mass (Fig. 6.1). In contrast, only 46% of the variation in bill length between male penguins of different species can be explained by differences in their body size (Table 6.1). While there is some allometric covariance of body size with bill size, bill size is less likely to affect the hydrodynamics of swimming to the same extent as flipper size and is potentially freer to respond to selective pressures from sexual selection independent of body size. Bills are used in fights as weapons and, in particular, the sturdiness of the bill, as measured by bill depth, has been shown to be most discriminating in morphometric analyses (Scolaro *et al.* 1983, Murie *et al.* 1991, Renner *et al.* 1998, Renner and Davis 1999) of many species. The bill of males could well have been subject to selective pressures for an increase in sturdiness through intrasexual competition. The likelihood that male-male competition is important to the mating system of penguin species probably varies with the degree to which males can compete before the arrival of females. In some species like the Yellow-eyed Penguin, males and females are resident at the site all year round and there is no real difference in arrival dates of males and females; in

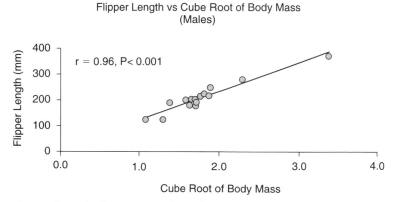

*Figure 6.1. Relationship between mean flipper length and mean body mass in different species of male penguins.*

Pygoscelid penguins the males typically arrive a few days before the females (1–5), while in Eudyptids and Magellanic Penguins the males can arrive anywhere from one to two weeks or more ahead of the females. Hence, it might be predicted that sexual dimorphism in bill size will be highest in those species where the males arrive most asynchronously from the females. Although there is a trend for sexual dimorphism in bill depth to be greatest in those species where the males arrive most before the females,[2] available data are too poor to test this adequately.

While bill size may differ as a result of male-male competition, females when exercising choice should pick males most likely to provide adequate parental care. In this instance, bill size is probably a less effective indicator of a male's ability to supply paternal care than is a variable like body size or condition. While parental care could include food provisioning rates, for most species, a crucial element to their breeding success is dictated by the male's ability to attend the nest during the female's absences at sea to forage (Chapter 7). This is especially so for offshore foragers: it has been predicted that body size dimorphism is related to the period of fasting the males must undergo (Davis and Speirs 1990). In the inshore foraging species, nest reliefs take place every day or so, even during incubation (Croxall and Davis 1999, Numata *et al*. 2000). For offshore foraging species, the males can undergo fasts of more than one month even in the medium-sized penguins (Davis 1982b, Williams *et al*. 1992, Ulbricht and Zippel 1994) while Emperor Penguin males go without food for 3.5 months during the Antarctic winter (Le Maho *et al*. 1976, Groscolas 1982). Indeed there is a positive relationship of body mass dimorphism with the length of fast males must endure (Davis and Speirs 1990). However, it is more complex than just that. Females of offshore foraging penguins must also often undergo long fasts too, especially in those species where the female takes the first incubation spell in addition to producing the eggs (e.g. Macaroni Penguins). Although as a group offshore foragers are not more dimorphic than inshore foragers, there is a positive relationship between the ratio of the fast males and females endure from arrival and their dimorphism in body mass.[3] Body mass is notoriously variable throughout the season and it is important to compare the relative weights of males and females at comparable times. Typically the data in the literature are too poor to do this thoroughly, albeit here we have used body masses of birds arriving at the colony at the start of the breeding season where available.

## FIRST-TIME BREEDERS

There has been very little work on the selectivity of female penguins that are breeding for the first time. In large part this is because of the lack of studies with known-age birds observed in sufficient detail to determine when breeding takes place for the first time. The best such study is the longitudinal study of Adelie Penguins at Cape Crozier, Ross Island (77°20′S, 169°15′E) from 1961 to 1975 (Ainley *et al*. 1983).

Sladen (1958) recognized that in Adelie colonies, young individuals initially attended the colony in seasons before they bred and wandered through it, unattached to any specific nest site or sub-colony. These 'wanderers' were confirmed to be young prebreeders (Le Resche and Sladen 1970), mainly 2–4 years of age (Ainley *et al.* 1983). While natal site influences place of first breeding, with most Adelie Penguins likely to nest close to or within 100 m of where they hatched (Ainley *et al.* 1983), wandering does have some effect on the eventual site chosen for breeding. Wandering begins near the natal site and becomes progressively more localized around the site that will be used for breeding the first time. Males are "the primary prospectors within the population" (Ainley *et al.* 1983), spending more time wandering than do females and are likely to breed significantly further from their natal site. For males, in the seasons leading up to breeding for the first time, a period of wandering typically leads to lone occupation of a nest site (or sites), to "keeping company" (Richdale 1951) with a female at a nest site, and, eventually to breeding. Females are inclined to keep company at a younger age than are males, so that the sequence they usually follow leading up to breeding goes: wandering to keeping company to breeding.

Despite this, there is no information available on either the specific nest site characteristics chosen by males when establishing their first territory or the characteristics of individual males that females initially pair with. Most first-time breeding males end up nesting in peripheral nests (Le Resche and Sladen 1970, Ainley *et al.* 1983) but this probably reflects a simple lack of availability of, or lack of ability to compete for, central sites, rather than representing any selectivity or preference for such sites. In Yellow-eyed Penguins, young females often pair with older males (Richdale 1957), but Adelies typically have partners about the same age (Ainley *et al.* 1983). What characteristics females are using to select their initial partner remain a mystery. However, based on prominence of calling in their mating behaviour, they seem likely to include vocal cues.

## DELAYED BREEDING

While in some respects the process of wandering, tending a nest site, and keeping company can be viewed as learning activities whereby young penguins get to practise aspects of breeding before engaging in the real thing (Ainley *et al.* 1983), the terrestrial side of breeding is not the only element that must be learnt. Penguins are relatively long-lived (e.g. Yellow-eyed Penguins can live at least 21 years in the wild (Massaro et al. in press); however, their age at first breeding is quite variable, with many delaying breeding well beyond the time of being physiologically capable of breeding. Delayed breeding is common in many seabirds, but in penguins, offshore foragers have the longest delay to breeding (Croxall and Davis 1999). The mean age of first breeding for offshore foragers (6.2 years) is almost double that of inshore foragers (3.3 years), suggesting that there is an aquatic component to breeding, namely foraging efficiency, that needs to be acquired before breeding is likely to be successful.

# MATE SELECTION

The mating strategies of males and females are quite different. As alluded to above, males are predicted to be the least discriminating sex and having established a nest site could be expected to court any female that comes within range of the nest. In Adelie Penguins, that is exactly what they do (Fig. 6.2a) (Davis and Speirs 1990). In contrast, females are predicted to be much more selective. The 24-hour daylight that characterizes the breeding season of Adelie Penguins at high latitudes (Davis 1995) enables continuous observation of their breeding behaviour once they arrive at the colony. Courtship patterns of females over two breeding seasons, from the time of their arrival at the colony until they were finally paired with the mate with which they shared incubation duties, can all be described by a model that depicts the females' behaviour as a series of conditional responses to the situation they encountered at their sub-colony (Fig. 6.2b) (Davis 1991). These conditional responses can be mimicked by a few simple rules of thumb (N.B. this is not to say that females consciously make these decisions, merely that their behaviour can be replicated using them):

(i)     Return to the previous season's nest site.

(ii)    If the previous season's mate is there and you were 'successful' with him in either of the two preceding seasons, pair with him again. If he is already paired, drive out the other female.

(iii)   Otherwise, choose a new male. But, if your previous mate returns within 7 days and you had been successful with him in either of the two preceding seasons, leave the new male for him.

(iv)    Leave the new male also if a 'better' male arrives at the sub-colony within 2 days. You will be forced to leave, too, if the new male's previous partner subsequently returns to the sub-colony and they had been successful in either of the two preceding seasons.

This pattern illustrates two things. Firstly, it suggests that for penguins, or Adelie Penguins at least, while they may be described as monogamous they are only monogamous to the extent that it means having only one partner at a time. It is more accurate to describe them as serially monogamous. A proportion of females (and consequently, males too) engage in mate switches, with up to 30% or more having two or even three partners during the courtship period (Davis and Speirs 1990). Secondly, females exercise the choice, whereas males are the passive pawns in the mating game. The nest site provides the focal point for reuniting with previous partners, and also the starting point for beginning the search for a new one. Females would appear to attach a high priority to reuniting with a male with which

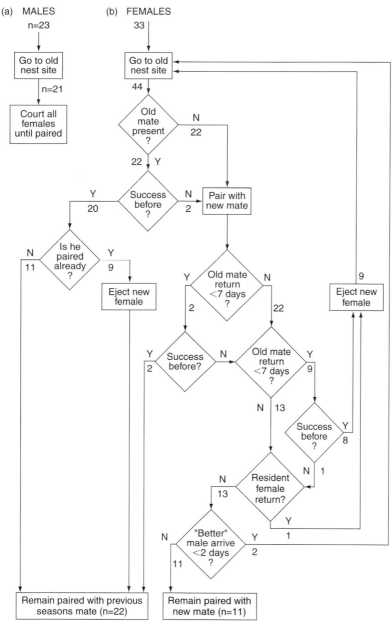

*Figure 6.2. Mating patterns of Adelie Penguins returning to their colony to breed: (a) pattern adopted by 23 males returning to breed within a single season (after Davis (1988b)); (b) pattern adopted by 33 instances of returning females over two seasons (after Davis (1991)). Mating "decisions" are represented as diamonds, while squares indicate outcomes. Key: Y = yes, N = no, numbers = numbers of females.*

they have been previously successful. Such bonds can be broken, however, if the previous male is too late arriving at the colony (i.e. more than a week after the female has arrived and paired with a new male), suggesting that the strength of attachment of females to a new male develops with time spent together. In contrast, no matter how late a female is returning to the colony, if her old partner is already paired and she was previously successful with him, she will usurp the new female, underscoring the strength of the bond that is forged between previously successful partners (Davis 1991).

To what extent is this pattern duplicated in other species of penguins? Although there have been relatively few studies that have observed penguins continuously throughout courtship (allowing mating patterns and mate switches to be monitored), the few that have done so would seem to support this general pattern. Fiordland Penguins exhibit mate switching within the courtship period, albeit at a much less frequent level than Adelie Penguins, and when doing so, they often switch to a previous partner. Two instances have also been observed where mate switching resulted from a female driving out another female from her previous partner's nest (St. Clair *et al.* 1999). Observations on 142 nests of Erect-crested Penguins revealed 11 instances of mate switching, 8 of which involved returning females ousting a female that was already paired with the male (Davis, Renner and Houston, unpubl. data). It appears that in crested penguins mate switching (within a season) occurs at low levels and mate fidelity (between seasons) tends to be reasonably high and constant. A study of Macaroni Penguins found mate fidelity rates of 71–79% over three years, in contrast to Gentoo Penguins where mate fidelity was highly variable, ranging from 0–89% (Williams and Rodwell 1992).

*Gentoo Penguins fighting over mates and nest sites (Photo: Martin Renner)*

Humboldt Penguins frequently copulate with more than one partner in a breeding season (19.2% of males and 30.7% of females), but these are the result of extra-pair copulations (EPCs—see below) rather than mate switching (Schwartz *et al.* 1999).

## DIVORCE

Even though penguins are not the mate-for-life types of popular fiction (Davis 2001a), they do appear to place a high priority on renewing pair bonds from year to year. Where both partners survive and return to the colony the next season, rates of reuniting can range from a high of 93.3% for Galapagos Penguins (calculated from Boersma (1976)) to lows of 15% in Emperor Penguins (Jouventin 1971) and 19% in King Penguins (Olsson 1998). The latter two species are unique among penguins in that they lay only a single egg, which they carry upon their feet in lieu of a nest site. From the observations on Adelie Penguins (see above), it is clear that penguins use the nest site as a rendezvous point; a place where male and female can meet up again. This will be particularly important for offshore breeders, which tend to be migratory and, therefore, absent from the colony between breeding seasons. As the migratory Emperor and King Penguins lack fixed nest sites, they lack the mechanism that could enhance the prospects for reunification and, as a consequence, the *divorce* rate (i.e. the proportion of pairs that do not reunite the following season even though both survive and are present in the colony) is high (Croxall and Davis 1999). However, it is grasping at the wrong end of the stick completely to conclude from this, as do Bried *et al.* (1999), that divorce is *adaptive*. Divorce occurs not because 'the costs of mate retention are high' but because King and Emperor Penguins lack a mechanism that would facilitate reunification. Penguin biologists are not alone in being tempted to ascribe adaptive functions to every little facet of morphology or behaviour, but understanding evolutionary outcomes requires recognition of constraints as much as adaptive design (Gould and Lewontin 1979).

The thrust of Bried *et al.*'s (1999) argument had nothing to do with the previous success or otherwise of the partnership. Divorce to get rid of an unsatisfactory mate is an entirely different proposition: because of the potential advantages, in terms of reproductive output, that could result from a successful pairing. From 68–88% of unsuccessful pairs of Adelie Penguins do not reunite the following season even though both are present, compared with only 20% or less of successful pairs (Spurr 1977, Davis 1988a). Higher rates of divorce in unsuccessful pairs have also been observed in Little Penguins (Reilly and Cullen 1981) and King Penguins (Olsson 1998). (N.B. 'Success' is defined somewhat differently by different authors, but the crucial aspect included in all definitions is that the pair have successfully managed to co-ordinate their pattern of nest reliefs—their foraging and fasting cycles—throughout at least the incubation period (Davis 1988a)).

It seems likely that mate attachment develops from the reinforcement that occurs during nest reliefs, when male and female greet each other with a 'mutual display'

*A pair of Adelie Penguins greet each other with a mutual display, which serves to reinforce the pairbond (Photo: Lloyd Spencer Davis)*

(Jouventin 1982). The long absences of offshore foragers mean that a male and female may experience only two or three nest reliefs over the course of the more than month-long incubation. Frequent nest reliefs (usually daily or thereabouts) occur once the chicks hatch and need to be fed. Hence, the degree of reinforcement of the pairbond (and probably, site attachment too) will be greater for pairs that successfully manage through to chick rearing, compared with those that fail before hatching. In contrast, inshore foragers have much more frequent nest reliefs during incubation and, as a consequence, might be expected to develop stronger pair bonds, even in failed breeders, and therefore show higher levels of mate fidelity.

Whether a pair reunites or not is strongly influenced by the degree of synchrony in arrival of the male and female at the colony the following breeding season. Pairs of Adelie Penguins that reunite arrive on average within 3 days of each other, whereas those that divorce arrive nearly a week apart (Davis and Speirs 1990). Similarly, the median arrival synchrony is only 3.5 days for King Penguins that reunite, compared with 8 days for those that do not; and none reunite if they are more than two weeks apart (Olsson 1998). This suggests that pairs that cannot co-ordinate their movements to and from the colony during the breeding season are also unlikely to be able to co-ordinate their arrival at the colony the following season (Davis and Speirs 1990). Or perhaps it is simply that if nesting failure occurs early in the breeding season, there will have been little opportunity for partners to reinforce their pair-bond (Davis 1991) and develop site attachment, making it less likely that they will return to a particular site and mate. Divorce rates are lowest in migratory species where the female spends the longest time at the nest during the initial part of the breeding season (Croxall and Davis 1999), providing greater opportunity for developing site and mate attachments.

In essence, the propensity for asynchronous arrival to lead to divorce reflects time constraints on breeding. Whatever the advantages of reuniting, birds faced with a limited period in which conditions are suitable to breed successfully cannot afford to wait around too long for a partner, no matter how successful they might have been together previously. Seasonality is more pronounced at high latitudes (Davis 1995), dictating that penguins that breed there must be migratory and, typically, will need to forage quite a way offshore for at least part of the season. Indeed, average divorce rates in offshore-foraging, migratory species (39.7%) are much higher than those in inshore-foraging, residential species (11.3%) (Croxall and Davis 1999). The extended breeding seasons of the latter permit them to wait for Mr Right or Ms Right, as the case may be. Also, the fact that they are residential and a pair may remain together throughout much of the non-breeding season aids re-pairing, reducing the importance of the nest site as a rendezvous point compared to migratory species. For example, Yellow-eyed Penguins and the northern subspecies of Gentoo Penguins often move nest sites between seasons, but as the pair remain together, this need not lead to separation and divorce rates are relatively low: 13% (Richdale 1957) and 3–38% (Williams and Rodwell 1992), respectively.

The effect of time constraints on mating patterns can be seen within the Adelie Penguin, where the imperative to mate quickly is most apparent at the highest latitudes within its range. The courtship period for females (i.e. the time from arriving at the colony at the beginning of the season until they have completed laying) is more than a week shorter than for those breeding at the other end of their range, and there is an indication that divorce is correspondingly higher (Fig. 6.3). Such a pattern could well hold for other species, too, if there were sufficient data available to test it.

## ADVANTAGES OF REUNITING

The mating patterns of penguins clearly indicate that, given the chance, they place a premium upon reuniting with previously successful partners. Yet, while on the one hand it may seem ludicrous that there should be an adaptive advantage to breaking up a successful partnership (a là Bried *et al.* 1999), it is not so straight-forward to demonstrate an advantage to mate retention. Again, the best data available come from Adelie Penguins. A two-year study at Wilkes Station (66°15′S) found that while 81% and 86% of penguins that reunited were successful at rearing chicks in the respective years, somewhat less, 74%, of birds that took a new partner managed to do likewise (Penney 1968, Wienecke *et al.* 2000). However, the much more detailed study of Ainley *et al.* (1983) at Cape Crozier (77°20′S), which examined percentage of pairs fledging at least one chick from 1963 to 1974, found only a slight and non-significant difference between those that retained their mates

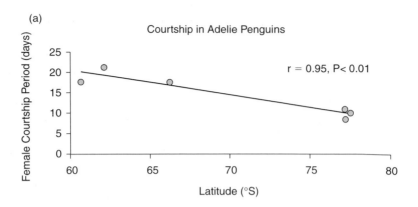

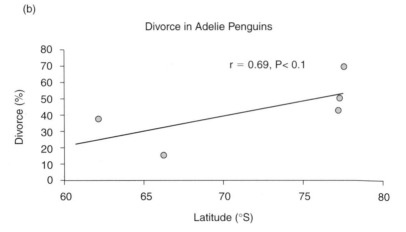

*Figure 6.3.    Relationship of (a) courtship period and (b) divorce rate to latitude in Adelie Penguins. Data derived from, Stonehouse (1963), Penney (1968), Davis (1982b), Ainley et al. (1983), Lishman (1985a), Trivelpiece and Trivelpiece (1990).*

(73.2%) and those that took a new one (68.9%). Furthermore, if any advantage was apparent it was only for birds breeding in their "third (or more) season with the same mate" (Ainley *et al.* 1983).

The chief advantage to penguins of reuniting with their previous partner may come from avoiding the costs of finding a new mate (Croxall and Davis 1999). Failure of a partner to show up the next year resulted in 11% of Adelie Penguins not breeding in Penney's (1968) study. The effect is even more pronounced in Adelie pairs where one member is a young breeder (< 7 years): fully 47.1% of males and 42.5% of females failed to breed if their previous partner failed to return (Ainley *et al.* 1983, Tables 8.13 and 8.14). Following divorce in Macaroni Penguins, 6% of females and 39% of males failed to breed, with the latter taking from 2–4 years to get another mate (Williams and Rodwell 1992). Also, 36% of Gentoo females failed to find a mate after getting divorced (Williams and Rodwell 1992).

The potentially high cost of missing out on getting a partner is probably the reason why penguins exhibit such high levels of nest site fidelity, given that the nest site provides the mechanism for reunification (see above). Seemingly, it should pay penguins to move to better nest sites, given the disparity in productivity between certain sites (Davis and McCaffrey 1986, Seddon and Van Heezik 1991a, Frere *et al.* 1992, Renner and Davis 2001). However, once a pair has nested at a site, the male especially displays a reluctance to shift; and this is most apparent in the migratory offshore-foraging species. Near Admiralty Bay (62° 10'S) on King George Island, South Shetlands, all three species of Pygoscelid penguin breed sympatrically: the offshore-foraging and migratory Adelie and Chinstrap males exhibit extremely high levels of nest site fidelity from one season to the next, 99% and 94% respectively, whereas the inshore-foraging, more residential Gentoo males used the same site only 63% of the time (Trivelpiece and Trivelpiece 1990). While Gentoo Penguins breeding on Bird Island, South Georgia (54°0'S) are more inclined to reuse their old nest site, even there, male Gentoo Penguins are as liable to shift sites as the females (Williams and Rodwell 1992), a result observed on King George Island also (Trivelpiece and Trivelpiece 1990). Furthermore, on the latter, more than two-thirds of Gentoo Penguins changing nest sites moved to different sub-colonies, whereas this rarely happened with Adelie and Chinstrap Penguins (Trivelpiece and Trivelpiece 1990). When Adelie Penguins do change nest sites, males typically move only as far as an adjacent nest site whereas females move further, 2.5 nest sites away on average (Davis and Speirs 1990). The implication is that the costs of shifting, which will include the increased risk of failing to get a mate, must offset the advantage that would accrue from shifting to a better site. Even so, there must be a mechanism that permits birds to recognize their previous site. Pairs that successfully co-ordinate their nest attendance patterns, at least as far as the end of incubation, are less likely to shift (Davis 1988a). Attachment to a site, like that to a mate, will be strengthened by the repeated reinforcement (journeys back to the nest, time spent at the nest) that is a corollary of successful breeding. Successful pairs of Little Penguins, too, seem more likely to breed at the same site (Bull 2000).

MATE CHOICE

Annual adult survival rates are somewhat related to body size, with the largest species tending to live longest (Croxall and Davis 1999). Nevertheless, most adult mortality in migratory species takes place outside of the breeding season during the migratory period. Return rates can be very variable, for example, ranging from 35–73% in Macaroni Penguins and 20–79% in the southern subspecies of Gentoo Penguins (Williams and Rodwell 1992). The failure of birds to return to the colony the following season cannot be entirely attributed to overwinter mortality as, at least in some species, there is growing evidence that birds will sometimes take a year off from breeding or 'sabbaticals' (e.g. Fiordland (St. Clair *et al.* 1999), Yellow-eyed (Darby, pers. comm.), Macaroni and Gentoo Penguins (Williams and Rodwell 1992)). The reasons for this are likely to be due to either the effects of food or climatic conditions (Ainley and LeResche 1973, Hays 1986) affecting the condition of birds prior to breeding (Cullen *et al.* 1992).

Irrespective of the advantages or otherwise of mate retention, then, because of the death or disappearance of a previous partner, or its asynchronous return, many penguins must seek a new partner at the beginning of the breeding season. While pairbonds can endure for many years in the inshore-feeding and largely residential Yellow-eyed Penguin (the record to date is one pair which have bred together for 12 consecutive years (Darby, pers. comm.)), for Adelie Penguins breeding at Cape Crozier, none breed with the same partner for more than three years and most get a new partner just about every year (Ainley *et al.* 1983).

As noted above, males are expected to be none too discriminating and their behaviour conforms to this—they may even try mating with other males (Davis *et al.* 1998). What, on the other hand, are the characteristics that a female penguin seeks when choosing a new partner? Female Magellanic Penguins breeding at Punta Tombo, Argentina (44°02′S), exhibit a preference for males in nests with good cover (D. Stokes and P.D. Boersma in litt.) that provide protection from the sun. However, the basis for female choice is likely to differ according to the species and ecological circumstances. One advantage to studying Adelie Penguins that breed at high latitudes during the austral summer is that, given a certain amount of masochism on the observers' part, the behaviour of the penguins can be monitored

*Confused or just not fussy? a male Rockhopper Penguin attempts to court a female Erect-crested Penguin on the Antipodes Islands (Photo: Lloyd Spencer Davis)*

around-the-clock. This, combined with the fact that both males and females return to their previous nest site and rarely breed outside of their sub-colony (Trivelpiece and Trivelpiece 1990), means that it is possible to study their courtship behaviour in more detail than has been possible for virtually any other species of bird.

A female Adelie Penguin when arriving at the colony at the start of the breeding season returns to her previous nest site where, if her partner is already there, she will pair with him (Davis and Speirs 1990). If, however, her previous mate is absent, she will form a partnership with an unpaired male, typically within minutes or, almost certainly, hours of arriving at her breeding group (sub-colony). Therefore, by knowing which males are unpaired within the sub-colony at the time each female arrives, it is possible to compare the characteristics of males that females choose with those of males that were available to them but they did not choose (Davis 1991).

Perhaps somewhat surprisingly, given the negative impact that skua predation has on the productivity of peripheral nests (Davis and McCaffrey 1986), nest location does not affect the likelihood of males being chosen (Davis 1991) (Fig. 6.4a). Neither does their breeding history, as males that have bred successfully the year before are no more likely to be chosen than males that have not (Davis 1991) (Fig. 6.4b). There is, however, a tendency for females to prefer familiar males that have bred in the sub-colony the previous season from those of new recruits (Fig. 6.4c). The latter are likely to be young, inexperienced breeders going through the process of prospecting for sites (see above). Adelie Penguins are perfectly capable of distinguishing the calls of their sub-colony neighbours from those of unfamiliar individuals (Speirs and Davis 1991).

Indeed, given that vocalizations of penguins are individually distinct (Penney 1968, Nordin 1988, Robisson *et al.* 1989, Bremond *et al.* 1990, Davis and Speirs 1990, Proffitt and McLean 1990, Robisson *et al.* 1993, Bustamante and Marquez 1996, Jouventin *et al.* 1999, Lengagne *et al.* 1999a), aspects of calls could potentially be used by females as indicators of male quality. The call associated with the

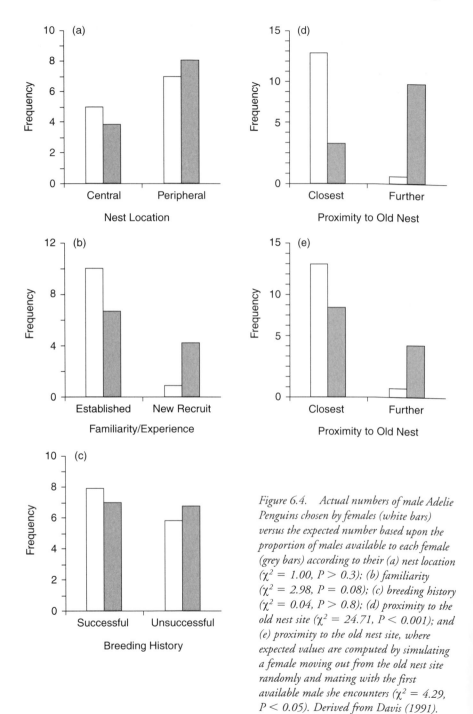

*Figure 6.4. Actual numbers of male Adelie Penguins chosen by females (white bars) versus the expected number based upon the proportion of males available to each female (grey bars) according to their (a) nest location ($\chi^2 = 1.00$, $P > 0.3$); (b) familiarity ($\chi^2 = 2.98$, $P = 0.08$); (c) breeding history ($\chi^2 = 0.04$, $P > 0.8$); (d) proximity to the old nest site ($\chi^2 = 24.71$, $P < 0.001$); and (e) proximity to the old nest site, where expected values are computed by simulating a female moving out from the old nest site randomly and mating with the first available male she encounters ($\chi^2 = 4.29$, $P < 0.05$). Derived from Davis (1991).*

*ecstatic display* (Sladen 1958), or its equivalent (Jouventin 1982), is confined to only males during the courtship period. Unpaired male Adelie Penguins, especially, perform this display in the presence of unpaired females (Davis and Speirs 1990) as well as spontaneously, often in response to other males calling (Davis 1995).

The fundamental frequency of a call is likely to be affected by body size, with largest individuals having the deepest voices. While the probability of a male Adelie Penguin being chosen by a female did not seem to relate to the fundamental frequency of his ecstatic call (Davis 1991), males selected by females had lower frequency calls (using a weighted average) than did males that were not chosen (Davis and Speirs 1990). Given the strong association of the ecstatic call with courtship behaviour (i.e. it is a sexually dimorphic trait, it is elicited by the presence of unpaired females, and females appear to pay particular attention to it, often moving between two ecstaticing males (Davis, pers. observation)), it seems inconceivable that it does not play a role in mate selection. However, just what that role is, is much harder to deduce: the relationship between call characteristics and choice is likely to be a complex one. In essence, a male's ability to provide adequate parental care (the probable basis for female choice) will be determined by his ability to remain on the nest fasting, attending to the eggs or chicks, during the periods when the female is absent. This will be a function of condition and not simply body size (to some extent body size may correlate with fasting ability, as larger males will tend to have larger fat stores). It is entirely possible that the amount of fat may be detectable from the call. A primary storage area for fat occurs around the upper chest overlying the syrinx, the structure that produces the call. It has been proposed that the more fat there is overlying the syrinx, the more it is likely to attenuate the higher frequencies of the call (Davis 2001a). So to a penguin, a sexy voice may well be a deep flat one. More research is needed in this area to pin down the acoustic side of mate selection in penguins.

Be all that as it may, the one feature that distinguishes the likelihood that an Adelie male will be chosen is his proximity to the female's old nest site (Fig. 6.4d). Of course, because females initially return to their old nest site and, if their previous mate is not there, begin their search for a new one from there, it might be that females are simply pairing up with the first unpaired male they encounter and, therefore, exercising no choice. By calculating expected values that each female had of encountering each male available to her (this was done by running 500 iterations of a model whereby the female moved randomly from her nest site and paired with the first available male she encountered) it is apparent that females are mating with the nearest available male to their old nest significantly more often than could be expected by chance (Fig. 6.4e). The advantage to the female of doing this is that it would seemingly enable her to switch back to her previous partner (Davis 1991), which is consistent with the high level of mate switching observed in this species and the premium females seemingly attach to previously successful partners.

# SPERM COMPETITION

While mate switching may well offer benefits for females, it poses a potentially huge problem for males. If females regularly copulate with more than one male during the courtship period *and* males must invest heavily in rearing the offspring: how can males ensure that they are not rearing another male's offspring? Just as there can be sexual selection for attributes that provide advantages in intrasexual competition for mating opportunities, so too there can be selection for attributes post-copulation that enhance competition between the ejaculates of different males for fertilization of the female's ova (Birkhead and Møller 1992). Sperm competition, then, is really just an extension of sexual selection.

Adelie Penguins are particularly suited to sperm competition studies because the 24-hour daylight that characterizes their breeding season means that *all* copulations a female engages in can be recorded. Furthermore, not only is it possible to observe whether a copulation has been successful (i.e. one that led to ejaculation), but also whether insemination occurred (i.e. whether sperm is transferred to the female's reproductive tract) (Hunter *et al.* 1996).

Hunter *et al.* (1995) found that not only did 14.9% of females switch mates during the courtship period (leading to copulating successfully with two or more partners), but 9.8% of females engaged in successful extra-pair copulations, whereby they left their partner briefly to copulate with another male before returning to their partner. While the latter is a phenomenon that has been previously unrecorded in the penguin literature, detecting extra-pair copulations is extraordinarily difficult because of the need to have all individuals readily identifiable from a distance, the brevity of the act and the intensity of observations needed to pick it up. Extra-pair copulations have subsequently been found to be frequent in Humboldt Penguins, where 30.7% of females engage in them (Schwartz *et al.* 1999).

There are two main mechanisms by which the pair male (i.e. the male that provides the parental care) could potentially help ensure that it is his sperm that fertilize the eggs. He could either try to increase the proportion of his own sperm in the female's reproductive tract relative to that of other males—a mechanism known as Proportional Representation—or he could do something that increases the likelihood that, being the last male, his sperm will have precedence—a mechanism called, with all the originality for which biologists are famous, Last Male Sperm Precedence. These two mechanisms are not mutually exclusive. Male Adelie Penguins copulate extremely frequently with their partners throughout the courtship period (an average of 34.4 times for pairs copulating with only one partner (Hunter *et al.* 1996)). However, while ovulation and fertilization are estimated to occur 24 hours prior to laying (Astheimer and Grau 1985), and there is an interval of three days between the laying of the first and second eggs, males typically stop copulating with their partners once the first egg is laid (Hunter *et al.* 1995). In contrast, males of females that had switched partners late in the pre-laying period, continued to copulate with them until the second egg was laid (Hunter *et al.* 1995), which is consistent with increasing the proportion of the pair male's sperm in the female's reproductive tract. It was predicted last male sperm precedence could be enhanced by increasing the copulation rate around the time of fertilization (i.e. 24 hours before laying), but no relationship between the timing of successful copulations and laying was apparent (Hunter *et al.* 1995).

One of the interesting things about courtship in Adelie Penguins is that very often copulation attempts are unsuccessful. A quarter of copulation attempts fail prior to cloacal contact being made, either because the male falls off or dismounts from the female; the female does not assume the appropriate position or stands, throwing the male off; or from disruption by neighbours (F. Hunter and L. Davis, unpubl. data). Even when cloacal contact is made between the male and female (i.e. a behaviourally successful copulation attempt), sperm may not be transferred to the female's reproductive tract either because the male misses the target (18.2% of behaviourally successful copulations) or the male fails to ejaculate (22.9%) (F. Hunter and L. Davis, unpubl. data). Swabs taken from the reproductive tracts of females confirm that when no ejaculate is seen, no sperm is transferred (Hunter *et al.* 1996). Males, it seems, are maintaining high copulation rates to the point that they deplete their semen supply. The interval between a successful ejaculate and the next ejaculation is greater if the second ejaculate is also successful (275 minutes) compared with if it is not (239 minutes) and, furthermore, the interval between successive successful ejaculates increases through the courtship period (F. Hunter and L. Davis, unpubl. data).

Why should males copulate if they are not able to transfer sperm? It may help to ensure that the female remains with the male, or, it could be that males are strategically allocating sperm to copulations. In evidence of the latter, extra-pair copulations are less likely to result in failed ejaculation than are copulations with the female a male is already paired with (F. Hunter and L. Davis, unpubl. data).

An interesting aside to all this is that female Adelie Penguins that are already paired occasionally engage in sex with an unpaired male in exchange for a stone (Hunter and Davis 1998). While the media picked upon this as being an example of prostitution, that is to miss the main point of this behaviour. Stones are important for lining Adelie Penguin nests to protect the contents from meltwater. Appropriate stones can be in short supply around a penguin colony and they are often stolen from other nests and fought over. Typically at the beginning of the breeding season it is the male that does most of the nest building but, before the female departs for sea after completing egg-laying, she often goes to find more stones to shore up the nest. It seems that a few females have learnt that they can dupe unpaired males out of their stones by acting as if they are going to have sex with them. Typically these males are on the periphery of sub-colonies late in the courtship period and, therefore, they are probably young males going through the process of establishing a site (see above).

The female approaches the male on his nest with her head bowed down, in the posture used as a precursor to sex by established couples. The male moves aside and, in a normal copulation, the female would move onto his nest and lie down for the act. In this case, what normally happens is that the female then stoops down, picks up a stone and takes it back to her own nest. If there is an analogy to be made with prostitution, it is much more like they take the money and run!

The males are slow learners because the female may go back to the same male repeatedly and continue to dupe him out of his stones. While attention has focussed on the fact that occasionally the female may actually assume the coital position and the male may get to mount her, it seems unlikely that this has much relevance for sperm competition (because the females are typically post-laying), and it is more likely that this behaviour is actually an alternative form of stone collecting, as noted by Derksen (1975). From the male's perspective, it could be argued that he has little to lose: he does not have a partner, so giving up a few stones matters little even with such slim odds of success. It is much harder to see what could be in it for the female beyond an easy means of collecting stones (although it is possible that extra-pair copulations could be a strategy to insure against male infertility given that 8.9% of Adelie Penguin eggs do not develop (Hunter *et al.* 1996)).

Despite the fact that mate switching and extra-pair copulations may be common in penguins, whatever the mechanisms of sperm competition, it seems that they are effective. DNA fingerprinting, albeit carried out on a fairly small scale to date, has revealed that only rarely does the male providing the care get cuckolded. In studies on Adelie Penguins (Hunter and Davis, unpubl. data) and the Royal subspecies of Macaroni Penguins (St. Clair *et al.* 1995), only a single individual has been found in each study that was not related to the putative father (i.e. the male providing the care). Offspring of Fiordland (McLean *et al.* 2000) and Humboldt (Schwartz *et al.* 1999)Penguins have proved to belong to the putative father in all cases, even though rates of extra-pair copulations are high in the latter.

Given the high level of investment male penguins must make in the care of the young, all this is just as well.

CHAPTER 7

# Parental investment

While the need to lay eggs has tied penguins to the land, this has given them one advantage over their mammalian counterparts. They may more readily adjust the level of their parental investment to the prevailing conditions or circumstances and they may do so at an earlier stage in the breeding attempt.

## THE INITIATION OF BREEDING

There has been little work on what factors initiate breeding in penguins. It is likely, as for most birds (Cockrem 1995), that photoperiod (daylength) is one of the most important—if not *the* most important—proximal cues that penguins use to determine when to breed. But beyond that, nutritional status is likely to play a part. For inshore feeding species such as the African Penguin, where food can be available near to the colonies for large parts of the year, it is possible for breeding to occur in all months of the year (Cooper 1980), although there still tends to be peaks in breeding (Crawford *et al.* 1999). For more seasonal breeders the start of the breeding season will be delayed in years of poor food supply (e.g. Little Penguins (Numata 2000), Magellanic Penguins (Boersma *et al.* 1990)). For Antarctic Penguins, ice conditions can also influence the timing of breeding, with arrival at the colony and breeding being later in years when the ice cover is heavy, necessitating slow, energy-sapping treks across the frozen sea-ice (Ainley and LeResche 1973, Chapter 4). Although this, too, is likely to be related to nutritional status, with birds arriving at the colonies in poor condition for breeding.

*Antarctic penguins, such as these Adelie Penguins, must undertake long energy-sapping treks across the frozen sea ice in years when ice cover is heavy (Photo: Lloyd Spencer Davis)*

If penguins have insufficient fat reserves at the start of a breeding season (i.e. if they do not reach a minimum threshold), it seems that they will refrain from breeding altogether. While heavy ice years may precipitate this in Adelie Penguins, it appears that poor food supplies result in the same effect in lower latitudes in penguins such as Yellow-eyed (Darby and Seddon 1990), King (Jiguet and Jouventin 1999) and African Penguins (Crawford and Dyer 1995). However, J. Darby and D. Fletcher (in litt.) caution against attributing skipped breeding seasons by Yellow-eyed Penguins to the direct effects of food supply on breeding condition: their analysis suggests that while this may occur occasionally, most missed breeding opportunities can be put down to the death or divorce of a partner.

Whatever, given adequate nutrition, penguins are physiologically annual breeders. This even applies to King Penguins (Jiguet and Jouventin 1999), where although they take about 14–16 months to rear a chick successfully (Jouventin and Lagarde 1995), birds will attempt to breed late in the following season. This late laying reduces the likelihood that the chick will have accumulated sufficient reserves to survive the long winter fasts (Cherel *et al.* 1987), and those late-laying birds that are unsuccessful at rearing a chick will lay early the next year (Jiguet and Jouventin 1999). Hence, while King Penguins can potentially produce two chicks every three years (Stonehouse 1960), they are more likely to be able to produce only one chick every two years (Weimerskirch *et al.* 1992). Uniquely, King Penguins have managed to reconcile a breeding cycle that takes more than a year while remaining responsive to annual changes in their environment.

## EGG FORMATION

Female Adelie Penguins begin the process of follicular development while they are still at sea and heading back to the colony to begin breeding (Astheimer and Grau 1985). While the clutch size is typically two, from 56.3% (Astheimer and Grau 1985) to 65% (Taylor 1962) of females will lay a third egg if the first is removed or lost within 24 hours (Davis and Miller 1990). However, none lay a fourth egg, suggesting that no more than three follicles develop during a single season (Astheimer and Grau 1985). Interestingly, obligate brood reducers like the Macaroni Penguin (which rear only one of the two eggs they lay) must also produce three follicles as they will occasionally lay three eggs (Gwynn 1993). After the clutch of two eggs is laid by penguins usually the third yolk becomes atretic and is reabsorbed (Astheimer and Grau 1985).

Depending upon the latitude (the courtship period is shorter the further south one goes), female Adelie Penguins come ashore for an average of 7.1 days at Cape Royds (77°33′S) (Stonehouse 1963) to over two weeks on Signy Island (60°42′S) (Sladen 1958, Lishman 1985a) before the first egg is laid. Yolk deposition takes between 14–17 days for Adelie (Astheimer and Grau 1985) and Fiordland Penguins (Grau 1982). In the Adelie, yolk deposition begins while the female is still at sea (Astheimer and Grau 1985), whereas in the Fiordland Penguin, yolk formation begins soon after the birds come ashore (Grau 1982). Given that penguins must fast when on land, this means that for the Fiordland females, the nutrients for their eggs must be derived wholly from their own body reserves (i.e. they are capital breeders) (Meijer and Drent 1999). Even Adelie Penguins get 96% of the protein and 99% of the lipids for their eggs from endogenous sources (Meijer and Drent 1999).

In Adelies, the eggs are laid an average of three days apart (Spurr 1975b), with the laying interval being a consequence of a regular three-day spacing in the onset of follicular development. This interval appears to be set at the follicular level and is not affected by the nutritional status of the female at the time of laying (Astheimer and Grau 1985) or latitude (Sladen 1958, Taylor 1962, Stonehouse 1963, Reid 1965, Spurr 1975b, Lishman 1985a, Davis and McCaffrey 1986).

So, too, the yolk content of the eggs appears to be more-or-less fixed. In Adelie Penguins, egg mass decreases with laying order; but while the amount of albumin decreases, yolk mass stays approximately constant between first and second eggs, and even in third eggs where the female has been induced to lay another (Astheimer and Grau 1985). Conversely, in Fiordland Penguins, egg mass is greater for the second egg and this is mainly due to increases in albumin (Grau 1982).

While the energy content of the materials used to form the eggs is relatively low compared with the energy expended while fasting—a Fiordland Penguin's clutch of two eggs represents only about 6% of the female's body mass at the start of breeding (Grau 1982)—it seems naïve to suggest, as does Grau (1982), that materials derived from the body's reserves are not in some way limiting for egg production. While only 4% of the lipids utilized during the courtship fast of Adelie females are actually used for the eggs (Astheimer and Grau 1985), at least 40% of the muscle catabolized during this period is used to provide the proteins for the eggs; and Meijer and Drent (1999) calculated that the eggs require 56% of the protein used by females during the laying period. Protein makes up a much higher proportion of the albumin (about 70–80%) than the yolk (about 32–35%) in penguin eggs (Williams *et al.* 1982). Boersma (1982) noted that in Fork-tailed Storm Petrels *Oceanodroma furcata* it is the simple proteins in the albumin that contribute to the growth of the embryo, leading to larger chicks at hatching.

In sum then, when, or even whether, penguins breed is partly determined by their condition. Penguin eggs vary in the amount of albumin; much, if not all, of which must be manufactured from the female's endogenous sources. Investment by females, whereby they mobilize proteins from their own muscles, could potentially result in larger chicks with presumably greater survival prospects. While mobilizing lipid may well not be difficult, we suggest that the same is unlikely to be true for proteins. Traditionally, availability of food to feed chicks has been seen as the limiting factor affecting investment in clutches, but recent studies of seabirds are showing that limitations on parental investment in reproduction can occur during the courtship and pre-breeding period (Davis and Cuthbert 2001).

Intraclutch egg-size variation in Black Kites *Milvus migrans* is partially a consequence of nutritional limitations at the time of laying, and egg size can affect both hatchability and survival of last-hatched chicks (Viñuela 1997). Even when the effects of parental quality are controlled for, larger egg size in Magellanic Penguins does correlate with increased size, mass and survivability of chicks during the first 10 days after hatching (Reid and Boersma 1990). Examination of egg-size in Yellow-eyed Penguins has shown that females invest more into their eggs as they get older and more experienced, up until they are 9–10 years old (Massaro *et al.* 2002).

## THE HORMONAL CONTROL OF REPRODUCTION

The breeding cycle of penguins can be broken into a number of phases: Courtship, Egg-laying (often this is included within authors' definitions of the Courtship Period), Incubation, and Chick Rearing. The latter may also be divided into a Guard phase and a Post-guard phase, depending upon whether a parent is continuously in attendance at the nest or not.

Penguins conform to the generalized pattern of changes in reproductive hormones found in most breeding birds (McQueen *et al.* 1999). That is, plasma levels of oestradiol (in females) and testosterone (in males) are very high during the courtship period, but fall precipitously by the time of clutch completion and remain at low basal levels throughout incubation and chick-rearing (Fig. 7.1). Similar patterns have been observed in Adelie (Groscolas *et al.* 1986, Davis *et al.* 1995, McQueen *et al.* 1999), Emperor (Groscolas *et al.* 1986), Fiordland (McQueen *et al.* 1998), Gentoo (Williams 1992, Mauget *et al.* 1995), King (Mauget *et al.* 1994), Macaroni (Williams 1992), Magellanic (Fowler *et al.* 1994), and Yellow-eyed Penguins (Cockrem and Seddon 1994). The peak in these gonadal steroid hormones during courtship is typically preceded by or coincident with peak levels in luteinizing hormone (LH) (Groscolas *et al.* 1986, Williams 1992, Mauget *et al.* 1995), a hormone secreted by the pituitary gland and responsible for stimulating gonadal growth and the secretion of gonadal steroids in birds.

In species that do not re-lay, such as the Macaroni Penguin and the southern sub-species of the Gentoo Penguin, LH levels usually follow a similar pattern to the gonadal hormones (Williams 1992), with a rapid decrease in plasma LH levels following laying being associated with gonadal regression. However, in the northern populations of Gentoos—such as those breeding at Crozet Island (46°S, 51°E), where laying a replacement clutch can occur—while LH levels decrease after courtship they do not drop to basal levels (Mauget *et al.* 1995). Interestingly, there is a similar disassociation of LH levels and gonadal hormones in Emperor Penguins, which never lay second clutches (Groscolas *et al.* 1986). Emperor Penguins are unusual in that their single egg and, ultimately, their chick is carried on their feet and protected by the brood pouch. LH levels are maintained at quite high levels in

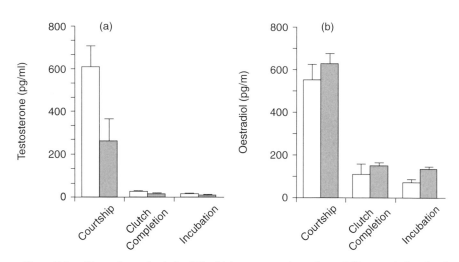

*Figure 7.1.   Mean plasma levels (± SE) of (a) testosterone in males and (b) oestradiol in females of Adelie Penguins (white bars) and Fiordland Penguins (grey bars) during courtship, at clutch completion and during incubation. Data derived from McQueen* et al. *(1998) and McQueen* et al. *(1999).*

Emperors until late in chick-rearing, when the chick is emancipated from the brood pouch, and Groscolas *et al.* (1986) wonder whether it has a parenting function in this species. Certainly LH levels rise in female Emperors during the brooding (guard) phase of chick rearing and decrease significantly in females that have lost their chicks, suggesting that there is a link between brooding behaviour and elevated LH levels (Lormée *et al.* 1999).

The hormone most associated with parental care, but notoriously difficult to assay in birds, is prolactin. In King Penguins, prolactin secretion rises dramatically during courtship, initially faster in females, but remains at similarly high levels in both sexes from incubation through to the end of the first period of chick rearing, while still maintaining quite high levels during the winter and later periods of chick-rearing (Garcia *et al.* 1996). In Emperor Penguins, prolactin levels are basal in both sexes upon arriving at the colony and only start to rise once mating has occurred (Lormée *et al.* 1999). The male is responsible for all the incubation in Emperor Penguins and the rise in prolactin secretion occurs earlier in males than females (Lormée *et al.* 1999).

## LAYING AND BROOD PATCH FORMATION

Under the influence of LH and other hormones then, a clutch of either one *(Aptenodytes)* or two eggs (all other species) is laid. In those species that typically lay two eggs, one-egg clutches are sometimes produced by young first-time breeders (Ainley *et al.* 1983).

Clutch mass varies from species to species and when corrected for body size, clutch mass as a proportion of body mass is smaller for the larger penguins (Fig. 7.2). There is a tendency for clutch mass to be proportionately smaller in off-shore foragers compared with inshore foragers,[1] but as offshore foragers also tend to be larger this could account for the differences (Table 7.1). Considering just off-shore foragers, there is a suggestion that clutch mass (as a proportion of body mass) gets smaller the longer the female is ashore fasting during the pre-laying/courtship period;[2] although, again, such a pattern may simply be a product of a trend for larger penguins to endure longer fasts during courtship. So while it is possible to draw an inference from all this that for offshore foragers, at least, the costs of pro-ducing eggs may be limiting, it could simply reflect constraints on the reproductive system of larger birds.

All penguins are colonial to some degree and coloniality can affect both the tim-ing of egg laying and the extent to which females invest in the eggs. Colonies of Adelie Penguins are highly synchronous in their egg-laying, but the degree of syn-chrony can vary between sub-colonies (Davis 1980). An experiment by Waas (1995), whereby social stimulation in colonies of the Royal subspecies of Macaroni Penguins was increased by playing back recordings of penguin calls, showed that such playbacks hastened the laying of eggs and increased the synchrony of colonies.

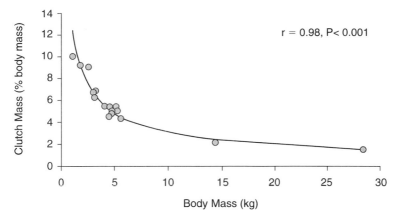

*Figure 7.2. Clutch mass as a percentage of female body mass in relation to body mass. Data from Table 7.1.*

*Table 7.1 Courtship period, body mass of females, clutch mass and laying interval of penguins. Data derived from Williams (1995)*

| Species | Courtship Period for Females (d) | Body Mass of Females (Kg) | Clutch Mass (g) | Clutch mass (% body mass) | Laying Interval (d) |
|---|---|---|---|---|---|
| **Offshore** | | | | | |
| King | 14 | 14.30 | 319 | 2.23 | |
| Emperor | 40 | 28.40 | 469 | 1.65 | |
| Adelie | 8.4 | 4.74 | 239 | 5.04 | 3 |
| Chinstrap | 17.4 | 4.77 | 228 | 4.78 | 3.2 |
| Rockhopper | 11.6 | 3.08 | 192 | 6.23 | 4.4 |
| Fiordland | | 4.03 | 220 | 5.46 | 4.1 |
| Snares | 13.5 | 2.48 | 227* | 9.14 | 4.4 |
| Erect-crested | | 5.43 | 234 | 4.31 | 5.4† |
| Macaroni | 10.5 | 5.31 | 243 | 4.58 | 4.2 |
| Magellanic | 8 | 4.59 | 250 | 5.45 | 3.8 |
| **Inshore** | | | | | |
| Little | 30 | 1.05 | 106 | 10.11 | 2.8 |
| Gentoo | 25 | 5.15 | 258 | 5.01 | 3.4 |
| Yellow-eyed | 30 | 5.10 | 276 | 5.41 | |
| African | | 3.10 | 212 | 6.84 | 3.1 |
| Humboldt | | 4.50 | 203* | 4.51 | |
| Galapagos | | 1.73 | 161* | 9.31 | 3.5 |

\* clutch mass estimated from length and breadth measurements according to Warham (1975)
† laying interval for Erect-crested from Davis, Renner and Houston (Unpubl. data)

Females exposed to exaggerated levels of calls, by playing back calls from their own colony, reduced the time from pairing until laying their first egg to just five days, compared with the eight days taken by control females and females exposed to the calls from different colonies (Waas 1995). Female Erect-crested Penguins that arrive late in the courtship period (when colony numbers are highest and the amount of calling is maximal), show a tendency to produce larger first eggs (Fig. 7.3). One explanation for the latter could be that late-arriving females are in a more advanced state of reproductive preparedness by the time they get to the colony (Ainley 1975).

The incubation period for penguins is long, ranging from just over a month in most to over 2 months for Emperor Penguins (Chapter 6). The chicks hatch in a semi-precocial state, which means that they still require brooding by a parent for a couple of weeks or more to assist them to thermoregulate and to protect them from predators. All this is too much for the female to endure on her own, and males are forced to contribute to incubation and chick rearing, making biparental care a necessity for penguins. This means that not only must the female undergo the physiological changes necessary to induce parental care at the time of laying, but males must also.

Penguins incubate the eggs by covering them with the brood patch, an area of bare skin on the belly that becomes infused with a plexus of blood vessels during incubation. Not all penguins begin to incubate properly as soon as the first egg is laid. While selection for immediate incubation has probably been strong in colder climates to keep eggs viable, in other species there appears to have been selection for only partial or no proper incubation of the first egg until the second egg is laid. This has the effect of reducing hatching asynchrony, such as in Yellow-eyed Penguins (Seddon and Darby 1990), or even helping to reverse it in crested penguins (St. Clair 1992). Development of the brood patch seems to be related to

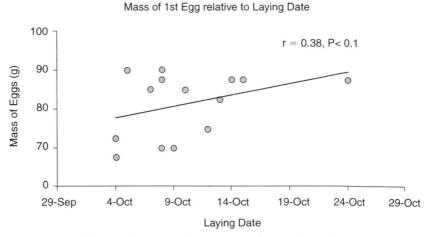

Figure 7.3.   *Mass of first eggs of Erect-crested Penguins in relation to laying date. Data from Davis, Renner and Houston (unpubl. data).*

when penguins start incubating effectively: brood patches probably develop in response to prolactin secretion, but the development of a brood patch can be artificially hastened by placing an egg in the nest of Yellow-eyed Penguins before egg-laying occurs, suggesting that the sight of an egg stimulates prolactin secretion (Massaro, pers. comm.).

The exact timing of brood patch development, then, varies from species to species and is also complicated by the fact that the sex taking the first incubation shift varies: in some species it is the male, in others the female, and in Chinstraps, it can be either (Table 7.2).

Due to their longer foraging trips, incubation spells are considerably longer for offshore foragers (1–2.5 weeks, even excluding the 2 months of Emperor Penguins) compared with the 1–2 days typical of inshore foragers (Table 7.2).

*Table 7.2. Incubation patterns for females. Data derived from Williams (1995) and Croxall and Davis (1999)*

| Species | Sex taking 1st Incubation Shift | 1st incubation Shift (d) | 2nd incubation Shift (d) | Incubation Period (d) |
|---|---|---|---|---|
| **Offshore** | | | | |
| King | male | 18.6 | 18.7 | 53.8 |
| Emperor | male | 64.4 | | 64.4 |
| Adelie | male | 16.6 | 12.3 | 33.2 |
| Chinstrap | female* | 6 | 9.8 | 33.4 |
| Rockhopper | female | 11.3 | 13.9 | 34.2 |
| Fiordland | male | 13 | 13 | 33.5 |
| Snares | female | 12.1 | 12 | 33.5 |
| Erect-crested | female | | | 35 |
| Macaroni | female | 12.8 | 10.4 | 35.5 |
| Magellanic | female | 14.9 | 17.4 | 40 |
| **Inshore** | | | | |
| Little | male | 2 | 2 | 33.4 |
| Gentoo | male | 1.4 | 1.3 | 35.6 |
| Yellow-eyed | male | 2 | 1.8 | 43.5 |
| African | male | 2.1 | 2 | 37.2 |
| Humboldt | male | 1 | 1 | 40.7 |
| Galapagos | male | 1.09 | 2 | 39 |

* Lishman (1985a) states that female Chinstrap Penguins always take the first incubation spell; however, Trivelpiece et al. (1983) maintain that either sex can.

# EGG AND CHICK MORTALITY: THE EFFECT OF
# PROLONGED FORAGING TRIPS

Traditionally, to examine causes of breeding failure, researchers monitored penguin nests at regular intervals that were typically spaced 5–10 days apart. The problem with doing this was that very often researchers were confronted with eggs or chicks that had simply disappeared from one nest visit to the next (Spurr 1975b). In such instances, while it may be reasonable to conclude that some animal (such as a skua) has taken the egg or chick, it is not possible to distinguish between predation (where the animal is responsible for the death of the embryo) and scavenging (where the fate of the embryo has already been determined by other events). This meant that for many years, the importance of losses resulting from prolonged foraging trips—which can result in desertion of eggs and starvation of chicks—went unrealized. It was only by keeping nests under frequent surveillance, so that causes of loss could be ascribed accurately, that the significance for the breeding success of penguins of delayed return from foraging trips was appreciated (Davis 1982b).

Regular monitoring of nests at frequent intervals has another benefit: it allows the application of powerful statistical procedures, known as survival analyses, to identify any significant periods of risk for eggs and chicks from each type of hazard they face (Davis and McCaffrey 1986). These techniques were initially developed for the medical sciences to evaluate the survival of patients. When first applied to penguins, survival analysis revealed that penguins could be amongst their own worst enemies (Davis and McCaffrey 1986). For Adelie Penguins breeding at Cape Bird, Antarctica, many breeding failures were a consequence of the failure of a foraging bird to return in time to the nest to relieve its incubating partner or to feed its chicks. The former caused desertions, the latter, starvations (Davis and McCaffrey 1986) (Fig. 7.4).

An offshore forager can be away from the nest for two weeks or more during the incubation period, necessitating long periods of fasting by its partner left on the nest. Anything that prolongs the forager's absence increases the risk of its not getting back before its partner's reserves are exhausted and the latter is forced to abandon the nest to seek food for itself. Losses due to desertions tend to be highest in offshore foragers and may affect as many as 15–20% of nests (Davis and McCaffrey 1986), or even more (Ainley *et al.* 1983), in a given season. However, the likelihood of desertion will be a function of both the time taken by the foraging bird and the fat reserves of the incubating bird, both of which are likely to vary with foraging conditions. Hence, the prevalence of desertions is highly variable from year to year (Yorio and Boersma 1994b).

As the absence from the nest is shorter for inshore foragers, desertions are less of a problem, but may still account for 3% and 5% of eggs in Yellow-eyed and African Penguins, respectively (Wilson 1985b, Seddon 1989).

Little Penguins tend to be intermediate in their foraging patterns, varying their foraging strategy according to the local ecological conditions (see Chapter 4). In

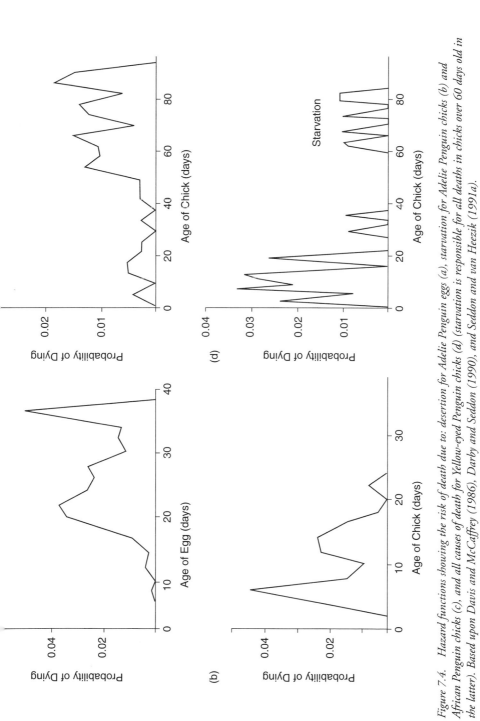

Figure 7.4. Hazard functions showing the risk of death due to: desertion for Adelie Penguin eggs (a), starvation for Adelie Penguin chicks (b) and African Penguin chicks (c), and all causes of death for Yellow-eyed Penguin chicks (d) (starvation is responsible for all deaths in chicks over 60 days old in the latter). Based upon Davis and McCaffrey (1986), Darby and Seddon (1990), and Seddon and van Heezik (1991a).

situations where they adopt an inshore foraging strategy, such as at Oamaru, deser-tions may account for only 9% of eggs (Numata 2000, Numata *et al.* 2000), but where they forage offshore at places like Motuara Island, desertions were responsi-ble for the loss of 27.5% of eggs over two years (Renner 1998).

Although there is some evidence that experience plays a role in influencing the threshold at which a bird will desert—experienced King Penguins will run their reserves lower before deserting than will inexperienced birds (Olsson 1997)—for the most part, it is the fat reserves of the incubating partner that set the limits on how long the foraging bird may be away during the incubation period. In contrast, once the chicks hatch, they set the limit to how long a foraging bird may be away before compromising its reproductive success: chicks need to be fed regularly.

## SURVIVAL OF CHICKS

Survival analyses have revealed that the chief menaces that penguin chicks must face are predation, starvation and, in the case of burrow-nesting penguins especially, rain. Nests of African Penguins can become flooded or collapse as a result of rain. This may affect chicks up to 34 days of age—killing them by drowning, hypother-mia, or smothering—but chicks are particularly vulnerable during the first 10 days of their lives (Seddon and van Heezik 1991a). Nests used by Little Penguins are also subject to flooding, and although Renner and Davis (2001) found no chicks drowned, chicks were at risk of dying due to hypothermia up to 18 days of age.

Predation was always going to be an issue for a bird that nests on the ground and cannot fly, especially where it nests in the open at higher latitudes. Penguins probably evolved their flightless lifestyle in the absence of any serious threat from terrestrial predators (Chapter 2) and they continue to maintain a toehold at breeding sites throughout the Southern Hemisphere because they are largely free of mammalian predators. It is not so much the adults that are vulnerable, but their young. Certainly, where mammalian predators such as mustelids, cats and foxes have been introduced, they have had devastating effects on penguins (Chapter 9). Nevertheless, in the higher latitudes, the threats are mainly from other birds, especially skuas, giant petrels, sheathbills and gulls. Predation by South Polar Skuas *Catharacta maccormicki* is the greatest source of loss of Adelie Penguin chicks; in one study they took 23.2% of chicks within a single season (Davis and McCaffrey 1986). The risk skuas pose to Adelie Penguin chicks is fairly constant until they begin crèching at about three weeks old, and is pretty much nonexistent by the time they are 30 days old and able to fend for themselves (Davis and McCaffrey 1986).

Interestingly, starvation can be a threat to all penguin chicks, but its pattern of risk is quite different for inshore and offshore foragers. Inshore foragers tend to take short foraging trips (<2 days) during incubation and chick rearing. As such, there is little probability that a newly hatched chick will miss a meal or fail to be fed enough to satisfy the modest food requirements for growth at that stage. As they get older, food demands become greater and that is where starvations are likely to be a factor, indicative of the parents struggling to return sufficient resources in the face of either increased demand and/or diminished supplies. Chicks of African Penguins are most at risk from starvation from 42–90 days after hatching (Seddon and van Heezik 1991a), and for Yellow-eyed Penguin chicks the risk does not become significant until they are 60 days old (Darby and Seddon 1990) (Fig. 7.4).

In contrast, for offshore foragers like Adelie Penguins, their chicks are particularly susceptible to starvation at about 6 days of age (Davis 1982b, Davis and McCaffrey 1986) (Fig. 7.4). As the remnants of the yolk sac are capable of sustaining chicks for a few days after they hatch, the likelihood of dying of starvation during the first few days of their lives is nil (Davis and McCaffrey 1986). Newly hatched Adelie Penguin chicks can survive for an average of 6.4 days (range: 5.5–8 days) on their yolk reserves (Reid and Bailey 1966). Hence, the observed peak in starvation risk at 6–8 days (Davis and McCaffrey 1986) suggests that these chicks have not been fed since hatching as a result of the brooding parent not being relieved. Davis and McCaffrey (1986) found that 12.9% of Adelie Penguin chicks died of starvation, much of it due to the failure of a foraging parent to return to the nest around the time of hatching (the parent on the nest is unable to feed the chicks because it will have digested all the food since it last fed).

On Motuara Island in New Zealand's Marlborough Sounds, Little Penguins adopt an offshore feeding strategy with parents taking average foraging trips of 6–7 days during incubation (Numata *et al.* 2000). Failure of an adult to return to the nest to feed chicks at the time of hatching killed 16.8% of chicks and accounted for 34% of all chick deaths (Renner 1998).

Starvation is a major cause of mortality for chicks of crested penguins, especially Snares, Fiordland and Rockhopper Penguins. While this, too, could potentially result from the non-return of a parent (in which case all chicks within a brood would die), the vast majority of the starvation is the result of asymmetrical feeding of offspring, resulting in brood reduction (see below).

Male Emperor Penguins are exceptional in that they incubate the single egg by themselves for over 2 months. It is critical that the female return at the time of hatching to relieve the male and feed the chick. Yet remarkably, the male Emperor has some insurance, being able to manufacture a 'milk' for its chick by breaking down its own oesophageal tissues (Prevost and Vilter 1963). The first detailed study of Emperor Penguins (Stonehouse 1953) concluded that females did not return to specific partners, but passed from one to another until they found a bird willing to surrender its chick. We now know that to be incorrect: they return only to their own.

King Penguins are also a special case, taking over a year to fledge their chicks. This means that the chicks must be left to fast for long periods over winter (in some cases for up to 5 months (Cherel *et al.* 1987)) while their parents go in search of food. Hence, late winter is a time when the chicks are malnourished and prone to starvation (Moore *et al.* 1998). In a way, this mimics what happens to inshore feeders on a much larger scale (i.e. the food supply in the immediate vicinity of inshore foragers is adequate for them to rear young chicks but finding enough food becomes harder as the demands of the chicks increase and the season wears on).

*During winter, chicks of King Penguins are left alone for long periods—sometimes up to 5 months—while their parents forage for food (Photo: Lloyd Spencer Davis)*

## TIMING OF RETURN

Given the critical need for offshore foragers to get back to the nest around the time of hatching to feed their chicks, it is perhaps not surprising that many do. What is surprising is that it appears that penguins possess some sort of timer that tells them when to return to the nest.

It was initially noted that male Adelie Penguins curtailed their time at sea if the hatching of their chicks were imminent (Davis 1982b). Subsequently, the ability of foraging birds to return to the nest about the time of hatching has been confirmed in other studies of Adelies (Davis 1988a, Davis and Miller 1990), other penguins such as Magellanic Penguins (Scolaro 1984), and even flying seabirds that take long foraging trips during incubation such as the Grey-faced Petrel *Pterodroma macroptera gouldi* (Johnstone and Davis 1990).

It is likely that any timing ability will have a hormonal basis to it. Adelie Penguins returning to the colony within five days of their chicks hatching have elevated levels of progesterone (Davis *et al.* 1995). While it is possible that progesterone acts as a stimulus that triggers the return of the foraging parents, it is more likely any observed elevation in progesterone levels is a consequence of other changes occurring in the body at that time. Hormonal studies of Adelie (McQueen *et al.* 1999)and Fiordland Penguins (McQueen *et al.* 1998) did not observe elevated peaks in progesterone just before hatching, although they did not examine that period around hatching in fine detail.

All birds, indeed all animals, have endogenous biological clocks. Typically these clocks are entrained or synchronized by the 24-hour day/night cycle. However, the Adelie Penguin, which breeds during the summer at very high latitudes, is subject to continuous daylight. Preliminary evidence indicates that their internal clocks are free-running (i.e. they are not entrained exactly to 24 hours) with periodicities somewhere between 27–30 hours (Davis 1995). It may be that an entrained circadian clock is of less relevance to their being able to co-ordinate breeding successfully than is a hormonally-based interval timer.

## CRÈCHING BEHAVIOUR

At a certain point in the growth of their chicks, one parent foraging alone cannot cater adequately for the energy demands of their chicks, and it is advantageous for both parents to forage simultaneously. Before chicks can be left unguarded, however, there are a number of conditions that must be satisfied.

Penguin chicks are hatched in a semi-precocial state (Furness and Monaghan 1987), which means that although they are covered in down and can move around, they are still dependent upon their parents for thermoregulation, feeding and protection. Hence, the three conditions that must be satisfied before parents can leave their chicks unattended are: (i) an ability to thermoregulate independently of the parents; (ii) natal site recognition (so as to be able to get back to the nest site to rendezvous with parents returning from the sea with food), and (iii) parent-offspring recognition (ability of parents and offspring to recognize each other so that parental care is not misdirected).

By the time Adelie Penguin chicks are 2 weeks of age they can thermoregulate (Goldsmith 1962) and locate their nest (Spurr 1975a). Parent-offspring recognition is accomplished by learning to recognize each other's calls (Penney 1968). Cross-fostering experiments have shown that adult Adelie Penguins learn to discriminate their own offspring by the time they are 17 days of age (Thompson and Emlen 1968, Davis and McCaffrey 1989), whereas it seems that chicks may learn to recognize their parents by the time they are 11–15 days old (Davis and McCaffrey 1989). Similarly, chicks of African Penguins learn to recognize the features of their nest sites between 12–16 days old, when they begin to explore outside the nest bowl, and their parents are able to recognize them from 17 days onwards (Seddon and van Heezik 1993b). This is consistent with studies of other animals, where selection leads to the development of recognition abilities at the times just before young might normally mix in the wild so that proximity can no longer be used as an unambiguous guide to relationships.

The age at which parents will leave their chicks unguarded seems to be governed by the energetic demands placed on the adults by the chicks. Parents of single chicks will guard them for longer than parents of two-chick broods (31 days versus 21 days, respectively, for chicks of Adelie Penguins) (Davis 1982a). Little Penguins faced with a food shortage as a result of a pilchard die-off left their chicks unguarded three days sooner (15.2 days old) than the next year when there was no die-off (18.4 days) (Renner 1998).

Date of hatching can also influence when chicks are left unguarded in some species. In Chinstrap Penguins, hatching date is negatively correlated with age of crèching, so that chicks hatched later in the season are left unguarded at an earlier age (Viñuela *et al.* 1996). In a clever cross-fostering experiment, Moreno *et al.* (1997) demonstrated that this effect had nothing to do with the provisioning ability of the parents. It is more likely that in crèching species like Chinstrap Penguins, parents of early-hatched offspring must continue to guard them until there is a threshold number of chicks available to form crèches, whereas parents of late-hatched offspring have the luxury of being able to leave their offspring in the care of the crèche as soon as the advantages of having two parents foraging become apparent.

This raises the following questions: what is the function of crèches and why don't all penguins crèche? While being left unguarded is a feature of the upbringing of all penguin chicks, whether they form crèches when left alone depends largely on the species and the situation. A crèche is the aggregating of chicks within a colony and, typically, chicks of surface-nesting penguins that nest at high density will congregate together when left alone. This can include the chicks of penguins belonging to the genera *Aptenodytes*, *Pygoscelis* and *Eudyptes* (Davis 1982a). Yellow-eyed Penguins nest many metres apart, and while in the forest habitat typical of their natural environment they do not crèche, in higher densities associated with flax plantings, chicks from two or more nests may come together occasionally. Burrowing species of penguins belonging to the genera *Spheniscus* and *Eudyptula* are less likely to crèche routinely, although in situations where they breed together on the surface or in caves, aggregations of chicks may occur. African Penguins traditionally breed in burrows dug into the guano cap on islands that host breeding seabirds, but the commercial harvesting of guano has increased the incidence of surface nesting and, with it, the incidence of crèching behaviour (Seddon and van Heezik 1993a).

There have been two main functions ascribed to crèching behaviour, albeit these are not mutually exclusive: (i) protection from predators, and (ii) reducing heat loss and protection from the cold (Davis 1982a). A third possibility—especially in the case of African Penguins where thermoregulation is not so much an issue—is that the crèche protects chicks from intraspecific aggression from adult penguins (Seddon and van Heezik 1993a). In the case of chicks of Emperor Penguins, which must survive in the Antarctic in extremely cold conditions, chicks clearly huddle together for warmth at the end of the Antarctic winter (Jouventin 1975). But for other species it must be recognized that there is a difference between coming together (forming a crèche) and maintaining contact.

For Adelie Penguin chicks, crèching is dependent upon the number of adults in the colony. Adults, by their mere presence, deter skuas, and they may sometimes chase skuas. This is particularly true of 'unemployed birds' (failed breeders or non-breeders that typically return to the colony coincident with the period when the parents are beginning to leave their chicks unguarded), which tend to stand around the periphery of the colony and will often chase skuas attacking chicks (Davis 1982a). This influx of adults without chicks is known as the Re-occupation Period and it has been suggested that by pairing up and forming attachments to nest sites at this time, it increases the probability that these birds will breed more successfully the following season (Spurr 1977). The ratio of adults to chicks in the colony is inversely related to the proportion of the chicks in crèches, with chicks more likely to aggregate when there are fewer adults present (Davis 1982a). In fact, during two seasons at Cape Royds when there was an abundance of young adult penguins present during the Re-occupation Period, crèching did not occur at all (Yeates 1975).

There is a difference between crèching and contact however. While Davis (1982a) showed that the incidence of crèching behaviour for Adelie Penguins was not correlated with environmental conditions, contact behaviour was, with chicks more likely to maintain contact when temperatures were lower and wind speed, cloud cover and humidity were higher. Thermoregulatory costs for chicks when they have just been left unguarded are much higher than for older chicks and, consequently, contact behaviours are more prevalent in chicks that have just begun to crèche (Lawless *et al.* 2001). In sum then, chicks aggregate for protection (usually from predators, but possibly also as a consequence of intraspecific aggression) but they maintain contact with each other to reduce heat loss.

# PARENT-OFFSPRING RECOGNITION

During the post-guard period of chick rearing, parents come ashore frequently to feed their chicks. For species nesting in burrows or in isolated nests (like the Yellow-eyed Penguin), the nest site serves as the meeting place. The nest site is also the rendezvous point in other species (apart from the Emperor, which does not maintain a nesting territory), but as the chicks may be dispersed—especially in those species that form crèches—returning parents announce their arrival by calling when approaching the vicinity of the breeding area.

Mutual recognition is mediated by recognition of calls that the adults and their chicks exchange. For Emperor Penguins, it is the sole means of reuniting, but it is important for all penguins as a way of not only re-uniting with their chicks but also avoiding misdirected parental care.

Penguin calls are individually distinct, with calls of individuals being significantly less variable than the variation that exists between individuals (Bustamante and Marquez 1996, Lengagne *et al.* 1997). Chicks recognize their parents by their calls. Playback experiments demonstrated that post-guard chicks of Snares Penguins were more responsive to calls of their own parents than those of other adults nesting in the colony or calls of Little Penguins (Proffitt and McLean 1990). A problem chicks face, however, is how to discern their own parents' calls from the hubbub of the colony about them. King Penguins respond to windy conditions, which reduce signal to noise ratios in colonies, by increasing the number of calls they emit and the number of syllables per call (Lengagne *et al.* 1999b). Even so, King Penguin chicks demonstrate a remarkable sensory capacity to differentiate their own parents' calls from masking background noise, a phenomenon described as the "cocktail party effect" (Aubin and Jouventin 1998).

# FEEDING CHASES

In Pygoscelid Penguins during the crèching phase of chick rearing, when parents come ashore to feed their chicks they often engage in feeding chases, whereby a parent runs and is closely followed by its begging chicks. Limited forms of feeding chases (where a chick follows its parent before or after being fed) have also been reported at times in species of the genera *Aptenodytes* and *Eudyptes*, penguins that nest in the open and whose chicks form crèches (Bustamante *et al.* 2002). However, the thing to note here is that the crested penguins (see below), King and Emperor Penguins all rear but a single chick, and the half-hearted nature of feeding chases in these species should suggest a clue as to the function or cause of feeding chases. Indeed, in situations where Adelie (Boersma and Davis 1997) and Chinstrap parents (Bustamante *et al.* 1992) have only one chick, feeding chases are much less likely to occur.

*An Adelie Penguin feeds its two competing crèche-stage chicks following a feeding chase that has led them away from the relative safety of the colony and crèche (Photo: Lloyd Spencer Davis)*

There have been a number of different hypotheses put forward to explain feeding chases because, on the surface at least, there would seem to be some cost associated with them: by running from the protection of the colony/crèche, chicks are more exposed to predation (Young 1994, Boersma and Davis 1997). It was initially thought that feeding chases were a means of avoiding competition or interference from chicks that were not the parent's own (Sladen 1958, Penney 1968). In Pygoscelids, when a parent returns to the sub-colony to feed its chicks, other chicks from the crèche—as well as its own—often crowd around begging for food.

However, if feeding chases were primarily to avoid harassment from foreign chicks, then they should be as likely in one-chick broods as two-chick broods, which is not the case.

The best-supported explanation for feeding chases (Bustamante *et al.* 2002) is that they are a means employed by the parents to reduce sibling competition and, therefore, deliver food more equitably to their chicks (Thompson 1981, Boersma and Davis 1997). The feeding chase serves to separate siblings and there is more likely to be a switch in the chick being fed after a feeding chase (Boersma and Davis 1997). If only one chick of a two-chick brood is present (Moreno *et al.* 1996), or the siblings are separated (Boersma and Davis 1997), chasing intensity and the likelihood of chases is much reduced. During feeding chases, Chinstrap parents keep running until their chicks are separated. While it has been implied that a weakness of this hypothesis is that it does not explain how species of penguins raising two chicks, apart from Pygoscelids, reduce sibling competition (Bustamante *et al.* 2002), it should not have to. That is like saying we cannot accept birds' feathers are an adaptation for flight because that does not explain how bats fly. Other penguins do use different mechanisms for reducing sibling competition. Magellanic Penguins use their flippers to keep one chick from monopolizing all the feeds, alternating feeds from side to side (Boersma 1991a). On the other hand, when food is not limiting, asymmetries in sibling competition for food may actually result in a more efficient transfer of food to offspring, as has been suggested for African Penguins (van Heezik and Seddon 1996).

While a negative consequence of size asymmetries and sibling competition is that the smaller chick may not get enough food and die of starvation (van Heezik and Seddon 1991), it is naïve to suggest that feeding chases function to facilitate brood reduction (Lundberg and Bannasch 1983). This can be countered in several ways: (i) while it may be in the individual chick's best interest to monopolize resources, chicks are equally valuable to their parents, (ii) should circumstances dictate that there was some advantage to the parents to reducing the brood (see below), it would be advantageous for that adjustment to occur earlier when the chicks are younger and before the parents have invested too much in the doomed chick, and (iii) the evidence indicates that feeding chases distribute food to the smaller chick compared with situations where there are no feeding chases (van Heezik and Seddon 1996, Boersma and Davis 1997).

## HATCHING ASYNCHRONY AND BROOD REDUCTION

Hatching asynchrony, as the term suggests, occurs when chicks within a nest hatch at different times. Hatching asynchrony is ubiquitous in orders of altricial birds (Stoleson and Beissinger 1995), leading to a size hierarchy amongst the siblings and, in many species, to subsequent brood reduction. David Lack proposed that hatching asynchrony is an adaptation that permits the size of broods to be adjusted to the prevailing food supply (Lack 1947, 1954, 1968). As first-hatched chicks gain a head start on last-hatched chicks, this enables them to outcompete their younger siblings—either by being aggressive towards them or monopolizing food when it is scarce—resulting in the starvation of the smallest chick. Lack's hypothesis predicts that in situations of poor food supply asynchronously hatching broods will produce more chicks than synchronously hatching broods.

With the exception of Emperor and King Penguins—which lay only a single egg—penguins lay a clutch of two eggs with a laying interval that averages 3–4 days (Croxall and Davis 1999). For all crested penguins, the average is on the high side of 4 days (Lamey 1990a) and recent data on Erect-crested Penguins reveals an average laying interval of 5.4 days (Davis, Renner and Houston, unpubl. data). As long as incubation is initiated before clutch completion, then hatching asynchrony is likely.

However, it is extremely controversial as to whether hatching asynchrony really is an adaptation to facilitate brood reduction (Forbes 1994). For penguins, the data are not convincing. In a study of Chinstrap Penguins, Moreno *et al.* (1994) found that any size asymmetries between chicks that resulted from hatching asynchrony disappeared by the crèche stage and that they were not stable (i.e. relative size reversals occurred within broods). Furthermore, where brood reduction occurred it did not improve the growth or survival of the remaining chick. Similar results were obtained from Gentoo Penguins, where chick survival and fledging weights did not vary between synchronous and asynchronous broods in any of five years (Williams and Croxall 1991b). For penguins breeding in colder climates, it has been suggested that hatching asynchrony is simply an inevitable non-adaptive by-product of the need to keep the eggs warm once they are laid (Williams and Croxall 1991b, Moreno *et al.* 1994). Such thermal imperatives are likely to be less important for penguins breeding in temperate to tropical climates, especially burrow-dwelling penguins. Nevertheless, hatching asynchrony does occur in Little Penguins and will induce brood reduction; but it seems doubtful whether the costs of losing the second chick could be compensated for by the slightly larger fledging size of the surviving chick (Renner 1998).

As a consequence of the equivocal data emerging from studies on a variety of birds (e.g. Hahn 1981, Magrath 1989, Hillström and Olsson 1994), numerous new hypotheses have been put forward to explain the adaptive value of hatching asynchrony (Clark and Wilson 1981, Magrath 1990, Stoleson and Beissinger 1995, Stenning 1996). These can be summarized as either adaptations to save time or adaptations—like Lack's hypothesis—to induce a size hierarchy in response to local food supply. Alternatively, some suggest that, as with the penguin examples above, hatching asynchrony may not be adaptive at all (Mead and Morton 1985, Stoleson and Beissinger 1995) or may even be maladaptive (Amundsen and Slagsvold 1991).

On one point there seems to be agreement. Whatever the cause of hatching asynchrony, it can lead to brood reduction. Penguins exhibit the complete range of variation in brood reduction: from no brood reduction in the synchronously-hatching broods of Yellow-eyed Penguins (Seddon 1989, van Heezik and Davis 1990, Edge *et al.* 1999); through facultative brood reduction (where one chick sometimes dies, usually in seasons of poor food supply) in the genera *Spheniscus* (Seddon and van Heezik 1991b, Boersma and Stokes 1995b), *Eudyptula* (Renner 1998) and *Pygoscelis* (Williams and Croxall 1991b, Moreno *et al.* 1994); to the obligate brood reduction in the genus *Eudyptes*, where two eggs are laid but only one chick fledges (Warham 1975, Lamey 1990b, St. Clair *et al.* 1995). This continuum is broadly associated with how far the birds must travel to get their food (Table 7.3). That is, the further a bird must travel to get food, the more difficult it is going to be to bring back enough food to support two chicks until, eventually, as in the case of Emperor and King Penguins, they do not even try to rear two chicks. Even were such a simplistic explanation sufficient to explain why crested penguins were physically incapable of provisioning two chicks, that does not explain why they should lay two eggs.

*Table 7.3.  Foraging distances of penguins in relation to chick rearing ability*

|  | 2 Eggs–2 Chicks | 2 Eggs– sometimes 2 Chicks | 2 Eggs–1 Chick | 1 Egg–1 Chick |
|---|---|---|---|---|
| Foraging Distance (km) during Incubation | <20 | 20–300 | 300–400 | up to 3000 |
| Foraging Distance (km) during Guard Stage | <20 | <100 | up to 120 | up to 300 |
| Examples | Yellow-eyed Gentoo | Adelie Magellanic | Crested penguins | Emperor King |

## BROOD REDUCTION IN CRESTED PENGUINS

The obligate brood reduction of crested penguins remains one of the great unsolved mysteries in the animal kingdom: why would a bird bother investing in two eggs if there was never any likelihood of rearing two chicks? Furthermore, the clutches of crested penguins are notable in other ways too. They exhibit the most extreme intraclutch egg-size dimorphism of any birds and, remarkably, it is the second egg that is larger. The surviving chick tends to be derived from this large second egg. While an increase in egg mass over the laying order is common in small altricial birds, the opposite is typical of seabirds (Clark and Wilson 1981). Yet the second eggs of crested penguins are up to 85% larger than first eggs (first eggs of Erect-crested Penguins average 81.6 g compared with 150.9 g for second eggs, Davis, Renner and Houston, unpubl. data) (Plate 19). Furthermore, while the

laying interval is amongst the longest for any bird, the second egg hatches up to 4 days or more before the small first-laid egg (Lamey 1990a). As a consequence, if both chicks hatch,[3] the chick from the large second egg gets a head start and is able to push its smaller sibling out of the way when competing for food brought back to the nest by the mother (another unique feature of the breeding of crested penguins is that during the three weeks or so of the guard stage, the female does all the provisioning while the male stays at the nest). What could be the possible reason for such a bizarre breeding strategy?

If one accepts that crested penguins cannot successfully provision two chicks to fledging,[4] then an often cited reason for laying two eggs is that the spare egg has an insurance function in the event that the other egg is lost (to predation or other factors) or is infertile. However, this does not explain why it should be the second egg that is favoured. Furthermore, in Macaroni and Erect-crested Penguins, the first egg is typically lost on or before the day the second egg is laid. There is even some suggestion that the first eggs may be deliberately ejected, although work on Erect-crested Penguins suggests that the eggs are more likely to be lost due to neglect rather than deliberate ejection (Davis 2001c). In those species at least, the first egg can have minimal insurance value.

Another hypothesis that has gained a considerable amount of press is that parents reduce investment in the first egg because fighting associated with the courtship period means that eggs are likely to get knocked out of nests and it is the first-laid eggs that are most vulnerable (Johnson *et al*. 1987). The intuitive appeal of this hypothesis is that it offers an explanation for why it should pay females to reduce investment in their first egg and favour their second egg. Williams (1995) rejected this hypothesis, but for the wrong reasons. He dismissed it because the number of fights in crested penguin colonies is on the wane when egg laying peaks (i.e. the peaks of fighting and egg laying do not coincide). But that is not the point. From an evolutionary perspective, the issue is whether first-laid eggs suffer differential mortality as a result of fighting; it does not matter that 'it could have been worse'. The fighting hypothesis can be dismissed because there is little evidence of fighting-induced mortality (St. Clair 1992, Davis 2001c).

So we are left with a situation where we have a mysterious form of breeding but no satisfactory explanation for how it came about.

To begin with, it might be instructive to determine whether the egg-size dimorphism of crested penguins is the result of investment being reduced in the first egg, investment being increased in the second egg, or investment being put into the second egg at the expense of the first egg. For non-crested penguins that lay two eggs, clutch mass averages 6.3% of female body mass, which is only slightly lower in crested penguins (5.9%), suggesting that investment is increased in the second egg at the expense of the first egg. However, clutch mass in the two species of crested penguins with the most extreme egg-size dimorphism, Erect-crested and Macaroni, averages only 4.4% of female body mass, which may indicate that there are resource limitations that affect the way the birds invest in their eggs.

Crested penguins tend to have long courtship periods, where females are ashore for two weeks or more before egg-laying. This means that much of the resources put into the eggs must be mobilized from the female's body reserves (i.e. they are capital breeders (Meijer and Drent 1999)), rather than obtained directly through feeding (i.e. income breeders). While it is true that most other penguins are largely capital breeders too (Meijer and Drent 1999), they tend to arrive at the colony, it would seem, more primed for breeding. In contrast, crested penguins, such as the Erect-crested Penguin, take a less intense approach to courtship. Whereas a female Adelie Penguin will typically form a partnership and copulate within minutes of returning to the colony at the start of the breeding season, Erect-crested females will often reject the initial mating attempts of their partners. Adelie Penguins copulate on average once every three hours throughout the courtship period; by contrast Erect-crested Penguins copulate an order of magnitude less (once every 30 hours) (Fig. 7.5). It seems that the reproductive systems of crested penguins are influenced by the social stimulation they receive from being in the colony. The Royal subspecies of Macaroni Penguins lay more synchronously and more quickly if exposed to playback of other penguins' calls (Waas 1995). Not only do the penguins produce eggs more quickly in response to calls of conspecifics, but the first eggs of Macaroni (Williams 1990) and Erect-crested Penguins that lay later in the courtship period (when the colony is fuller) tend to be larger than those of early breeders (Fig. 7.3). This further suggests that social stimulation affects how readily they can mobilize resources for egg production.

The lack of readiness of crested penguins for breeding is apparent from their demeanour once the first egg is laid. Erect-crested Penguins show little nest building behaviour, may not incubate or, if they do, they do so half-heartedly (Davis 2001c). Williams (1990) has argued that the cost of egg production is low. However, if crested penguins favour the second egg and hatching asynchrony really

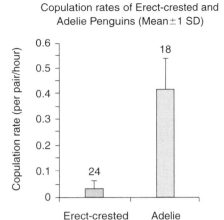

Copulation rates of Erect-crested and
Adelie Penguins (Mean±1 SD)

*Figure 7.5. Copulation rates of Adelie and Erect-crested Penguins. Numbers of pairs are given atop the bars. Data from Davis and Hunter (unpubl. data) and Davis, Renner and Houston (unpubl. data).*

does serve to facilitate brood reduction, then presumably selection should lead to a shorter laying interval (to advantage the second egg) if the process of egg production were not in some way limiting. A.J. Williams (1981) has suggested that laying intervals in penguins are limited by the time required for mobilization and deposition of mineral elements, particularly calcium, to form the heavy eggshell.

If laying intervals become so long that the second egg cannot be relied upon to hatch sufficiently before the first-laid egg for hatching asynchrony to provide an efficient means of brood reduction, then selection might lead to other means of reducing the brood, even if that meant doing away with any insurance function that having another egg may hold. This could lead to neglect or deliberate rejection of the first-laid egg (St. Clair *et al.* 1995). The problem with this argument is that the hormonal mechanisms that induce egg laying are the same as those that induce incubation behaviour and parental care (Mead and Morton 1985). Continuous observation of Erect-crested Penguins during daylight hours over the egg laying period revealed that there was a high probability of the first egg being lost from the nest on the day the second egg was laid (Fig. 7.6), a feature also noted by St. Clair *et al.* (1995) for the Royal subspecies of Macaroni Penguins. However, rather than deliberate rejection—females still displayed a retrieving response if a displaced first egg was placed close to the nest—it seems that most were lost simply as a consequence of mechanical difficulties associated with trying to incubate two such disparate eggs on sites with very little nesting material. Females responded to the greater stimulus offered by the large bright-white second-laid egg, pushing it into the posterior position of their brood patch and then attempted to draw the small, greenish and, by this stage, somewhat dirty first-laid egg into the anterior part of the brood patch. They seemed to find difficulty getting comfortable, because the females would constantly stand up, try to readjust the eggs, turning around in the nest as they did so. To use an analogy, it must be like trying to lie prone across a football and a tennis ball at the same time, making it more difficult for the female to gain a purchase on the small egg. Inevitably, this leads to the small egg being knocked out of the nest. But it was not deliberate ejection. If females were genetically programmed to eject eggs deliberately (and it is hard to imagine how the hormonal mechanisms for egg laying and egg care could be decoupled when they are controlled by the same hormones), it seems extraordinary that they should mainly eject on the day that the second egg is laid.

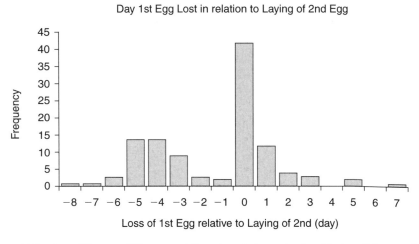

*Figure 7.6.   Loss of first egg of Erect-crested Penguins relative to the day of laying of the second egg (0 = day second egg laid). Data from Davis, Renner and Houston (unpubl. data).*

To come to terms with all this, we need to seek answers in phylogeny. Forgetting about the reversed hatching order of crested penguins for the moment, it seems that hatching asynchrony in semi-precocial birds is the ancestral condition as a consequence of incubation being initiated before egg laying is complete (Stoleson and Beissinger 1995). Indeed, this is true for most penguins. The real question of interest, then, is not why some penguins have hatching asynchrony, but why some might have hatching synchrony.

Here we must examine the Yellow-eyed Penguin. Despite Lack's hypothesis, it seems that hatching asynchrony does have costs associated with it when conditions are good because the smaller chick is put at a disadvantage through the resulting size asymmetries and sibling competition even though feeding conditions may be sufficient (Forbes 1994). Yellow-eyed Penguins, presumably in the face of consistently adequate feeding conditions for parents to provision two chicks, have coun-

tered the effects of the laying asynchrony by getting their chicks to hatch synchronously. They do this by delaying incubation and the onset of brood patch formation. The brood patch does not start to form until after the first egg is laid.
Experiments using artificial eggs have demonstrated that brood patches in both
male and females are stimulated to develop by the presence of an egg in the nest
(Massaro, pers. comm.). As brood patches take more than the length of the laying
interval to develop fully, this means that the clutch does not receive complete incubation until after the second egg is laid, leading to both chicks typically hatching
on the same day.

While some aspects of the phylogeny of penguins are controversial and unre-
solved, there is little doubt that *Megadyptes* are closely related to crested penguins
and basal to them (Edge 1996). In other words, crested penguins are exploiting offshore food sources but are derived from ancestors that probably shared the synchronously hatching adaptations of the inshore-feeding Yellow-eyed Penguins.
Given that the offshore feeding strategy of crested penguins meant that they were
unlikely to be able to provision two chicks and, therefore, needed to reduce brood
size, then the delayed brood patch formation that they inherited from their Yellow-
eyed Penguin-like ancestors (St. Clair 1992), would give the second eggs an
advantage. In part, at least, this is because they are exposed to risk factors for fewer
days. Hence, it seems reasonable that, under those circumstances, selection should
favour a reduction in investment in the first egg. However, even if it were possible
to get rid of it completely and produce a clutch size of only one (and developmen-
tally it may not be possible to favour a second egg without retaining a first egg), it
may not pay crested penguins to do so because the first egg functions to prime the
development of the brood patch and, therefore, initiate full incubation for the
second egg after it is laid.

Maybe it is not such a mystery after all?

## Mate Guarding?

If the eggs of crested penguins were not bizarre enough, their uniqueness continues after the eggs are laid. At that point, in all other penguins, either the male or
female will go to sea to feed, it being necessary to have only one parent on the nest
at a time to incubate the eggs. However, despite the long courtship fast endured by
both male and female crested penguins, both sexes remain together at the nest for
up to 10 days after the completion of the clutch. Typically it is the male that will
eventually leave, with the female remaining to incubate alone; although in
Fiordland Penguins it is the female that will go to sea first (Warham 1975).

In the case of Erect-crested Penguins, by the time the eggs are laid the males have
been present at the colony for well over a month. To say they are starving is not to
put too fine a point on it. And yet, they remain with the female after the eggs are
laid. How long they remain is a function of when the eggs are laid. Males of early
layers stay around for longer than those of later breeders (Fig. 7.7) so that the nett

*An incubating female Erect-crested Penguin is attacked on her nest by two non-breeding birds*
*(Photo: Lloyd Spencer Davis)*

result is that the colony is essentially emptied of breeding males over a very short period of some three days or so. At this point, non-breeding birds, often operating in pairs, will attack females left incubating the eggs. They move from nest to nest, pecking the females and hitting them with their flippers. In some instances, the attacks may be so sustained as to drive the females from the nest. Could it be that the males hang around as a form of mate and progeny guarding?

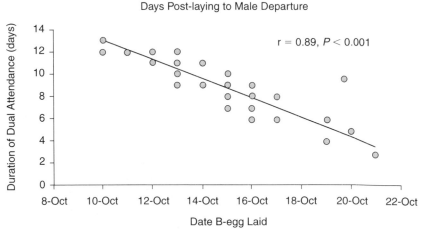

*Figure 7.7.    The period male Erect-crested Penguins remain at the nest after laying relative to the date of laying of the second egg. Data from Davis, Renner and Houston (unpubl. data).*

# FLEDGING

At a certain point chicks depart from the colony and go to sea to feed themselves. Originally, it was thought that the adults initiated this by refraining from feeding the chicks. However, while feeding frequency may decline, adult penguins feed chicks right up until they fledge and it is, in fact, usually the chicks that abandon the adults of their own accord and leave the colony (Burger 1980). Timing of fledging is in part influenced by body mass of the chicks, which, in turn, is influenced by food availability (Bost and Jouventin 1991). There is little doubt that fledging mass is a major, if not the major, predictor of fledgling survival in penguins and the likelihood that they will be recruited into the breeding population (Dann 1988).

For offshore foragers the feeding season and, hence, fledging period, is constrained by latitude; with seasons and fledging periods being shorter at high latitudes (Croxall and Davis 1999). On the other hand, the fledging periods of penguins adopting an inshore foraging strategy increase as the latitude increases. It is as if the more seasonal nature of the food supply at higher latitudes reduces the efficiency of an inshore foraging strategy for transferring food to chicks. Gentoo and Yellow-eyed Penguins, the most southerly-breeding inshore foragers, take 89 and 106 days to fledge their chicks respectively: up to a month longer than the time taken by comparably-sized offshore foragers breeding at similar latitudes. As Croxall and Davis (1999) suggest, perhaps the different feeding and breeding tactics of penguins are not so paradoxical after all, with an inshore feeding strategy suiting the consistent food supplies of the lower latitudes and an offshore strategy suiting the pulsed and more variable food supplies of the higher latitudes.

*A pair of Adelie Penguin chicks at the water's edge ready to fledge. Note the white chin compared to the black chin of the adult plumage (Photo: Lloyd Spencer Davis)*

## CHAPTER 8

# Moult and migration

## MOULT

The very feature that allows penguins to be marine creatures forces them ashore no less than do the demands of breeding. The feather survival suits of penguins wear out and the feathers must be replaced if they are to retain their insulative properties. The problem for the penguins is that the process of moulting is a debilitating one, requiring huge amounts of energy to manufacture the new feathers but, as the effectiveness of the insulation is much reduced while the old feathers fall out and the new ones grow, this means that the birds must be confined to land or ice. As a consequence, they cannot eat and, therefore, must rely on their fat reserves to sustain them through this period of 2–5 weeks as well as powering the growth of the new feathers (Groscolas and Cherel 1992). Energetically, moulting is more demanding than courtship, incubating eggs or brooding chicks. Yet, penguins typically moult after breeding when they have been drained by the demands of rearing chicks. The exceptions are Galapagos and Humboldt Penguins, which moult before breeding, and African and King Penguins, which may moult either before or after breeding (Adams and Brown 1990). Of course, in the case of the low latitude, resident, inshore-feeding Galapagos, Humboldt and African Penguins, where breeding may take place in all months of the year, nature affords such flexibility and what is before and what is after becomes a little academic. For King Penguins, which take more than one calendar year to fledge their young, it depends where they are in their cycle whether, in a given year, moulting takes place before or after breeding. The main point is that moulting is interspersed with breeding.

This means that the parents must engage in a balancing act. They must ensure that there is enough food brought to their chicks to enhance their fledging and survival prospects (fledgling mass is a good predictor of a chick's potential to become a breeder (Dann 1988)), yet they must make sure that there is food enough for them to fatten themselves sufficiently to get through moult. This balancing act is likely to be most critical at highly seasonal, high-latitude breeding locations, where migratory offshore-feeding penguins are typically faced with an abundance of food for a strictly limited period. At a certain point, such parents must make the decision to abandon their offspring and look after their own survival prospects (Moreno *et al.* 1997).

Adult penguins undergo pre-moult periods at sea for anywhere from less than 2 weeks in the case of Antarctic-breeding Gentoo and Adelie Penguins (N.B. Gentoos at lower latitudes take 7 weeks (Adams and Brown 1990)) to 10 weeks for Snares and Fiordland Penguins (Williams 1995). The pre-moult periods of inshore-feeding penguins tend to be quite variable, whereas moulting by penguins at high latitudes tends to be highly synchronous, suggesting that local food availability constrains the timing of moult (Adams and Brown 1990). In non-migratory inshore-feeding species like the Yellow-eyed Penguin, in years of poorer than normal food supply, parents may continue to invest in chicks, delaying the onset of moulting by weeks or even months (van Heezik and Davis 1990). The same luxury is not afforded penguins where their food supply is highly seasonal.

Fat constitutes the major source of energy for fasting penguins while they moult, providing up to 85% of the total energy expenditure for moulting King Penguins, with most of that being derived from subcutaneous fat stores (Cherel *et al.* 1994). Consequently, penguins must use the pre-moult foraging trip to fatten up and they lay down fat at a prodigious rate. The Royal subspecies of Macaroni Penguins increase their body weight by 2–3 kg (Hindell 1988b, Hull *et al.* 2001) during a pre-moult foraging trip of about 36 days, putting on weight at 83.3 g/day (Hull *et al.* 2001). This is necessary because during the four weeks of moult, Royal Penguins lose almost half (46–47%) of their pre-moult body mass (Hull *et al.* 2001). Macaroni Penguins breeding on Bird Island, South Georgia, take only 12–14 days on their pre-moult foraging trips—presumably in response to excellent feeding conditions—putting on weight at an astonishing 178.6 (males) to 208.3 (females) g/day (Williams and Croxall 1991a). King Penguins put on 5.6 kg during their pre-moulting foraging trip, increasing their body weight by 47% at a rate of 328 g/day (Cherel 1995).

While many penguins moult at their breeding sites (e.g. 99% of "Royal Penguins" do so (Hull *et al.* 2001)), this is not always the case. Adelie Penguins breeding on the Antarctic Peninsula moult amongst the pack-ice, whereas sympatrically breeding Chinstrap Penguins moult in or near breeding colonies (Trivelpiece *et al.* 1987). Interestingly, Eudyptid penguins tend to moult at their breeding sites and engage in allopreening if paired (i.e. one bird preens another): moulting Macaroni and Rockhopper Penguins in pairs are more likely to be free of ticks than their unpaired neighbours within the colony (Brooke 1985a).

PATTERN OF MOULT

Moulting in penguins is characterized by all the feathers being renewed simultaneously, thereby requiring the penguins to fast ashore for 2–5 weeks (Groscolas and Cherel 1992). Feather synthesis begins while the penguins are still at sea on their pre-moult foraging trip (Cherel *et al.* 1994). Once ashore, the moulting fast can be characterized by three phases. Phase I, during the first few days ashore, is marked by a decrease in basal metabolic rate (resulting in a rapid decrease in daily body mass loss), mobilization of fat stores and a reduction in protein use (Cherel and Freby 1994). Phase II is a long period of low and steady daily mass loss in keeping with a more or less constant utilization of fat reserves, while Phase III is a period of increasing daily body mass loss due mostly to an increase in protein catabolism as fat reserves become exhausted (Groscolas and Robin 2001). While Phase III may be observed towards the end of the moult fast in King Penguins (Cherel *et al.* 1988), it seems that under normal conditions penguins may complete their moult before their fat reserves reach such a low threshold that increased utilization of body proteins is triggered: at least that is the case for the Macaroni Penguin (Williams *et al.* 1992).

Compared with fasts associated with breeding (when ashore for courtship or incubation), metabolic rates during moult are much higher, being 39% higher for Gentoo Penguins and 63% higher for Macaronis (Davis *et al.* 1989) (although this premium seems to be substantially less in the smallest penguin, the Little Penguin (Gales *et al.* 1988)). Partly this is due to the costs of synthesizing the feathers and partly due to the reduced thermal efficiency. New feathers begin developing under the skin before the penguins return from their pre-moult foraging trip. In Macaroni, Rockhopper and King Penguins, new feathers start to protrude after four or five days ashore when they are already about half their final length (Brown 1986, Cherel *et al.* 1994) and feather synthesis continues for the first three weeks of the fast (Brown 1986), or until day 24 in the case of King Penguins (Cherel *et al.* 1994). In the latter, old feathers begin to fall out on day 12 and it takes until day 21 for this process to be complete (Cherel *et al.* 1994). Hence, for some nine days the penguins are in something of a state of undress with new feather synthesis and old feather loss overlapping. Comparison of moulting and daily mass loss in King, Emperor, Macaroni and Rockhopper Penguins suggests that peak energy demands are associated with a reduction in thermal insulation associated with feather loss rather than feather growth per se (Adams and Brown 1990, Cherel *et al.* 1994), with increased thermoregulatory demands as insulation is reduced. Time to complete moult can be variable, depending upon the season, and in the case of King Penguins, the time of year (Weimerskirch *et al.* 1992), suggesting that environmental conditions may influence the rate at which energy can be devoted to synthesizing feathers.

While a reduction in the thermal effectiveness of their feather survival suits would seem to be reason enough for penguins not to venture into the water when moulting, there is a less obvious reason also. In fact, it should not be assumed that penguins will not go into the water when moulting. Certainly *Spheniscus* penguins breeding in hot climates can sustain at least brief periods in the water: at Punta Tombo, Argentina, Magellanic Penguins will often go to sea before completing the moult (Davis, pers. observation). However, not only does feather loss interfere with the insulation of the penguins, the loose uplifted layer of feathers interferes with the penguin's streamlining. Travelling speeds of pre-moult African Penguins drop from 13.5 kph to only 4 kph during moult: which means that the penguins are probably forced to suspend feeding because they are too slow to catch prey (Wilson 1985a).

While most energy is provided by oxidation of fat reserves, a proportion of the energy is derived from protein (about 15% in King Penguins (Cherel *et al.* 1994)), with moulting birds utilizing protein at about twice the rate of breeding birds. Compared with pre-breeding birds, pre-moulting King Penguins have larger breast and leg muscles. Muscle protein metabolism seems to be influenced by high levels of circulating thyroxine in moulting penguins (Groscolas and Cherel 1992). Penguin feather proteins are rich in the sulphur-containing amino acids, having more cystine than other body tissue proteins or most proteins in their food. A bottleneck in keratin synthesis during the moulting fast is, therefore, the availability of cystine (Murphy *et al.* 1990). Certainly, the plasma levels of several biochemical elements change during the moult fast, suggesting that the birds may need to selectively accumulate nutrients through dietary specialization prior to moulting (Ghebremeskel *et al.* 1989). It seems that King Penguins on their pre-moult foraging trips target myctophid fishes (Raclot *et al.* 1998).

# MIGRATION

The six inshore-feeding species of penguins (African, Galapagos, Gentoo, Humboldt, Little and Yellow-eyed) may remain at their breeding sites all year round. While access to a close year-round food supply will be a prerequisite to remaining resident, Croxall and Davis (1999) posed the question: why should inshore-feeders remain resident?

It seems clear that for penguins breeding at moderate to high latitudes, seasonal changes in productivity, reflected in food supply, are the main stimulants to migration (Croxall and Davis 1999, Putz *et al.* 2000). Additionally, Antarctic species are forced to migrate because their sites become surrounded by impenetrable sea-ice (Croxall and Davis 1999).

Determining where penguins go during their winter migration has proved to be a difficult task especially as the conditions for tracking their movements at sea are often bleak (made more so in the case of the Antarctic-breeding penguins by the winter darkness and presence of pack-ice and ice-bergs). Observations from aboard ships, while limited in their ability to track penguins, have been useful for identifying that Adelie Penguins spend the winter in the pack-ice (Ploetz *et al.* 1991). Aircraft have been used to locate migrating Little Penguins equipped with radio transmitters, which stay reasonably close to shore and do not travel too far from the colony (Weavers 1992). Nevertheless, the only real hope for following the migratory route of penguins rests with satellite telemetry and, recently, the advent of GPS (Global Positioning System) loggers small enough to be fitted to penguins.

Even then, the path has not been an easy one. Apart from issues about device effects, the main obstacle has been developing a means of attaching the transmitters to penguins that will last sufficiently long to cover the entire period of migration (Davis *et al.* 2001), which can be up to 6–8 months depending upon the species. It seems that the feathers to which the devices are attached pull out with the persistent drag and while implantation of devices may be an option (Davis *et al.* 2001), the increasing miniaturization of devices may offer the best prospects of a solution (Ballard *et al.* 2001).

Satellite telemetry of migrating Adelie Penguins that had moulted at two distant colonies in the Ross Sea region of Antarctica (Cape Bird and Cape Hallett) suggest that the birds travel along a common path close to the coastline of the Antarctic continent to an overwintering feeding ground in pack-ice north-west of the Balleny Islands (Fig. 8.1). If the penguins moulting at Cape Bird had bred there *and* data from the limited sample size can be generalized, it suggests that some penguins breeding on Ross Island may need to migrate twice as far as those breeding around Cape Hallett (around 6000 km round-trip versus 3000 km, respectively) (Davis *et al.* 1996, Davis *et al.* 2001). If the costs of migration are in some way related to the distance travelled, then this should have an impact upon life history parameters.

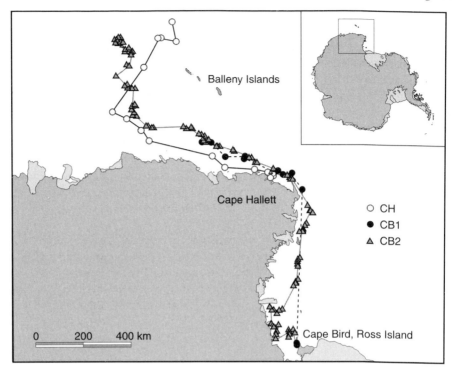

*Figure 8.1.   Migratory routes taken by two Adelie Penguins (CB1 and CB2) from Cape Bird in 1991 and an Adelie Penguin from Cape Hallett (CH) in 1998 (after Davis et al. 2001).*

On the other hand, satellite tracks of two Adelie Penguins known to have nested at Ross Island's Cape Crozier Colony and another two from nearby Beaufort Island travelled to the eastern Ross Sea, consistent with concentrations of Adelies seen there during winter from onboard ships (Ainley, pers. comm.). Two explanations may account for these anomalies. Firstly, it may be that some Adelies from the north-western Ross Sea colonies, such as Cape Hallett and Cape Adare, may—for whatever reason—travel to Ross Island to moult, before returning to overwinter west of the Balleny Islands with other penguins from the north-western Ross Sea colonies. Alternatively, Adelie Penguins breeding on Ross Island are derived from two distinct lineages (Lambert *et al.* 2002), and it is possible that traditional overwinter feeding grounds are different for the two groups.

Most mortality of adult penguins occurs outside the breeding period, suggesting that migration is a time when penguins are most vulnerable. Average annual survival estimates for adult penguins range from 75% for the smallest, Little Penguin, to 95% for the largest, Emperor Penguin (Williams 1995). However, there is a good deal of variation between years and localities. For example, while Adelie Penguins may average 89.4% (Ainley *et al.* 1983), in some years as many as a quarter or more do not return from their overwinter migration (Davis 1988a). If strenuous migration lowers life expectancy, penguins that have to undertake long migrations might be expected to breed at a younger age and have lower levels of mate retention (i.e. not risk forgoing mating while waiting for a previous partner to return) than those taking shorter migrations (Davis 1997). This hypothesis has yet to be tested adequately.

Whereas the Antarctic-breeding Adelie Penguins are away from their breeding colonies for over 8 months, Magellanic Penguins, which breed at more temperate latitudes such as Punta Tombo (44°02′S) in Argentina, endure a migration of some 5–6 months (Stokes *et al.* 1998). They too head north, hugging the South American coastline as they head to winter feeding grounds off the coast of southern Brazil (Stokes *et al.* 1998). Magellanic Penguins breeding considerably further south, at Seal Bay (51°38′S) in the Falkland Islands, appear to follow a similar migratory path, heading for the same anchovy-rich waters found from the River Plate estuary to southern Brazil (Putz *et al.* 2000).

Satellite telemetry of Humboldt Penguins breeding on Pan de Azúcar Island (26°09′S) in northern Chile, revealed that during winter most stayed within a 90 km radius of the island, although one travelled 640 km to the north (Culik and Luna-Jorquera 1997a). However, during periods of food shortages resulting from strong El Niño Southern Oscillation events—when a layer of warm surface water hampers up-welling of cold nutrient-rich waters—Humboldt Penguins from Pan de Azúcar migrated *south*, as far as 895 km down the Chilean coast (Culik *et al.* 2000).

*Pan de Azúcar Island in northern Chile, where Humboldt Penguins breed under desert conditions and are subject to periodic food shortages resulting from strong El Niño Southern Oscillation events (Photo: Loyd Spencer Davis)*

Little Penguins breeding on Phillip Island (38°31'S), Australia, may be present at the colony throughout the year, but during winter many undergo long-term trips away from the colony. The most popular destination is Port Phillip Bay (about 60 km away to the west) and trips averaged 16 days. However, some birds continue to travel westwards along the south Australian coastline, with one reaching 710 km from the breeding colony in under 4 weeks (Weavers 1992).

So to answer the question originally posed by Croxall and Davis (1999): because of the high costs of migration, penguins remain in the vicinity of their colony year-round if they can. While predictable seasonal food shortages force off-shore feeding penguins at temperate and high latitudes to migrate, even inshore-feeding resident penguins will migrate in response to a lack of food brought about by El Niño or other environmental conditions. Penguins are not the fluffy creatures that toy manufacturers would have us believe; rather, they are plastic creatures—at least in terms of their behaviour and how they respond to their environment.

CHAPTER 9

# Conservation

It is one thing to be plastic, quite another to be indestructible. While penguins are able to respond within limits to changes in their environment, this does not make them impervious to environmental perturbations or other threats. And, it seems that it is the inshore feeding penguins, relying on a sustained and localized food supply, that are likely to be most vulnerable to such shocks.

The history of flightless birds coming into contact with humans, especially Europeans, has not been a good one: generally a wave of extinction has followed — from the Madagascan Elephant Bird, to flightless rails on many Pacific islands, to the Dodo (Flannery 1994, Quammen 1997). Yet, remarkably, there are no confirmed extinctions of penguins that have occurred in recent times coincident with the exploration and invasion of the Southern Hemisphere by Europeans.

Unlike other flightless birds, penguins spend most of their lives at sea. Nevertheless, they must still come ashore for breeding, relying on a strip of accessible ground near suitable food sources to raise their young. When on land penguins would seem to be at least as vulnerable as any terrestrial bird: they are easy to capture, their demography renders them slow to react to population crashes, and they congregate in colonies. Combine this with, in some cases, a small population size and you have all the ingredients for an extinction recipe.

Viewed in this light, it is nothing short of incredible that penguins have been so resilient. But we must not be complacent. The well-being of penguins has never been more under threat; their future has never looked so grim.

# DEMOGRAPHY

Some features of the life history of penguins would seem to stand them in good stead for resisting the worst that the world can throw at them. They are long-lived and the extraordinary ability of all penguins to withstand long periods of fasting (Croxall and Davis 1999) makes them well equipped to handle periods when food is difficult to find. A particular breeding attempt may have to be abandoned, but as long as the adults survive, the potential to maintain the population is retained.

On the negative side, penguins have low rates of reproduction. All lay only one or two eggs, and few produce replacement clutches or second clutches. While annual survival rates of adults is quite high—ranging from 75% to 95% (Chapter 8)—post-fledging survival rates tend to be low. Together with what can be substantial losses owing to egg and chick mortality (Chapter 7), this means that most eggs do not produce additions to the adult population. Furthermore, even should they survive to adulthood, penguins do not begin breeding right away. Age of first breeding varies from 2–3 years in Little (Dann and Cullen 1990) and Yellow-eyed Penguins (Richdale 1957) through to 5–6 years in Emperor and King Penguins, and 7–8 years in some of the crested penguins (Croxall and Davis 1999). Average age of first breeding in offshore foraging species (6.2 years) is nearly twice that of inshore foragers (3.3 years) (Croxall and Davis 1999, Chapter 6). Additionally, long-term banding studies of penguins are revealing that the chicks of a few 'super pairs' contribute disproportionately to the next generation, with most other pairs failing to produce even a single chick that will survive to reproduce (Dann and Cullen 1990).

# CONSERVATION

All this means that penguins have a relatively slow capacity to respond to population crashes, with recovery, even if conditions are favourable, likely to take several years. Also, once a population becomes low in number it becomes particularly vulnerable. Small populations have reduced genetic diversity and are more likely to be susceptible to unpredictable fluctuations in the environment. Similarly, a restricted distribution makes penguin populations vulnerable to localized events such as a reduction in food supply, disease, predation or pollution.

The threats to penguins have never been more dangerous to their long-term survival and they have never occurred on so many fronts simultaneously.

EXPLOITATION

Although much less of a problem now, for the better part of the 19th and 20th Centuries, humans exploited penguins directly for their oil, their eggs, and their feathers.

As stocks of Right Whales *Eubalaena glacialis* and fur seals *Arctocephalus sp.* became depleted, whalers and sealers turned their attention to penguins. King Penguins, especially, were harvested for their oil and feathers until they disappeared from Heard Island and colonies on the Falkland Islands (Boersma and Stokes 1995a). On Macquarie Island, King Penguins were commercially exploited for their oil from 1810 to 1911, with one breeding colony being completely extermi-nated by 1840: it took the King Penguins on Macquarie 60–80 years to recover (Rounsevell 1982). Cessation of their slaughter has seen King Penguins recover elsewhere too, re-establishing former colonies (Conroy and White 1973). At Gough Island in the south Atlantic, there is even some evidence that Rockhopper Penguins were used by local fishermen to bait crayfish pots (Williams 1984).

While the harvesting of adult penguins was stopped, the harvesting of their eggs was more persistent. In this regard, it was those penguins that lived most closely in association with human populations that suffered most: the penguins that inhabit the lower latitudes. At the turn of the 20th century there were an estimated 575,000 African Penguins; by the 1990s their numbers had decreased by nearly 70% to 180,000. Although there are a number of factors that have influenced this dramatic decline, excessive egg harvesting is one of the main culprits (Crawford *et al.* 1995). Collecting eggs was suspended in 1969, but in one area alone, more than 13 million eggs were taken over a 30-year period (Frost *et al.* 1976b). Declines in Humboldt Penguin numbers were also initiated by exploitation of their eggs, as well as harvest-ing the adults for food, oil and skins (Hays 1984). But it would be wrong to conclude that harvesting of eggs was an experience weathered by only the inshore foraging penguins of the lower latitudes: Rockhopper Penguin eggs have long been important sources of food on Tristan da Cunha and the Falkland Islands, where they continue to be harvested even today (up to 62,000 eggs are taken annually from Nightingale Island, Tristan da Cunha (Williams 1984)); Gentoo eggs on South Georgia and the Falkland Islands were commonly taken to provide nourishment for the crews of ships; and even Adelie eggs were collected in their thousands (Cott 1953).

HABITAT DESTRUCTION

In some cases, it was the effects of harvesting other seabird products that had a negative impact upon penguins. Again, amongst the hardest hit were the African and Humboldt Penguins, which often made their burrows by digging into the build-up of guano deposited on islands and the like by the masses of other seabirds that bred there, such as pelicans and boobies. Burrows dug into sand are more prone to collapse and birds breeding above ground in the open suffer low breeding success (Seddon and Van Heezik 1991a). In Peru, since the mid-19th century, commercial removal of guano down to bare rock has occurred, making it impossible for penguins to excavate burrows (Paredes and Zavalaga 2001). As a consequence, guano harvesting in South Africa and Peru has been at least partially responsible for the collapse of the African (Cooper 1980) and Humboldt Penguin populations (Paredes and Zavalaga 2001), respectively.

The viability of Yellow-eyed Penguins nesting on New Zealand's South Island has been threatened by the destruction of their coastal forest habitat (Darby and Seddon 1990). While Yellow-eyed Penguins exhibit a strong preference for overhead vegetative cover to protect their nests from insolation (Seddon and Davis 1989), in some areas where farming practices have cleared the land they are increasingly nesting in the open (McKay *et al.* 1999).

*Farming practices impinge on the habitat of penguins, such as these King Penguins on the Falkland Islands (Photo: Lloyd Spencer Davis)*

For Little Penguins breeding in Australia it has been land subdivision for housing (Norman *et al.* 1992) and resort development (Dunlop *et al.* 1988) that has reduced their available breeding habitat. Nine of ten breeding colonies on Phillip Island disappeared during the 20th century and the area occupied by penguins decreased by 60–80% (Dann 1992, Norman *et al.* 1992).

But destruction of habitat is not just a consequence of the juxtaposition of penguins and the populated world of humans. Even in the Antarctic, Adelie Penguin colonies have had their habitat taken over for bases (Wilson *et al.* 1990) and even airstrips (Micol and Jouventin 2001). The construction of an airstrip from 1984–1992 to service the French base at Pointe Géologie (66°S, 140°E) destroyed two islands (Ile du Lion and Ile Buffon) and 10% of the Adelie Penguin nests in the Pointe Géologie archipelago. While the population of Adelie Penguins breeding in the general area has increased significantly since then (Micol and Jouventin 2001), this is likely due to increases either in food availability or in habitat availability (more ice-free areas as a consequence of global warming) rather than the beneficence of the French.

## PREDATION

Being flightless and ground-nesters makes penguins potentially vulnerable to land-based predators and it seems that they must have evolved in areas relatively free of predators (Chapter 2). Habitat destruction by humans and the introduction of foreign predators have often gone hand in hand.

Foxes *Vulpes vulpes* first appeared on Australia's Phillip Island at the beginning of the 20th century (Lade *et al.* 1996), where they have become the major land-based threat to Little Penguins (Norman *et al.* 1992). On Penguin Island in Western Australia, Little Penguins make use of human structures to nest under but these are also favoured basking sites for King Skinks *Egernia kingii*, which prey on their eggs (Meathrel and Klomp 1990). Feral cats *Felis domesticus* used to kill at least 9% of African Penguin chicks produced on Dassen Island each year (Berruti 1986).

Mariners, sealers and whalers, whose ships carried cats and rats, eventually reached the hitherto uninhabited sub-Antarctic islands. On Macquarie Island, predation by cats and rats threatens burrow-nesting seabirds, although they are not considered serious threats to the four species of penguin breeding on the island (Rounsevell and Brothers 1984). House Mice *Mus musculus* were introduced to Marion Island in the 19th century by sealers. When a meteorological station was established on the island in 1948, five cats were taken to the island to control mice in the kitchen: by 1975 there were estimated to be over 2000 cats on the island which consumed 400,000 small petrels annually (Williams 1984) but also were seen to take penguin chicks (Berruti 1981). The cats have subsequently been eradicated from Marion Island, with the last being caught in 1991 (Bester *et al.* 2000).

In many cases, once introduced predators have become established, options for removing them are unrealistic. Predation by ferrets *Mustela furo*, stoats *M. erminea* and feral cats has been identified as the major cause of chick mortality for Yellow-eyed Penguins breeding on the south-eastern coast of New Zealand's South Island (Darby and Seddon 1990, Ratz and Murphy 1999). Although the chicks are available to the predators for only a very limited period, populations of mustelids and cats are maintained in the area because the conversion of coastal forest to farmland has seen populations of rabbits *Oryctolagus cuniculus* flourish in the areas occupied by Yellow-eyed Penguins (Alterio and Moller 1997). There is controversy about the value of having ungrazed vegetation buffers around penguin colonies. It seems that these are just as likely to attract as deter mustelids and cats (Alterio *et al.* 1998, Ratz 2000) and an examination of faecal pellets suggested that rabbits and hares *Lepus europaeus* were as likely to use the ungrazed buffers as they were the grazed farmland (Moller *et al.* 1998). However, any relationship between rabbit numbers, predator numbers and levels of predation on penguins remains unclear. In the meantime, trapping of predators around penguin colonies remains the only effective way of controlling predation of chicks.

Domesticated animals can also provide problems for penguins. Predation by dogs is a major source of mortality for Little Penguins breeding in northern Otago, New Zealand. Of a sample of 181 autopsied birds for which the cause of death could be determined, 30 (17%) were killed by dogs (Hocken 2000).

## HUMAN DISTURBANCE

Even when humans are trying to be kind to penguins, we are at risk of disturbing them as scientist and tourist alike. Some penguins have long been known to panic when approached too closely by humans (Hockey and Hallinan 1981). Measurement of the heart rates of Adelie Penguins have illustrated that even if they show little overt reaction, penguins can exhibit increases in heart rates in response to human stimuli, such as the approach of a human or helicopter, which may be interpreted as an indicator of stress (Culik *et al.* 1990). The negative effects of low-flying planes and helicopters are undeniable, causing massive panic in penguin colonies, nest desertion and exposure to predation (Wilson *et al.* 1991). However, the impact on penguins from merely having humans approach them is much more equivocal. Whereas to measure heart rate, Culik *et al.* (1990) had to capture and handle penguins to fit them with ECG monitors—preconditioning their subjects by having such a stressful encounter with humans—Nimon *et al.* (1995) used eggs with infrared heartbeat sensors placed into nests of penguins, and found that although there might be some initial slight elevation of heart rate to a human visitor that approaches to 3 m from the nest and remains there for 5 minutes, mean rates during the approach and observation period (84.3 beats per minute) were not significantly different to the mean rates before the appearance of a visitor (83.8 beats per minute). Although, incredibly, this paper in *Nature* does not say what species this work was conducted on, presumably they were Gentoo Penguins based upon Nimon's rather small collection of published papers on penguins.

Issues remain about whether visitations by tourists or scientists to penguin colonies have negative impacts on them (Woehler *et al.* 1994). In carefully controlled experiments, Giese (1996) demonstrated that Adelie Penguins exhibited poorer breeding success in response to simulated visits by tourists and nest checking by researchers than did undisturbed colonies. But a lot depends upon the prior experience of penguins as to how stressful they find an approach by humans. Measurements of the stress hormone, corticosterone, demonstrate that the mere presence of humans is stressful for Magellanic Penguins not accustomed to seeing humans, but for birds previously exposed to high levels of human visitation, they do not become stressed by the approach of humans (Fowler 1999). A study of

African Penguins also suggested that they become desensitized to approaches by humans (van Heezik and Seddon 1990).

This capacity of penguins to become accustomed/acclimated to the presence of humans suggests that carefully managed tourism need not negatively affect penguin breeding success. Indeed, this has been demonstrated for Magellanic (Yorio and Boersma 1992), Yellow-eyed (Ratz and Thompson 1999) and Little Penguins (D. Houston, in litt.).

Of course, rather than going to the penguins, sometimes we bring them to us. Exportation of live penguins to zoos contributed to the decline of Rockhopper Penguins on Gough Island (Williams 1984) and Humboldt Penguins in Peru (Hays 1984), with more than 3500 penguins being exported from Peru between 1970 and 1978 (Boersma 1991b). Mortality rates of penguins in zoos were often high (Austin 1978), especially from disease (Flach *et al.* 1990). Advances in penguin husbandry techniques, which include better management of disease, better nutrition and dietary guidelines, and a better understanding of their behavioural requirements, now enables the zoo community to contribute to penguin conservation through captive breeding programmes and education (Diebold *et al.* 1999). Zoos must work towards maintaining self-sustaining populations of penguins if they are to fulfil their potential to be repositories for species to help augment wild populations and reintroduce species to restored habitats (Boersma 1991b).

## FISHERIES

Fishing by humans can pose a direct risk to penguins when there is a danger of them being taken as by-catch. This problem is likely to be most acute where gill-nets are used to catch fish. Autopsies of 185 Yellow-eyed Penguins, found that 21 had drowned after becoming entangled in gillnets and another 21 showed features consistent with having suffered a similar fate. A further 30 gillnet entanglements had been reported to government agencies and, considering the rarity of the Yellow-eyed Penguin on the South Island of New Zealand, Darby and Dawson (2000) considered gillnet entanglements as a significant threat to the viability of the population. For Magellanic Penguins breeding at Ría Gallegos on the Patagonian coast, the situation is even worse, with several thousand penguins being killed in gillnets each year and the numbers of breeding pairs in the colony decreasing by almost 60% between 1986 and 1998 (P. Gandini, E. Frere, S. Ferrari and M. Perroni, in litt.). In the Valparaíso region of central Chile, over 600 Humboldt Penguins and 58 Magellanic Penguins died due to entanglement in gillnets during a six-year period (Simeone *et al.* 1999).

Driftnet fishing, using gillnets in oceanic waters around the Tristan da Cunha group of islands in the South Atlantic, has been identified as causing considerable mortality of Rockhopper Penguins (Ryan and Cooper 1991). It seems that capture probabilities for drift gillnets are much higher than those for fixed gillnets: of 922 Humboldt Penguins caught in fisheries around Punta San Juan, Peru ($15°22'$ S,

75°12′W) between November 1991 and December 1998, most were caught during a 17-month period when fishermen switched from using fixed gillnets to drift gillnets (P. Majluf, B. Babcock and J. Riveros, in litt.). Even longline fisheries can be dangerous for some penguins, with 11 King Penguins being reported caught as by-catch by Japanese tuna longline vessels fishing off Africa between 1992 and 1996 (Ryan and Boix-Hinzen 1998).

Indirectly, fisheries can also pose a threat to penguins where they compete for the same species the penguins feed upon. Overfishing of pelagic shoaling fish by the South African purse-seine fisheries was at least partially responsible for a decline in numbers of African Penguins (Crawford and Shelton 1978). Diet studies of penguins, such as those of King Penguins breeding at Heard Island (Moore *et al.* 1998), Magellanic Penguins breeding in the Falklands (Thompson 1993) and Yellow-eyed Penguins breeding in New Zealand (van Heezik 1990b), suggest an overlap with commercial fisheries and the potential for competition. However, there is a paucity of adequate data available to really establish the extent to which penguins may be affected by fishing activities. While there is evidence that transient variability in krill biomass will be reflected in the breeding performance of upper trophic-level predators such as penguins (Boyd and Murray 2001), the relationship between fishing effort and krill biomass within an area is unclear. This is in part because the availability of krill is affected by age-structured stochastic recruitment (Mangel and Switzer 1998) and large-scale ocean transport pathways capable of moving krill over large distances (Murphy *et al.* 1998). However, modelling the effects of krill fisheries on Adelie Penguins indicates that reductions in breeding success and adult survival can be expected as krill catch increases (Mangel and Switzer 1998).

Ironically, because of the sensitivity of penguins to changes in food availability, it has been suggested that penguins can act as bioindicators of fish and krill stocks (Davis and Miller 1990, Trivelpiece *et al.* 1990, Miller and Davis 1993, Davis 1997). If competition from fisheries really does impact upon them negatively, it is probably the birds that are going to be able to tell us first.

## Pollution and Disease

Of course, it is not just what we take out of the oceans that is the problem, it is often what we put into them. And probably the worst offender in terms of causing problems for seabirds is oil (Camphysen and Heubeck 2001). Between 1981 and 1991, 4215 oiled African Penguins were taken to the South African National Foundation for the Conservation of Coastal Birds (SANCCOB) (Adams 1994). Extrapolating their data from the number of oiled carcasses of Magellanic Penguins found along beaches in Chubut, Argentina, Gandini *et al.* (1994) estimated that more than 20,000 adults and 22,000 juvenile Magellanic Penguins may be killed each year by oil pollution along a 3000 km stretch of the Argentine coast. The toxic effects of oil are also responsible for the deaths of Little Penguins (Harrigan 1992), with one oil spill in Apollo Bay, Australia, resulting in 152 being washed ashore dead and another 166 oiled penguins being recovered, of which only 55 survived (Jessop and Du Guesclin 2000). Even penguins in the Antarctic are not immune to getting oiled (Wilson 1979, Reid 1995).

In recent times African Penguins have had to endure two major oil spills. On 20 June 1994, a freighter, the *Apollo Sea*, sank north of Robben Island releasing about 2000 tons of fuel oil into the sea (Davis 2001a). Approximately 10,000 oiled penguins were collected and transported to a SANCCOB rescue centre where they were cleaned, with just over half surviving and being released eventually (Underhill *et al.* 1999). But worse was to come. On 23 June 2000, another ship, the *Treasure*, sank off the western South African coast between Dassen and Robben Islands with 1300 tons of fuel oil on board. More than 19,000 African Penguins were oiled and, amazingly, about 19,000 (only about 150 oiled adults were known to have died in the wild) were collected by SANCCOB and taken into captivity for cleaning and care (Crawford *et al.* 2000). An experiment to translocate penguins 360 km away from the area of an oil spill had been carried out in Tasmania, Australia, after the *Iron Baron* ran aground in 1995, resulting in 1894 oiled Little Penguins being taken into captivity (Hull *et al.* 1998). This proved to be an effective means of protecting the penguins as by the time most had travelled back to their colony the oil had been dispersed. Consequently, in response to the oil spill from the *Treasure*, 19,500 unoiled penguins were caught on Dassen and Robben Islands and transported to a release site at Port Elizabeth, 800 km to the east (Crawford *et al.* 2000). Satellite telemetry revealed that it took about 18 days for these penguins to swim back to the islands (Davis 2001a). More than 20% of the total population of the species was taken into captivity by SANCCOB during the rescue operation, with less than 2000 of the penguins being lost (Crawford *et al.* 2000). However, it would be naïve to expect that rescue efforts could be mounted on such a large and effective scale for penguins breeding in other locations and, sadly, even for the African Penguin, modelling indicates that low-level chronic oiling can have a greater impact than one catastrophic event (Shannon and Crawford 1999).

While oil is toxic for penguins when ingested, it also clogs their feathers, destroying the insulative and waterproofing properties of their survival suits. In what was perhaps an ethically questionable experiment, oiled penguins swam at slower speeds and had increased heart rates and metabolic rates compared with unoiled penguins (Culik *et al.* 1991). Also, oiled penguins taken into captivity may be more susceptible to disease (Graczyk *et al.* 1995a, Carrasco *et al.* 2001).

Relatively little is known about the prevalence of disease in penguins, irrespective of its relationship to pollution (Clarke and Kerry 1993). Antibodies for avian malaria have been detected in the blood of many penguin species (Graczyk *et al.* 1995b, Graczyk *et al.* 1995c). Antibodies for infectious bursal disease virus, a pathogen of domestic chickens, have been found in Adelie and Emperor Penguins in the Antarctic. It seems that the likely source of such pathogens was chicken taken to the Antarctic to feed humans, which was then disposed of poorly, making it available to scavenging skuas (Gardner *et al.* 1997). Such an infectious agent is suspected responsible for the mass mortality of hundreds of Adelie Penguin chicks.

Of course, penguins are also exposed to ubiquitous pollutants such as heavy metals (Norheim 1987, Kureishy *et al.* 1993, Szefer *et al.* 1993), PCBs and organochlorine pesticides (Monod *et al.* 1992, Sen Gupta *et al.* 1996). While levels found in penguins confined to the Antarctic may be many times lower than levels found in birds such as skuas that range beyond the Antarctic zone (Focardi *et al.* 1992), the low activity of certain liver enzymes suggest that Adelie Penguins may be particularly vulnerable to the toxicity of environmental pollutants (Wanwimolruk *et al.* 1999).

CLIMATE

Although the pollutants that humankind produces may affect penguins directly, their most insidious and threatening effects are much less direct. Historically, it seems that penguins have been responsive to climatic change, switching diet and altering their range (Emslie *et al.* 1998). However, the global warming that has occurred since the middle of the 20th century is seen largely as a consequence of human-induced pollution. On the Antarctic Peninsula, pronounced warming has occurred during the last 50 years, which has seen Gentoo and Chinstrap Penguins expand their ranges southwards (Emslie *et al.* 1998). Increases in the likes of Chinstrap Penguins were initially put down to increased krill availability as a result of the decimation of krill-eating whale stocks by humans (Croxall *et al.* 1984), but these have more recently been interpreted in light of changes in the physical environment, such as changes in sea-ice extent especially as it relates to climatic fluxes

*Global warming has affected colonies of Pygoscelid penguins breeding on the Antarctic Peninsula (Photo: Richard Cuthbert)*

(Croxall 1992). Fraser *et al.* (1992) put forward a hypothesis that changes in penguin numbers on the Antarctic Peninsula are related to environmental warming, which has reduced the frequency of cold years with extensive sea-ice cover during winter. One consequence of fewer cold winters has been to decrease the availability of krill, which, when young, rely on the insulation provided by sea-ice to survive the winters. This seems certain to affect Adelie Penguins and other vertebrate predators in the Antarctic marine food web (Loeb *et al.* 1997).

One analysis suggests that it is the insidious, gradual climate change caused by global warming that is responsible for the population decline of Yellow-eyed Penguins in New Zealand (Peacock *et al.* 2000). Yet there is no doubting that El Niño Southern Oscillation (ENSO) events can have immediate and catastrophic impacts upon penguins. This is especially true of the Galapagos (Valle *et al.* 1987, Boersma 1998) and Humboldt Penguins (Hays 1986, Paredes and Zavalaga 1998, Culik *et al.* 2000). During El Niño events the sea surface temperature increases, resulting in a band of warm water at the surface that prevents upwelling of nutrient-bearing colder currents. As a consequence, productivity is reduced, which ultimately limits the availability of food to the likes of penguins and other higher-level predators in the food web. A strong El Niño, lasting from October 1982 to July 1983 caused massive mortality of the Galapagos Penguin, reducing the population by 77% (Valle *et al.* 1987). The tragedy for the penguins that breed on the eastern side of the South Pacific Ocean is that the frequency of El Niño events has been increasing over the last quarter century. This factor, combined with the species' relatively small population size and limited distribution, places the entire species under real threat (Boersma 1998).

The effects of climatic change and ENSO are not limited to *Spheniscus* penguins. The breeding success of Little Penguins correlates with ENSO events (Perriman *et al.* 2000). Over the last 50 years, the population of Emperor Penguins in Terre Adelie, Antarctica, has declined by 50% because of a decrease in adult survival associated with a prolonged abnormally warm period and reduction in the extent of the sea-ice (Barbraud and Weimerskirch 2001). However, the news is not always bad: global climatic warming is suggested to have contributed to increases in Adelie Penguin numbers in the Ross Sea region of Antarctica (Taylor and Wilson 1990). On the other hand, rising sea surface temperatures associated with global warming are implicated in the massive decline in Rockhopper Penguins breeding on the sub-Antarctic Campbell Island (Cunningham and Moors 1994). Warmer water may also result in algal blooms that produce fatal biotoxins, such as those suspected of killing Yellow-eyed Penguins during 1990 (Gill and Darby 1993).

# OUTLOOK

Of the 16 species of penguins, half are classified as 'endangered' or 'vulnerable' using the criteria for the IUCN Red List categories (Chapter 3) (Ellis *et al.* 1998).

Inshore foragers are disproportionately at risk, with only the Gentoo and the Little Penguin being classified as of 'lower risk'. The limited feeding ranges of inshore foragers makes them particularly susceptible to localized perturbations, whereas offshore foragers have a wider scope for avoiding problems. Ironically, it is through mimicking the foraging flexibility of flying birds that offshore-feeding penguins have been able to protect themselves against some of the limitations that come from being flightless. It is just one way that penguins have evolved to live in their two worlds: the challenge remaining is to live in ours.

# Notes

## CHAPTER 2

1 The exact number of species is a matter of controversy, though most authorities cite 16–18. Much hinges on (i) the status of the subspecies of Rockhopper and Little Penguins, and (ii) the validity of claims that the following truly represent sister species: Little and White-flippered Penguins, Macaroni and Royal Penguins. See Chapter 3 for an evaluation of the evidence.

2 Galapagos Penguins breed on the Galapagos Islands, which straddle the equator. Although they feed in waters that are part of the Southern Hemisphere's currents and most breed on or below the equator, on at least one island the penguins are technically just inside the Northern Hemisphere.

3 N.B. There are some differences between the cytochrome $b$ sequences in the two sources, possibly due to sequencing or transcription errors.

## CHAPTER 3

1 Conservation status as determined by IUCN-The World Conservation Union in the Penguin Conservation Assessment and Management Plan (Ellis *et al.* 1998).

## CHAPTER 4

1 When chicks need to be fed a further factor, C (the amount of energy supplied to chicks), must be added to the energy that must be obtained: $G = I - (RMR + F + C)$.

2 Metabolic rates may vary between the sexes. Female Adelie Penguins, for example, use more energy incubating than do males (Chappell *et al.* 1992, B. Green and L. Davis unpubl. data).

3 $r = 0.81$, $P < 0.01$; data from Heath and Randall (1989).

4 Dense swarms of krill are characteristic of waters at higher latitudes, where upwellings of nutrients support a plankton bloom during the austral summer.

## CHAPTER 6

1   The incubation period of 34 days in Adelie Penguins (Davis and McCaffrey 1986) is exactly that expected based upon egg mass (Bucher *et al.* 1986). However, the incubation periods of Emperor Penguins (2 months) are 50% longer than expected from egg mass alone (Bucher *et al.* 1986), while those of Yellow-eyed Penguins are extremely variable, 39–51 days (Seddon 1989), which may reflect the intensity of incubation and periods when the eggs are left unattended, as is common in Procellariiformes (Boersma 1982).

2   $r = 0.56$, $P = 0.1$

3   $r = 0.74$, $P < 0.04$

## CHAPTER 7

1   Student's *t*-test, $t = 1.70$, $P = 0.06$, one-tailed.

2   $r = 0.55$, $P < 0.1$, one-tailed data in Table 7.1.

3   In Macaroni and Erect-crested Penguins, the small first egg is usually lost well before hatching.

4   While there is some evidence that Fiordland and Snares Penguins may occasionally fledge two chicks (McLean 2000), it seems that they are locked into a system where their ability to rear two chicks is not really tested against the prevailing conditions because hatch asynchrony leads to brood reduction in their young chicks before food becomes limiting.

# References

ADAMS, N. J. 1984. Utilization efficiency of a squid diet by adult King Penguins (*Aptenodytes patagonicus*). *Auk* 101: 884–886.

ADAMS, N. J. 1994. Patterns and impacts of oiling of African Penguins *Spheniscus demersus*: 1981–1991. *Biological Conservation* 68: 35–41.

ADAMS, N. J. & BROWN, C. R. 1990. Energetics of moult in penguins. In *Penguin Biology* (Ed. by Davis, L. S. and Darby, J. T.), pp. 297–316. Academic Press, Inc., San Diego, California.

ADAMS, N. J. & KLAGES, N. T. 1989. Temporal variation in the diet of the Gentoo Penguin *Pygoscelis papua* at sub-Antarctic Marion Island. *Colonial Waterbirds* 12: 30–36.

ADAMS, N. J. & WILSON, M.-P. 1987. Foraging parameters of Gentoo Penguins *Pygoscelis papua* at Marion Island. *Polar Biology* 7: 51–56.

AGNEW, D. J. & KERRY, K. R. 1995. Sexual dimorphism in penguins. In *The Penguins: Ecology and Management* (Ed. by Dann, P., Norman, I. and Reilly, P.), pp. 299–318. Surrey Beatty & Sons, Chipping Norton, NSW, Australia.

AINLEY, D. G. 1975. Development of reproductive maturity in Adelie Penguins. In *The Biology of Penguins* (Ed. by Stonehouse, B.), pp. 139–157. MacMillan, London.

AINLEY, D. G. & LeRESCHE, R. E. 1973. The effects of weather and ice conditions on breeding in Adelie Penguins. *Condor* 75: 235–239.

AINLEY, D. G., LeRESCHE, R. E. & SLADEN, W. J. L. 1983. *Breeding biology of the Adelie Penguin.* University of California Press, Berkeley, Los Angeles & London.

AINLEY, D. G., NUR, N. & WOEHLER, E. J. 1995. Factors affecting the distribution and size of Pygoscelid penguin colonies in the Antarctic. *The Auk* 112: 171–182.

AINLEY, D. G., WILSON, P. R., BARTON, K. J., BALLARD, G., NUR, N. & KARL, B. 1998. Diet and foraging effort of Adelie Penguins in relation to pack-ice conditions in the southern Ross Sea. *Polar Biology* 20: 311–319.

ALTERIO, N. & MOLLER, H. 1997. Diet of feral house cats *Felis catus*, ferrets *Mustela furo* and stoats *M. erminea* in grassland surrounding Yellow-eyed Penguin *Megadyptes antipodes* breeding areas, South Island, New Zealand. *Journal of Zoology* 243: 869–877.

ALTERIO, N., MOLLER, H. & RATZ, H. 1998. Movements and habitat use of feral house cats *Felis catus*, stoats *Mustela erminea* and ferrets *Mustela furo*, in grassland surrounding Yellow-eyed Penguin *Megadyptes antipodes* breeding areas in spring. *Biological Conservation* 83: 187–194.

AMUNDSEN, T. & SLAGSVOLD, T. 1991. Hatching asynchrony: facilitating adaptive or mal-adaptive brood reduction? In *Acta XX Congressus Internationalis Ornithologici* (Ed. by Bell, B. D., Cossee, R. O., Flux, J. E. C., Heather, B. D., Hitchmough, R. A., Robertson, C. J. R. and Williams, M. J.), pp. 1707–1719. New Zealand Ornithological Congress Trust Board, Wellington, New Zealand.

APPS, P. J. 1983. Aspects of the ecology of feral cats on Dassen Island, South Africa. *South African Journal of Zoology* 18: 393–399.

ASTHEIMER, L. B. & GRAU, C. R. 1985. The timing and energetic consequences of egg formation in the Adelie Penguin. *The Condor* 87: 256–268.

AU, D. & WEIHS, D. 1980. At high speeds dolphins save energy by leaping. *Nature* 284: 548–550.

AUBIN, T. & JOUVENTIN, P. 1998. Cocktail-party effect in King Penguin colonies. *Proceedings of the Royal Society of London Series B: Biological Sciences* 265: 1665–1673.

AUSTIN, W. A. 1978. Penguin management at the Detroit Zoo. *International Zoo Yearbook* 18: 66–70.

BALLARD, G., AINLEY, D. G., RIBIC, C. A. & BARTON, K. R. 2001. Effect of instrument attachment and other factors on foraging trip duration and nesting success of Adelie Penguins. *Condor* 103: 481–490.

BANNASCH, R. 1995. Hydrodynamics of penguins—an experimental approach. In *The Penguins: Ecology and Management* (Ed. by Dann, P., Norman, I. and Reilly, P.), pp. 141–176. Surrey Beatty & Sons, Chipping Norton, NSW, Australia.

BANNASCH, R. 1996. Advances in biomechanical studies of penguin swimming. Third International Penguin Conference, Cape Town. African Seabird Group, 2.

BANNASCH, R., WILSON, R. P. & CULIK, B. 1994. Hydrodynamic aspects of design and attachment of a back-mounted device in penguins. *Journal of Experimental Biology* 194: 83–96.

BARBOSA, A., MORENO, J., POTTI, J. & MERINO, S. 1997. Breeding group size, nest position and breeding success in the Chinstrap Penguin. *Polar Biology* 18: 410–414.

BARBRAUD, C. & WEIMERSKIRCH, H. 2001. Emperor Penguins and climate change. *Nature* 411: 183–186.

BARLOW, K. E., BOYD, I. L., CROXALL, J. P., REID, K., STANILAND, I. J. & BRIERLEY, A.S. 2002. Are penguins and seals in competition for Antarctic krill at South Georgia? Marine Biology 140: 205–213.

BARLOW, K. E. & CROXALL, J. P. 2002. Seasonal and interannual variation in foraging range and habitat of Macaroni Penguins at South Georgia. Marine Ecology Progress Series 232: 291–304.

BAUDINETTE, R. V., GILL, P. & O'DRISCOLL, M. 1986. Energetics of the Little Penguin, *Eudyptula minor*: Temperature regulation, the calorigenic effect of food, and moulting. *Australian Journal of Zoology* 34: 35–45.

BERKMAN, P. A. 1992. The Antarctic marine ecosystem and humankind. *Aquatic Science* 6: 295–333.

BERRUTI, A. 1981. The status of the Royal Penguin and Fairy Prion at Marion Island, with notes on feral cat predation on nestlings of large birds. *Cormorant* 9: 123–128.

BERRUTI, A. 1986. The predatory impact of feral cats *Felis catus* and their control on Dassen Island. *South African Journal of Antarctic Research* 16: 123–127.

BESTER, M. N., BLOOMER, J. P., BARTLETT, P. A., MULLER, D. D., VAN ROOYEN, M. & BUECHNER, H. 2000. Final eradication of feral cats from sub-Antarctic Marion Island, southern Indian Ocean. *South African Journal of Wildlife Research* 30: 53–57.

BIRKHEAD, T. R. & MØLLER, A. P. 1992. *Sperm competition in birds. Evolutionary causes and consequences*. Academic Press, San Diego.

BLACK, J. M. 1996. *Partnerships in birds: the study of monogamy*. Oxford University Press, Oxford.

BLAKE, R. W. & SMITH, M. D. 1988. On penguin porpoising. *Canadian Journal of Zoology* 66: 2093–2094.

BOERSMA, P. D. 1975. Adaptations of Galapagos Penguin for life in two different environments. In *The Biology of Penguins* (Ed. by Stonehouse, B.), pp. 101–114. MacMillan, London.

BOERSMA, P. D. 1976. An ecological and behavioral study of the Galapagos Penguin. *Living Bird* 15: 43–93.

BOERSMA, P. D. 1982. Why some birds take so long to hatch. *The American Naturalist* 120: 735–750.

BOERSMA, P. D. 1991a. Asynchronous hatching and food allocation in the Magellanic Penguin *Spheniscus magellanicus*. In *Acta XX Congressus Internationalis Ornithologici* (Ed.

by Bell, B. D., Cossee, R. O., Flux, J. E. C., Heather, B. D., Hitchmough, R. A., Robertson, C. J. R. and Williams, M. J.), pp. 961–973. New Zealand Ornithological Congress Trust Board, Wellington, New Zealand.

BOERSMA, P. D. 1991b. Status of wild and captive penguin populations. *Trends in Ecology and Evolution* 6: 381–382.

BOERSMA, P. D. 1998. Population trends of the Galapagos Penguin—impacts of el nino and la nina. *Condor* 100: 245–253.

BOERSMA, P. D. & DAVIS, L. S. 1997. Feeding chases and food allocation in Adélie Penguins, *Pygoscelis adeliae*. *Animal Behaviour* 54: 1047–1052.

BOERSMA, P. D. & STOKES, D. L. 1995a. Conservation: threats to penguin populations. In *The Penguins* (Ed. by Williams, T. D.), pp. 127–139. Oxford University Press, Oxford.

BOERSMA, P. D. & STOKES, D. L. 1995b. Mortality patterns, hatching asynchrony, and size asymmetry in Magellanic Penguin (*Spheniscus magellanicus*) chicks. In *The Penguins: ecology and management* (Ed. by Dann, P., Norman, I. and Reilly, P.), pp. 1 25. Surrey Beatty & Sons, Chipping Norton, NSW.

BOERSMA, P. D., STOKES, D. L. & STRANGE, I. J. 2002. Applying ecology to conservation: tracking breeding penguins at New Island South reserve, Falkland Islands. *Aquatic Conservation: Marine and Freshwater Ecosystems* 12: 63–74.

BOERSMA, P. D., STOKES, D. L. & YORIO, P. M. 1990. Reproductive variability and historical change of Magellanic Penguins (*Spheniscus magellanicus*) at Punta Tombo, Argentina. In *Penguin Biology* (Ed. by Davis, L. S. and Darby, J. T.), pp. 13–44. Academic Press, Inc., San Diego, California.

BOST, C. A. & JOUVENTIN, P. 1990. Evolutionary Ecology of Gentoo Penguins (*Pygoscelis papua*). In *Penguin Biology* (Ed. by Davis, L. S. and Darby, J. T.), pp. 85–112. Academic Press, San Diego, California.

BOST, C. A. & JOUVENTIN, P. 1991. Relationship between fledging weight and food availability in seabird populations: is the Gentoo Penguin a good model? *Oikos* 60: 113–114.

BOST, C. A., KOUBBI, P., GENEVOIS, F., RUCHON, L. & RIDOUX, V. 1994. Gentoo Penguin *Pygoscelis papua* diet as an indicator of planktonic availability in the Kerguelen Islands. *Polar Biology* 14: 147–153.

BOSWALL, J. 1972. The South American Sea Lion *Otaria byronia* as a predator on penguins. *Bulletin of British Ornithological Club* 92: 129–132.

BOYD, I. L. & MURRAY, A. W. A. 2001. Monitoring a marine ecosystem using responses of upper trophic level predators. *Journal of Animal Ecology* 70: 747–760.

BREMOND, J. C., AUBIN, T., NYAMSI, R. M. & ROBISSON, P. 1990. Song of the Emperor Penguin (*Aptenodytes forsteri*): Research of parameters likely to be used for individual recognition. *Comptes Rendus Des Sciendes* 311 serie III: 31–35.

BRIED, J., JIGUET, F. & JOUVENTIN, P. 1999. Why do *Aptenodytes* penguins have high divorce rates? *Auk* 116: 504–512.

BROOKE, M. 1985a. The effect of allopreening on tick burdens of molting Eudyptid penguins. *Auk* 102: 893–895.

BROOKE, M. D. L. 1985b. Skua predation on penguin eggs: the influence of egg quality and location. *The Wilson Bulletin* 97: 366–368.

BROOKE, R. K. & WALLER, T. S. 1976. Shark predation on seabirds in natal waters. *Ostrich* 47: 126.

BROWN, C. R. 1986. Feather growth, mass loss and duration of moult in Macaroni and Rockhopper Penguins. *Ostrich* 57: 180–184.

BROWN, C. R. & KLAGES, N. T. W. 1987. Seasonal and annual variation in diets of Macaroni (*Eudyptes chrysolophus chrysolophus*) and Southern Rockhopper (*E. chrysocome chrysocome*) Penguins at Sub-antarctic Marion Island. *Journal of Zoology* 212: 7–28.

BUCHER, T. L., BARTHOLOMEW, G. A., TRIVELPIECE, W. Z. & VOLKMAN, N. J. 1986. Metabolism, growth, and activity in Adélie and Emperor Penguin embryos. *Auk* 103: 485–493.

BULL, L. 2000. Fidelity and breeding success of the Blue Penguin *Eudyptula minor* on Matiu-Somes Island, Wellington, New Zealand. *New Zealand Journal of Zoology* 27: 291–298.

BURGER, A. E. 1991. Maximum diving depths and underwater foraging in alcids and penguins. In *Studies of high-latitude seabirds. 1. Behavioural, energetic, and oceanographic aspects of seabird feeding ecology.* (Ed. by Montevecchi, W. A. and Gaston, A. J.), pp. 9–15. Canadian Wildlife Service.

BURGER, J. 1980. The transition to independence and postfledging care in seabirds. In *Behaviour of Marine Animals, Vol 4: Marine Birds* (Ed. by Burger, J., Olla, B. L. and Winn, H. E.), pp. 367–447. Plenum Press, New York.

BURLEY, N. 1981. The evolution of sexual indistinguishability. In *Natural selection and social behavior, recent research and new theory* (Ed. by Alexander, R. D. and Tinkle, D. W.), pp. 121–137. Chiron Press, New York.

BUSTAMANTE, J., BOERSMA, P. D. & DAVIS, L. S. 2002. Feeding chases in penguins: begging competition on the run? In *The evolution of begging: competition, cooperation and communication* (Ed. by Wright, J. and Leonard, M. L.), pp. 303–318. Kluwer Academic Publishers, Dordrecht, The Netherlands.

BUSTAMANTE, J., CUERVO, J. J. & MORENO, J. 1992. The function of feeding chases in the Chinstrap Penguin, *Pygoscelis antarctica*. *Animal Behaviour* 44: 753–759.

BUSTAMANTE, J. & MARQUEZ, R. 1996. Vocalizations of the Chinstrap Penguin *Pygoscelis antarctica*. *Colonial Waterbirds* 19: 101–110.

CAMPHYSEN, C. J. & HEUBECK, M. 2001. Marine oil pollution and beached bird surveys: the development of a sensitive monitoring instrument. *Environmental Pollution* 112: 443–461.

CARRASCO, L., LIMA, J. S., HALFEN, D. C., SALGUERO, F. J., SANCHEZ-CORDON, P. & BECKER, G. 2001. Systemic aspergillosis in an oiled Magellanic Penguin (*Spheniscus magellanicus*). *Journal of Veterinary Medicine Series B-Infectious Diseases and Veterinary Public Health* 48: 551–554.

CHAPPELL, M. A., JANES, D. N., BUTCHER, T. L. & SHOEMAKER, V. H. 1992. Reproductive effort, diving behaviour, and foraging energetics in Adelie Penguins. *Antarctic Journal of the United States* 27: 145–146.

CHAPPELL, M. A., JANES, D. N., SHOEMAKER, V. H., BUCHER, T. L. & MALONEY, S. K. 1993a. Reproductive effort in Adelie Penguins. *Behavioural Ecology and Sociobiology* 33: 173–182.

CHAPPELL, M. A., SHOEMAKER, V. H., JANES, D. N., MALONEY, S. K. & BUCHER, T. L. 1993b. Energetics of foraging in breeding Adélie Penguins. *Ecology* 74: 2450–2461.

CHAPPELL, M. A. & SOUZA, S. L. 1988. Thermoregulation, gas exchange, and ventilation in Adelie Penguins (*Pygoscelis adeliae*). *Journal of Comparative Physiology B* 157: 783–790.

CHARRASSIN, J.-B., BOST, C. A., PÜTZ, K., LAGE, J., DAHIER, ZORN, T. & LE MAHO, Y. 1998. Foraging stategies of incubating and brooding King Penguins *Aptenodytes patagonicus*. *Oecologia* 114: 194–201.

CHARRASSIN, J. B., BOST, C. A., PÜTZ, K., LAGE, J., DAHIER, T. & LE MAHO, Y. 1999. Changes in depth utilization in relation to the breeding stage: a case study with the King Penguin *Aptenodytes patagonicus*. *Marine Ornithology* 27: 43–47.

CHEREL, Y. 1995. Nutrient reserve storage, energetics, and food consumption during the prebreeding and premoulting foraging periods of King Penguins. *Polar Biology* 15: 209–214.

CHEREL, Y., CHARRASSIN, J.-B. & CHALLET, E. 1994. Energy and protein requirements for molt in the King Penguin (*Aptenodytes patagonicus*). *American Journal of Physiology* 266: R1182–R1188.

CHEREL, Y. & FREBY, F. 1994. Daily body-mass loss and nitrogen excretion during moulting fast of Macaroni Penguins. *Auk* 111: 492–495.

CHEREL, Y. & KOOYMAN, G. L. 1998. Food of Emperor Penguins (*Aptenodytes forsteri*) in the western Ross Sea, Antarctica. *Marine Biology* 130: 335–344.

CHEREL, Y., LELOUP, J. & LE MAHO, Y. 1988. Fasting in King Penguin. II. Hormonal and metabolic changes during molt. *American Journal of Physiology* 254: R178–R184.

CHEREL, Y. & RIDOUX, V. 1992. Prey species and nutritive value of food fed during summer to King Penguin *Aptenodytes patagonica* chicks at Possession Island, Crozet Archipelago. *Ibis* 134: 118–127.

CHEREL, Y., RIDOUX, V. & RODHOUSE, P. G. 1996. Fish and squid in the diet of King Penguin chicks, *Aptenodytes patagonicus*, during winter at sub-Antarctic Crozet Islands. *Marine Biology* 126: 559–570.

CHEREL, Y., STAHL, J.-C. & LE MAHO, Y. 1987. Ecology and physiology of fasting King Penguin chicks. *Auk* 104: 254–262.

CLANCEY, P. A. 1966. On the penguins *Spheniscus demersus* (Linnaeus) and *Spheniscus magellanicus* (Forster). *Ostrich* 37: 237.

CLARK, A. B. & WILSON, D. S. 1981. Avian breeding adaptations: hatching asynchrony, brood reduction and nest failure. *The Quarterly Review of Biology* 56: 257–277.

CLARKE, J., MANLY, B., KERRY, K., GARDNER, H., FRANCHI, E., CORSOLINI, S. & FOCARDI, S. 1998. Sex differences in Adelie Penguin foraging strategies. *Polar Biology* 20: 248–258.

CLARKE, J. R. 2001. Partitioning of foraging effort in Adelie Penguins provisioning chicks at Bechervaise Island, Antarctica. *Polar Biology* 24: 16–20.

CLARKE, J. R. & KERRY, K. R. 1993. Diseases and parasites of penguins. *Korean Journal of Polar Research* 4: 79–96.

COCKREM, J. F. 1995. Timing of seasonal breeding in birds, with particular reference to New Zealand birds. *Reproduction, Fertility, & Development* 7: 1–19.

COCKREM, J. F. & SEDDON, P. J. 1994. Annual cycle of sex steroids in the Yellow-eyed Penguin (*Megadyptes antipodes*) on South Island, New Zealand. *General and Comparative Endocrinology* 94: 113–121.

COLLAR, N. J., CROSBY, M. J. & STATTERSFIELD, A. J. 1994. *Birds to watch 2: the world list of threatened birds*. Birdlife International, Cambridge, UK.

COLLINS, M., CULLEN, J. M. & DANN, P. 1999. Seasonal and annual foraging movements of Little Penguins from Phillip Island, Victoria. *Wildlife Research* 26: 705–721.

CONROY, J. W. H. & WHITE, M. G. 1973. The breeding status of the King Penguin (*Aptenodytes patagonica*). *British Antarctic Survey Bulletin* 32: 31–40.

CONWAY, W. G. 1971. Predation on penguins at Punta Tombo. *Animal Kingdom* 74: 2–8.

COOPER, A. & PENNY, D. 1997. Mass survival of birds across the Cretaceous-Tertiary Boundary: molecular evidence. *Science* 275: 1109–1113.

COOPER, J. 1980. Breeding biology of the Jackass Penguin with special reference to its conservation. In *Proceedings of the Fourth Pan-African Ornithological Congress held at Mahe, Seychelles, 6–13 November, 1976. South African Ornithological Society, South Africa*, pp. 227–231.

COOPER, J., BROWN, C. R., GALES, R. P., HINDELL, M. A., KLAGES, N. T. W., MOORS, P. J., PEMBERTON, D., RIDOUX, V., THOMPSON, K. R. & VAN HEEZIK, Y. M. 1990. Diets and dietary segregation of Crested penguins (*Eudyptes*). In *Penguin Biology* (Ed. by Davis, L. S. and Darby, J. T.), pp. 131–156. Academic Press, San Diego, California.

CORIA, N. R., SPAIRANI, H., VIVEQUIN, S. & FONTANA, R. 1995. Diet of Adélie Penguins *Pygoscelis adeliae* during the post-hatching period at Esperanza Bay, Antarctica, 1987/88. *Polar Biology* 15: 415–418.

COSTA, D. P. 1991. Reproductive and foraging energetics of high latitude penguins, albatrosses and pinnipeds: implications for life history patterns. *American Zoologist* 31: 111–130.

COTT, H. B. 1953. The exploitation of wild birds for their eggs. *Ibis* 95: 409–449.

CRACRAFT, J. 1973. Continental drift, paleoclimatology, and the evolution and biogeography of birds. *Journal of Zoology* 169: 455–545.

CRACRAFT, J. 1982. Phylogenetic relationships and monophyly of loons, grebes and hesperornithiform birds, with comments on the early history of birds. *Systematic Zoology* 31: 35–56.

CRACRAFT, J. 1985. Monophyly and phylogenetic relationships of the Pelecaniformes: a numerical cladistic analysis. *Auk* 102: 834–853.

CRAWFORD, R. J. M., DAVIS, S. A., HARDING, R. T., JACKSON, L. F., LESHORO, T. M., MEYER, M. A., RANDALL, R. M., UNDERHILL, L. G., UPFOLD, L., VAN DALSEN, A. P., VAN DER MERWE, E., WHITTINGTON, P. A., WILLIAMS, A. J. & WOLFAARDT, A. C. 2000. Initial impact of the Treasure oil spill on seabirds off western South Africa. *South African Journal of Marine Science* 22: 157–176.

CRAWFORD, R. J. M. & DYER, B. M. 1995. Responses by four seabird species to a fluctuating availability of Cape Anchovy *Engraulis capensis* off South Africa. *Ibis* 137: 329–339.

CRAWFORD, R. J. M., SHANNON, L. J. & WHITTINGTON, P. A. 1999. Population dynamics of the African Penguin *Spheniscus demersus* at Robben Island, South Africa. *Marine Ornithology* 27: 139–147.

CRAWFORD, R. J. M. & SHELTON, P. A. 1978. Pelagic fish and seabird interrelationships off the coasts of South West and South Africa. *Biological Conservation* 14: 85–109.

CRAWFORD, R. J. M., WILLIAMS, A. J., HOFMEYR, J. H., KLAGES, N. T. W., RANDALL, R. M., COOPER, J., DYER, B. M. & CHESSELET, Y. 1995. Trends of African Penguin *Spheniscus demersus* populations in the 20th Century. *South African Journal of Marine Science* 16: 101–118.

CROXALL, J. P. 1992. Southern Ocean environmental changes: effects of seabird, seal, and whale populations. *Royal Society of London. Philosophical transactions. Series B.* 338: 319–328.

CROXALL, J. P. & DAVIS, L. S. 1999. Penguins: paradoxes and patterns. *Marine Ornithology* 27: 1–12.

CROXALL, J. P. & DAVIS, R. W. 1990. Metabolic rate and foraging behaviour of *Pygoscelis* and *Eudyptes* penguins at sea. In *Penguin Biology* (Ed. by Davis, L. S. and Darby, J. T.), pp. 207–228. Academic Press, Inc., San Diego, California.

CROXALL, J. P., DAVIS, R. W. & O'CONNELL, M. J. 1988a. Diving patterns in relation to diet of Gentoo and Macaroni Penguins at South Georgia. *The Condor* 90: 157–167.

CROXALL, J. P. & FURSE, J. R. 1980. Food of Chinstrap Penguins *Pygoscelis antarctica* and Macaroni Penguins *Eudyptes chrysolophus* at Elephant Island Group, South Shetland Islands. *Ibis* 122: 237–245.

CROXALL, J. P. & GASTON, A. J. 1988. Patterns of reproduction in high-latitude Northern- and Southern-hemisphere seabirds. In *19th International Ornithological Congress*, pp. 1176–1194. University of Ottawa Press, Ottawa.

CROXALL, J. P. & LISHMAN, G. S. 1987. The food and feeding ecology of penguins. In *Seabirds: feeding ecology and role in marine ecosystems* (Ed. by Croxall, J. P.), pp. 101–131. Cambridge University Press, Cambridge.

CROXALL, J. P., McCANN, T. S., PRINCE, P. A. & ROTHERY, P. 1988b. Reproductive performance of seabirds and seals at South Georgia and Signy Island, South Orkney Islands, 1976–1987: implications for Southern Ocean monitoring studies. In *Antarctic Ocean and Resources Variability* (Ed. by Sahrhage, D.), pp. 261–285. Springer-Verlag, Berlin, Heidelberg.

CROXALL, J. P., PRINCE, P. A., BAIRD, A. & WARD, P. 1985. The diet of the Southern Rockhopper Penguin *Eudyptes chrysocome chrysocome* at Beauchene Island, Falkland Islands. *Journal of Zoology, London Series A* 206: 485–496.

CROXALL, J. P., PRINCE, P. A., HUNTER, I., McINNES, S. J. & COPESTAKE, P. G. 1984. The seabirds of the Antarctic Peninsula, islands of the Scotia Sea, and Antarctic Continent between 80°W and 20°W: their status and conservation. In *No 2, ICBP Seabird Conservation Symposium, 1982: Status and Conservation of the World's Seabirds* (Ed. by

Croxall, J. P., Evans, P. G. H. and Schreiber, R. W.), pp. 637–666. International Council for Bird Preservation. ICBP Technical Publication.

CROXALL, J. P., REID, K. & PRINCE, P. A. 1999. Diet, provisioning and productivity responses of marine predators to differences in availability of Antarctic krill. *Marine Ecology Progress Series* 177: 115–131.

CULIK, B., HENNICKE, J. & MARTIN, T. 2000. Humboldt Penguins outmanoeuvring El Nino. *Journal of Experimental Biology* 203: 2311–2322.

CULIK, B., WILSON, R. P. & BANNASCH, R. 1994. Underwater swimming at low energetic cost by Pygoscelid penguins. *Journal of Experimental Biology* 197: 65–78.

CULIK, B. M., ADELUNG, D. & WOAKES, A. J. 1990. The effect of disturbance on the heart rate and behaviour of Adélie Penguins (*Pygoscelis adeliae*) during the breeding season. In *Antarctic ecosystems. Ecological change and conservation* (Ed. by Kerry, K. L. and Hempel, G.), pp. 177–182. Springer, Berlin Heidelberg New York.

CULIK, B. M., LUNA-JORQUERA, G., OYARZO, I I. & CORREA, H. 1998. Humboldt Penguins monitored via VHF telemetry. *Marine Ecology Progress Series* 162: 279–286.

CULIK, B. M. & LUNA-JORQUERA, G. 1997a. The Humboldt Penguin *Spheniscus humboldti*—a migratory bird. *Journal fur Ornithologie* 138: 325–330.

CULIK, B. M. & LUNA-JORQUERA, G. 1997b. Satellite tracking of Humboldt Penguins (*Spheniscus humboldti*) in northern Chile. *Marine Biology* 128: 547–556.

CULIK, B. M., WILSON, R. P., A.T., W. & SANUDO, F. W. 1991. Oil pollution of Antarctic penguins: effects on energy metabolism and physiology. *Marine Pollution Bulletin* 22: 388–391.

CULLEN, J. M., MONTAGUE, T. L. & HULL, C. 1992. Food of Little Penguins *Eudyptula minor* in Victoria: comparison of three localities between 1985 and 1988. *Emu* 91: 318–341.

CUNNINGHAM, D. M. & MOORS, P. J. 1994. The decline of Rockhopper Penguins *Eudyptes chrysocome* at Campbell Island, Southern Ocean and the influence of rising sea temperatures. *Emu* 94: 27–36.

CUTHBERT, R. 1999. *The breeding ecology and conservation of Hutton's shearwater (*Puffinus huttoni*).* PhD thesis, University of Otago, Dunedin, New Zealand.

D'AMORE, W. A. & JESSOP, R. E. 1995. Causes of sickness and injury in Little Penguins (*Eudyptula minor*) rehabilitated at Phillip Island, Victoria, Australia. *Penguin Conservation* 8: 6–12.

DANN, P. 1988. An experimental manipulation of clutch size in the Little Penguin *Eudyptula minor. Emu* 88: 101–103.

DANN, P. 1992. Distribution, population trends and factors influencing the population size of Little Penguins *Eudyptula minor* on Phillip Island, Victoria. *Emu* 91: 263–272.

DANN, P. & CULLEN, J. M. 1990. Survival, patterns of reproduction, and lifetime reproductive output in Little Blue Penguins (*Eudyptula minor*) on Phillip Island, Victoria, Australia. In *Penguin Biology* (Ed. by Davis, L. S. and Darby, J. T.), pp. 63–84. Academic Press, Inc., San Diego, California.

DARBY, J. T. & DAWSON, S. M. 2000. Bycatch of Yellow-eyed Penguins (*Megadyptes antipodes*) in gillnets in New Zealand waters 1979–1997. *Biological Conservation* 93: 327–332.

DARBY, J. T. & SEDDON, P. J. 1990. Breeding biology of Yellow-eyed Penguins (*Megadyptes antipodes*). In *Penguin Biology* (Ed. by Davis, L. S. and Darby, J. T.), pp. 45–62. Academic Press, San Diego, California.

DAVIS, L. S. 1980. *Egg and chick survival of the Adelie Penguin (Pygoscelis adeliae) at Cape Bird, Antarctica.* MSc thesis, University of Canterbury, Christchurch.

DAVIS, L. S. 1982a. Creching behaviour of Adelie Penguin chicks (*Pygoscelis adeliae*). *New Zealand Journal of Zoology* 9: 279–286.

DAVIS, L. S. 1982b. Timing of nest relief and its effect on breeding success in Adelie Penguins (*Pygoscelis adeliae*). *Condor* 84: 178–183.

DAVIS, L. S. 1988a. Coordination of incubation routines and mate choice in Adélie penguins (*Pygoscelis adeliae*). *Auk* 105: 428–432.

DAVIS, L. S. 1988b. Mate choice in penguins. *Cormorant* 16: 126.

DAVIS, L. S. 1991. Mate choice and sexual dimorphism in penguins. In *Acta XX Congressus Internationalis Ornithologici* (Ed. by Bell, B. D., Cossee, R. O., Flux, J. E. C., Heather, B. D., Hitchmough, R. A., Robertson, C. J. R. and Williams, M. J.), pp. 1352–1360. New Zealand Ornithological Congress Trust Board, Wellington, New Zealand.

DAVIS, L. S. 1993. Penguins with a latitude problem. *Natural History* 102: 48–51.

DAVIS, L. S. 1995. The control of behaviour: free-running circadian rhythms in the Antarctic summer. In *The penguins: ecology and management* (Ed. by Dann, P., Norman, I. and Reilly, P.), pp. 56–72. Surrey Beatty & Sons, Chipping Norton, NSW, Australia.

DAVIS, L. S. 1997. Ecological constraints on parental investment by Adelie Penguins: can desertions be used as a biological indicator of environmental change? *Korean Journal Of Polar Research* 8: 63–67.

DAVIS, L. S. 2001a. *The Plight of the Penguin*. Longacre Press, Dunedin.

DAVIS, L. S. 2001b. Sphenisciformes. In *Encyclopaedia of Ocean Sciences* (Ed. by Steele, J. H., Thorpe, S. A. and Turekian, K. K.), pp. 2872–2880. Academic Press, London.

DAVIS, L. S. 2001c. A superlative penguin. *Natural History* 01/11: 46–55.

DAVIS, L. S., BOERSMA, P. D. & COURT, G. S. 1996. Satellite telemetry of the winter migration of Adélie Penguins (*Pygoscelis adeliae*). *Polar Biology*.

DAVIS, L. S., COCKREM, J. F., MILLER, G. D. & COURT, G. S. 1995. An incubation timer for seabirds: progesterone and its relationship to hatching in Adélie Penguins. *Emu* 95: 245–251.

DAVIS, L. S. & CUTHBERT, R. L. 2001. Reproductive ecology of seabirds. In *Encyclopaedia of Ocean Sciences* (Ed. by Steele, J. H., Thorpe, S. A. and Turekian, K. K.), pp. 2663–2669. Academic Press, London.

DAVIS, L. S., HARCOURT, R. G. & BRADSHAW, C. J. A. 2001. The winter migration of Adelie Penguins breeding in the Ross Sea sector of Antarctica. *Polar Biology* 24: 593–597.

DAVIS, L. S., HUNTER, F. M., HARCOURT, R. G. & MICHELSON HEATH, S. 1998. Reciprocal homosexual mounting in Adélie Penguins (*Pygoscelis adeliae*). *Emu* 98: 136–137.

DAVIS, L. S. & MCCAFFREY, F. T. 1986. Survival analysis of eggs and chicks of Adélie Penguins (*Pygoscelis adeliae*). *Auk* 103: 379–388.

DAVIS, L. S. & MCCAFFREY, F. T. 1989. Recognition and parental investment in Adelie Penguins. *Emu* 89: 155–158.

DAVIS, L. S. & MILLER, G. D. 1990. Foraging patterns of Adelie Penguins during the incubation period. In *Antarctic ecosystems: ecological change and conservation.* (Ed. by Kerry, K. R. and Hempel, G.), pp. 203–207. Springer-Verlag, Berlin Heidelberg.

DAVIS, L. S. & MILLER, G. D. 1992. Satellite tracking of Adélie Penguins. *Polar Biology* 12: 503–506.

DAVIS, L. S. & SPEIRS, E. A. H. 1990. Mate choice in penguins. In *Penguin Biology* (Ed. by Davis, L. S. and Darby, J. T.), pp. 377–398. Academic Press, San Diego, California.

DAVIS, L. S., WARD, G. D. & SADLEIR, R. M. F. S. 1988. Foraging by Adelie Penguins during the incubation period. *Notornis* 35: 15–23.

DAVIS, R. W., CROXALL, J. P. & O'CONNELL, M. J. 1989. The reproductive energetics of Gentoo (*Pygoscelis papua*) and Macaroni (*Eudyptes chrysolophus*) Penguins at South Georgia. *Journal of Animal Ecology* 58: 59–74.

DAWSON, C., VINCENT, J. F. V., JERONIMIDOS, G., RICE, G. & FORSHAW, P. 1999. Heat transfer through penguin feathers. *Journal of Theoretical Biology* 199: 291–295.

DAWSON, E. W. 1974. Adelie Penguins and Leopard Seals: illustrations of predation— history, legend and fact. In *21(1)*, pp. 36–39.

DAWSON, E. W. 1984. Adelie Penguins and Leopard Seals—a further note. *Notornis* 21: 379–389.

DE LEON, A., FARGALLO, J. A. & MORENO, J. 1998. Parental body size affects meal size in the Chinstrap Penguin (*Pygoscelis antarctica*). *Polar Biology* 19: 358–360.

DE QUEIROZ, K. & GOOD, D. A. 1997. Phenetic clustering in biology: a critique. *The Quarterly Review of Biology* 72: 3–30.

DEL HOYO, J., ELLIOT, A. & SARGATAL, J. (ed.). 1992. *Handbook of the Birds of the World*. Lynx Edicions for ICBP, Barcelona.

DELACA, T. E., LIPPS, J. H. & ZUMWALT, G. S. 1975. Encounters with Leopard Seals (*Hydruga leptonyx*) along the Antarctic Peninsula. *Antarctic Journal of the United States* 10: 85–91.

DERKSEN, D. V. 1975. Unreported method of stone-collecting by the Adelie Penguin. *Notornis* 22: 77–78.

DIEBOLD, E. N., BRANCH, S. & HENRY, L. 1999. Management of penguin populations in North American zoos and aquariums. *Marine Ornithology* 27: 171–176.

DU PLESSIS, C. J., VAN HEEZIK, Y. M. & SEDDON, P. J. 1994. Timing of King penguin breeding at Marion Island. *Emu* 94: 216–219.

DUNLOP, J. N., KLOMP, N. I. & WOOLLER, R. D. 1988. Penguin Island, Shoalwater Bay, Western Australia. *Corella* 12: 93–98.

EDGE, K.-A. 1996. *Parental investment in penguins: a phylogenetic and experimental approach*. PhD thesis, University of Otago, Dunedin.

EDGE, K. A., JAMIESON, I. G. & DARBY, J. T. 1999. Parental investment and the management of an endangered penguin. *Biological Conservation* 88: 367–378.

ELLIS, S., CROXALL, J. P. & COOPER, J. (ed.). 1998. *Penguin conservation assessment and management plan*. IUCN/SSC Conservation Breeding Specialist Group, Apple Valley, USA.

EMSLIE, S. D., FRASER, W., SMITH, R. C. & WALKER, W. 1998. Abandoned penguin colonies and environmental change in the Palmer Station area, Anvers Island, Antarctic Peninsula. *Antarctic Science* 10: 257–268.

EMSLIE, S. D., KARNOVSKY, N. & TRIVELPIECE, W. 1995. Avian predation at penguin colonies on King George Island, Antarctica. *Wilson Bulletin* 107: 317–327.

FELSENSTEIN, J. 1978. Cases in which parsimony and compatibility methods will be positively misleading. *Systematic Zoology* 27: 401–410.

FELSENSTEIN, J. 1985. Confidence limits on phylogenies: an approach using the bootstrap. *Evolution* 39: 783–791.

FLACH, E. J., STEVENSON, M. F. & HENDERSON, G. M. 1990. Aspergillosis in Gentoo Penguins (*Pygoscelis papua*) at Edinburgh Zoo, 1964–1988. *Veterinary Record* 126: 81–85.

FLANNERY, T. F. 1994. *The Future Eaters: an ecological history of the Australasian lands and people*. Reed Books, Chatswood, N.S.W.

FOCARDI, S., FOSSI, C., LEONZIO, C., LARI, L., MARSILLI, L., COURT, G. S. & DAVIS, L. S. 1992. Mixed function oxidase activity and chlorinated hydrocarbon residues in Antarctic seabirds: South Polar Skua (*Catharacta maccomicki*) and Adelie Penguin (*Pygoscelis adeliae*). *Marine Environmental Research* 34: 201–205.

FORBES, L. S. 1994. The good, the bad and the ugly: Lack's brood reduction hypothesis and experimental design. *Journal of Avian Biology* 25: 338–343.

FORDYCE, R. E. & JONES, C. M. 1990. Penguin history and new fossil material from New Zealand. In *Penguin Biology* (Ed. by Davis, L. S. and Darby, J. T.), pp. 419–446. Academic Press, San Diego, California.

FORTESCUE, M. E. 1995. Biology of the Little Penguin *Eudyptula minor* on Bowen Island and at other Australian colonies. In *The Penguins: Ecology and Management* (Ed. by Dann, P., Norman, I. and Reilly, P.), pp. 364–392. Surrey Beatty & Sons, Chipping Norton, NSW, Australia.

FOWLER, G. S. 1999. Behavioral and hormonal responses of Magellanic Penguins (*Spheniscus magellanicus*) to tourism and nest site visitation. *Biological Conservation* 90: 143–149.

FOWLER, G. S., WINGFIELD, J. C., BOERSMA, P. D. & SOSA, R. A. 1994. Reproductive endocrinology and weight change in relation to reproductive success in the Magellanic Penguin (*Spheniscus magellanicus*). *General and Comparative Endocrinology* 94: 305–315.

FRASER, W. R., TRIVELPIECE, W. Z., AINLEY, D. G. & TRIVELPIECE, S. G. 1992. Increases in Antarctic penguin populations: reduced competition with whales or a loss of sea ice due to environmental warming? *Polar Biology* 11: 525–531.

FRERE, E., GANDINI, P. & BOERSMA, D. 1992. Effects of nest type and location on reproductive success of the Magellanic Penguin *Spheniscus magellanicus*. *Marine Ornithology* 20: 1–2.

FROST, P. G. H., SIEGFRIED, W. R. & BURGER, A. E. 1976a. Behavioural adaptations of the Jackass Penguin, *Spheniscus demersus* to a hot arid environment. *Journal of Zoology* 179: 165–187.

FROST, P. G. H., SIEGFRIED, W. R. & COOPER, J. 1976b. Conservation of the Jackass Penguin (*Spheniscus demersus* (L.)). *Biological Conservation* 9: 79–99.

FROST, P. G. H., SIEGFRIED, W. R. & GREENWOOD, P. J. 1975. Arterio-venous heat exchange systems in the Jackass Penguin *Spheniscus demersus*. *Journal of Zoology* 175: 231–241.

FURNESS, R. W. & MONAGHAN, P. 1987. *Seabird ecology*. Glasgow, Scotland.

GALES, N. J., KLAGES, N. T. W., WILLIAMS, R. & WOEHLER, E. J. 1990a. The diet of the Emperor Penguin, *Aptenodytes forsteri*, in Amanda Bay, Princess Elizabeth Land, Antarctica. *Antarctic Science* 2: 23–28.

GALES, R. P. 1985. Breeding seasons and double brooding of the Little Penguin *Eudyptula minor* in New Zealand. *Emu* 85: 127–130.

GALES, R. P. 1987. Validation of the stomach-flushing technique for obtaining stomach contents of penguins. *Ibis* 129: 335–343.

GALES, R. P. 1988. The use of otoliths as indicators of Little Penguin *Eudyptula minor* diet. *Ibis* 130: 418–426.

GALES, R. P., GREEN, B. & STAHEL, C. 1988. The energetics of free-living Little Penguins *Eudyptula minor* (Spheniscidae), during moult. *Aust. Wildlife Res.* 36: 159–167.

GALES, R. P., WILLIAMS, C. & RITZ, D. 1990b. Foraging behaviour of the Little Penguin, *Eudyptula minor*: initial results and assessment of instrument effect. *Journal of Zoology, London* 220: 61–85.

GANDINI, P., BOERSMA, P. D., FRERE, E., GANDINI, M., HOLIK, T. & LICHTSCHEIN, V. 1994. Magellanic Penguins (*Spheniscus magellanicus*) affected by chronic petroleum pollution along coast of Chubut, Argentina. *Auk* 111: 20–27.

GARCIA, V., JOUVENTIN, P. & MAUGET, R. 1996. Parental care and the prolactin secretion pattern in the King Penguin—an endogenously timed mechanism. *Hormones and Behavior* 30: 259–265.

GARDNER, H., KERRY, K. & RIDDLE, M. 1997. Poultry virus infection in Antarctic penguins. *Nature* 387: 245.

GHEBREMESKEL, K., WILLIAMS, G., KEYMER, I. F., HORSLEY, D. & GARDNER, D. A. 1989. Plasma chemistry of Rockhopper (*Eudyptes crestatus*), Magellanic (*Spheniscus magellanicus*) and Gentoo (*Pygoscelis papua*) wild penguins in relation to moult. *Comparative Biochemistry and Physiology* 92: 43–47.

GIESE, M. 1996. Effects of human activity on Adelie Penguin *Pygoscelis adeliae* breeding success. *Biological Conservation* 75: 157–164.

GILL, J. M. & DARBY, J. T. 1993. Deaths in Yellow-Eyed Penguins (*Megadyptes antipodes*) on the Otago Peninsula during the summer of 1990. *New Zealand Veterinary Journal* 41: 39–42.

GOLDSMITH, R. 1962. Reproductive behaviour and adaptation in the Adelie Penguin (*Pygoscelis adeliae*). *Journal of Reproduction and Fertility* 4: 237–238.

GOULD, S. J. & LEWONTIN, R. C. 1979. The spandrels of San Marco and the Panglossian paradigm: a critique of the adaptationist programme. *Proceedings of the Royal Society, London* B 205: 581–598.

GRACZYK, T. K., BROSSY, J. J., PLOES, A. & STOSKOPF, M. K. 1995a. Avian malaria seroprevalence in Jackass Penguins (*Spheniscus demersus*) in South Africa. *Journal of Parasitology* 81: 703–707.

GRACZYK, T. K., COCKREM, J. F., CRANFIELD, M. R., DARBY, J. T. & MOORE, P. 1995b. Avian malaria seroprevalence in wild New Zealand penguins. *Parasite* 2: 401–405.

GRACZYK, T. K., CRANFIELD, M. R., BROSSY, J. J., COCKREM, J. F., JOUVENTIN, P. & SEDDON, P. J. 1995c. Detection of Avian Malaria infections in wild and captive penguins. *Journal of the Helminthological Society of Washington* 62: 135–141.

GRANT, W. S., DUFFY, D. C. & LESLIE, R. W. 1994. Allozyme phylogeny of *Spheniscus* penguins. *Auk* 111: 716–720.

GRAU, C. R. 1982. Egg formation in Fiordland Crested Penguins (*Eudyptes pachyrhynchus*). *Condor* 84: 172–177.

GROSCOLAS, R. 1982. Changes in plasma lipids during breeding, moulting and starvation in male and female Emperor Penguins (*Aptenodytes forsteri*). *Physiological Zoology* 55: 45–55.

GROSCOLAS, R. & CHEREL, Y. 1992. How to molt while fasting in the cold: the metabolic and hormonal adaptations of Emperor and King Penguins. *Ornis Scandinavica* 23. <?>

GROSCOLAS, R., JALLAGEAS, M., GOLDSMITH, A. R. & ASSENMACHER, I. 1986. The endocrine control of reproduction and molt in male and female Emperor (*Aptenodytes forsteri*) and Adelie (*Pygoscelis adeliae*) Penguins. 1. Annual changes in plasma levels of gonadal steroids and LH. *General and Comparative Endocrinology* 62: 43–53.

GROSCOLAS, R. & ROBIN, J. P. 2001. Long-term fasting and re-feeding in penguins. *Comparative Biochemistry and Physiology a-Molecular and Integrative Physiology* 128: 645–655.

GUINET, C. 1992. Hunting behaviour of Killer Whales *Orcinus orca* around the Crozet Islands. *Canadian Journal of Zoology* 70: 1656–1667.

GWYNN, A. M. 1993. Clutch size in *Eudyptes* penguins. *Emu* 93: 287–290.

HAHN, D. C. 1981. Asynchronous hatching in the Laughing Gull: cutting losses and reducing rivalry. *Animal Behaviour* 29: 421–427.

HARRIGAN, K. E. 1992. Causes of mortality of Little Penguins *Eudyptula minor* in Victoria. *Emu* 91: 273–277.

HAYS, C. 1984. The Humboldt Penguin in Peru. *Oryx* 18: 92–95.

HAYS, C. 1986. Effects of the 1982–83 El Nino on Humboldt Penguin colonies in Peru. *Biological Conservation* 36: 169–180.

HEATH, R. G. M. & RANDALL, R. M. 1989. Foraging ranges and movements of Jackass Penguins (*Spheniscus demersus*) established through radio telemetry. *Journal of Zoology* 217: 369–379.

HEDGES, S. B. & SIBLEY, C. G. 1994. Molecules vs. morphology in avian evolution: the case of the "pelecaniform" birds. *Proceedings of the National Academy of Sciences of the United States of America* 91: 9861–9865.

HENNICKE, J. & CULIK, B. 2000. Parental investment in Humboldt Penguins. 4th International Penguin Conference, Coquimbo, Chile.

HENNIG, W. 1950. *Grundzüge einer Theorie der Phylogenetischen Systematik*. Deutscher Zentralverlag, Berlin.

HILLSTRÖM, L. & OLSSON, K. 1994. Advantages of hatching asynchrony in the Pied Flycatcher *Ficedula hypoleuca*. *Journal of Avian Biology* 25: 205–214.

HINDELL, M. A. 1988a. The diet of the King Penguin *Aptenodytes patagonicus* at Macquarie Island. *Ibis* 130: 193–203.

HINDELL, M. A. 1988b. The diet of the Royal Penguin *Eudyptes schlegeli* at Macquarie Island. *Emu* 88: 219–226.

HINDELL, M. A. 1989. The diet of Gentoo Penguins *Pygocscelis papua* at Macquarie Island: winter and early breeding season. *Emu* 89: 71–78.

Ho, C. Y.-K., Prager, E. M., Wilson, A. C., Osuga, D. T. & Feeney, R. E. 1976. Penguin evolution: protein comparisons demonstrate phylogenetic relationship to flying aquatic birds. *J. Mol. Evol.* 8: 271–282.

Hocken, A. G. 1997. Plumage and bill morphology variations in a population of the Blue Penguin (*Eudyptula minor*). *Notornis* 44: 259–263.

Hocken, A. G. 2000. Cause of death in Blue Penguins (*Eudyptula m. minor*) in North Otago, New Zealand. *New Zealand Journal of Zoology* 27: 305–309.

Hockey, P. A. R. & Hallinan, J. 1981. Effect of human disturbance on the breeding behaviour of Jackass Penguins *Spheniscus demersus*. *South African Journal of Wildlife Research* 11: 59–62.

Hodgson, A. 1975. *Some aspects of the ecology of the Fairy Penguin* Eudypula minor novaehollandiae (forster) *in southern Tasmania*. PhD thesis, University of Tasmania. Hobart, Australia.

Hofman, R. J. 1973. Leopard Seal study at Palmer Station. *Antarctic Journal of the United States* 8: 196–197.

Hofmeyr, G. J. G. & Bester, M. N. 1993. Predation on King penguins by Antarctic Fur Seals. *South African Journal of Antarctic Research* 23: 71–74.

Holdaway, R. N. 1991. *Systematics and palaeobiology of Haast's eagle (*Harpagornis moorei Haast, *1872) (Aves: Accipitridae)*. PhD thesis, University of Canterbury, Christchurch, New Zealand.

Hui, C. A. 1987. The porpoising of penguins: an energy-conserving behavior for respiratory ventilation? *Canadian Journal of Zoology* 65: 209–211.

Hull, C. L. 2000. Comparative diving behaviour and segregation of the marine habitat by breeding Royal Penguins, *Eudyptes schlegeli*, and eastern Rockhopper Penguins, *Eudyptes chrysocome filholi*, at Macquarie Island. *Canadian Journal of Zoology* 78: 333–345.

Hull, C. L., Hindell, M. A., Gales, R. P., Meggs, R. A., Moyle, D. I. & Brothers, N. P. 1998. The efficacy of translocating Little Penguins *Eudyptula minor* during an oil spill. *Biological Conservation* 86: 393–400.

Hull, C. L., Hindell, M. A. & Michael, K. 1997. Foraging zones of Royal Penguins during the breeding season, and their association with oceanographic features. *Marine Ecology Progress Series* 153: 217–228.

Hull, C. L., Wilson, J. & le Mar, K. 2001. Moult in adult Royal Penguins, *Eudyptes schlegeli*. *Emu* 101: 173–176.

Hunter, F. M. & Davis, L. S. 1998. Female Adélie Penguins acquire nest material from extrapair males after engaging in extrapair copulations. *Auk* 115: 526–528.

Hunter, F. M., Davis, L. S. & Miller, G. D. 1996. Sperm transfer in the Adélie Penguin. *Condor* 98: 410–413.

Hunter, F. M., Miller, G. D. & Davis, L. S. 1995. Mate switching and copulation behaviour in the Adélie Penguin. *Behaviour* 132: 691–707.

Hunter, S. 1991. The impact of avian predator-scavengers on King Penguin *Aptenodytes patagonica* chicks at Marion Island. *Ibis* 133: 343–350.

Irvine, L. G., Clarke, J. R. & Kerry, K. R. 2000. Low breeding success of the Adelie Penguin at Bechervaise Island in the 1998/99 season. *CCAMLR Science* 7: 151–167.

Jacob, J. & Hoerschelmann, H. 1981. Verwandtschaftsbeziehungen bei Pinguinen (Sphenisciformes). *Journal fur Ornithologie* 122: 78–88.

Jenkins, R. J. F. 1974. A new giant penguin from the Eocene of Australia. *Palaeontology* 17: 291–310.

Jessop, R. & Du Guesclin, P. 2000. The effects of an oil spill at Apollo Bay, Victoria, on Little Penguins *Eudyptula minor* in May 1990. *Australian Bird Watcher* 18: 192–198.

Jiguet, F. & Jouventin, P. 1999. Individual breeding decisions and long term reproductive strategy in the King Penguin *Aptenodytes patagonicus*. *Ibis* 141: 428–433.

Johnson, K., Bednarz, J. C. & Zack, S. 1987. Crested Penguins: why are first eggs smaller? *Oikos* 49: 347–349.

JOHNSTONE, R. M. & DAVIS, L. S. 1990. Incubation routines and foraging trip regulation in the Grey-faced Petrel *Pterodroma macroptera gouldi*. *Ibis* 132: 14–20.

JONES, I.L. & HUNTER, F. M. 1998. Heterospecific mating preferences for a feather ornament in Least Auklets. *Behavioral Ecology* 9: 187–192.

JOUVENTIN, P. 1971. Comportement et structure sociale chez le Manchot Empereur. *Terre et la Vie* 25: 510–586.

JOUVENTIN, P. 1975. Mortality parameters in Emperor Penguins *Aptenodytes forsteri*. In *The Biology of Penguins* (Ed. by Stonehouse, B.), pp. 435–446. Macmillan Press, London.

JOUVENTIN, P. 1982. *Visual and Vocal Signals in Penguins, their Evolution and Adaptive Characters*. Paul Parey, Berlin.

JOUVENTIN, P., AUBIN, T. & LENGAGNE, T. 1999. Finding a parent in a King Penguin colony: the acoustic system of individual recognition. *Animal Behaviour* 57: 1175–1183.

JOUVENTIN, P. & LAGARDE, F. 1995. Evolutionary ecology of the King Penguin *Aptenodytes patagonicus*: the self regulation of the breeding cycle. In *The Penguins: Ecology and Management* (Ed. by Dann, P., Norman, I. and Reilly, P.), pp. 80–95. Surrey Beatty & Sons, Chipping Norton, NSW, Australia.

JOUVENTIN, P., STAHL, J. C., WEIMERSKIRCH, H. & MOUGIN, J. L. 1984. Seabirds of the French Subantarctic Islands and Adelie Land, their status and conservation. In *Status and Conservation of the World's Seabirds* (Ed. by Croxall, J. P., Evans, P. G. H. and Schreiber, R. W.), pp. 609–625. ICBP Technical Publication, Cambridge.

KERRY, K. R., CLARKE, J. R. & ELSE, G. D. 1995. The foraging range of Adélie Penguins at Berchervaise Island, MacRobertson Land, Antarctica as determined by satellite telemetry. In *The penguins: ecology and management* (Ed. by Dann, P., Norman, I. and Reilly, P.), pp. 216–243. Surrey Beatty & Sons, Chipping Norton, NSW, Australia.

KINSKY, F. C. 1960. The yearly cycle of the northern Blue Penguin (*Eudyptula minor novaehollandiae*) in the Wellington Harbour area. *Records of the Dominion Museum, Wellington* 3: 145–218.

KLAGES, N. T. W. 1989. Food and feeding ecology of Emperor Penguins in the eastern Weddell Sea. *Polar Biology* 9: 385–390.

KLAGES, N. T. W., BROOKE, M. L. & WATKINS, B. P. 1988. Prey of Northern Rockhopper Penguins at Gough Island, South Atlantic Ocean. *Ostrich* 59: 162–165.

KLOMP, N. I., MEATHREL, C. E. & WOOLLER, R. D. 1988. The protracted breeding regime of Little Penguins in Western Australia. *Cormorant* 16: 128–129.

KLOMP, N. I. & WOOLLER, R. D. 1991. Patterns of arrival and departure by breeding Little Penguins at Penguin Island, Western Australia. *Emu* 91: 32–35.

KLOMP, N. I. & WOOLLER, R. D. 1988. Diet of Little Penguins, *Eudyptula minor*, from Penguin Island, Western Australia. *Australian Journal of Marine and Freshwater Research* 39: 633–639.

KOOYMAN, G., HULL, C., OLSSON, O., ROBERTSON, G., CROXALL, J. & DAVIS, L. 1999. Foraging patterns of polar penguins. In *22nd International Ornithological Congress, Durban* (Ed. by Adams, N. J. and Slotow, R. H.), pp. 2021–2039. Birdlife South Africa, Johannesburg.

KOOYMAN, G. L. 1975. Behaviour and physiology of diving. In *The Biology of Penguins* (Ed. by Stonehouse, B.), pp. 115–137. MacMillan, London.

KOOYMAN, G. L. & DAVIS, R. W. 1987. Diving behavior and performance, with special reference to penguins. In *Seabirds: feeding ecology and role in marine ecosystems* (Ed. by Croxall, J. P.), pp. 63–75. Cambridge University Press, Cambridge.

KOOYMAN, G. L., DRABEK, C. M., ELSNER, R. & CAMPBELL, W. B. 1971. Diving behavior of the Emperor Penguin, *Aptenodytes forsteri*. *Auk* 88: 775–795.

KOOYMAN, G. L., GENTRY, R. L. & BERGMAN, W. P. 1972. Respiratory studies of seals and penguins. *Antarctic Journal of the United States* 7: 74–75.

KOOYMAN, G. L. & PONGANIS, P. J. 1990. Behaviour and physiology of diving in Emperor and King Penguins. In *Penguin Biology* (Ed. by Davis, L. S. and Darby, J. T.), pp. 229–242. Academic Press, San Diego, California.

KOOYMAN, G. L. & PONGANIS, P. J. 1994. Emperor Penguin oxygen consumption, heart rate and plasma lactate levels during graded swimming exercise. *Journal of Experimental Biology* 195: 199–209.

KUREISHY, T. W., SEN GUPTA, R., MESQUITA, A. & SANZGIRY, S. 1993. Heavy metals in some parts of Antarctica and the Southern Indian Ocean. *Marine Pollution Bulletin* 26: 651–652.

LA COCK, G. D. 1988. Effect of substrate and ambient temperature on burrowing African Penguins. *Wilson Bulletin* 100: 131–132.

LACK, D. 1947. The significance of clutch size. *Ibis* 89: 302–352.

LACK, D. 1954. *The natural regulation of animal numbers.* Oxford University Press (Clarendon), London.

LACK, D. 1968. *Ecological adaptations for breeding in birds.* Methuen, London.

LADE, J. A., MURRAY, N. D., MARKS, C. A. & ROBINSON, N. A. 1996. Microsatellite differentiation between Phillip Island and mainland Australian populations of the Red Fox *Vulpes vulpes. Molecular Ecology* 5: 81–87.

LAMBERT, D. M., RITCHIE, P. A., MILLAR, C. D., HOLLAND, B., DRUMMOND, A. J. & BARONI, C. 2002. Rates of evolution in ancient DNA from Adelie Penguins. *Science* 295: 2270–2273.

LAMEY, T. C. 1990a. Hatch asynchrony and brood reduction in penguins. In *Penguin Biology* (Ed. by Davis, L. S. and Darby, J. T.), pp. 399–416. Academic Press, San Diego, California.

LAMEY, T. C. 1990b. Snares Crested Penguin in the Falkland Islands. *Notornis* 37: 78.

LAUGKSCH, R. C. & ADAMS, N. J. 1993. Trends in pelagic fish populations of the Saldanha Bay region, southern Benguela upwelling system, 1980–1990: a predator's perspective. *South African Journal of Marine Science* 13: 295–307.

LAWLESS, R. M., BUTTEMER, W. A., ASTHEIMER, L. B. & KERRY, K. R. 2001. The influence of thermoregulatory demand on contact crèching behaviour in Adélie Penguin chicks. *Journal of Thermal Biology* 26: 555–562.

LE MAHO, Y. 1977. The Emperor Penguin: a strategy to live and breed in the cold. *American Scientist* 65: 680–693.

LE MAHO, Y., DELCLITTE, P. & CHATONNET, J. 1976. Thermoregulation in fasting Emperor Penguins under natural conditions. *American Journal of Physiology* 231: 913–922.

LE MAHO, Y., GENDNER, J.-P., CHALLET, E., BOST, C.-A., GILLES, J., VERDON, C., PLUMERE, C., ROBIN, J.-P. & HANDRICH, Y. 1993. Undisturbed breeding penguins as indicators of changes in marine resources. *Marine Ecology Progress Series* 95: 1–6.

LE RESCHE, R. E. & SLADEN, W. J. L. 1970. Establishment of pair and breeding site bonds by young known-age Adelie Penguins (*Pygoscelis adeliae*). *Animal Behaviour* 18: 517–526.

LENGAGNE, T., AUBIN, T., JOUVENTIN, P. & LAUGA, J. 1999a. Acoustic communication in a King Penguin colony: importance of bird location within the colony and of the body position of the listener. *Polar Biology* 21: 262–268.

LENGAGNE, T., AUBIN, T., LAUGA, J. & JOUVENTIN, P. 1999b. How do King Penguins (*Aptenodytes patagonicus*) apply the mathematical theory of information to communicate in windy conditions? *Proceedings Royal Society Of London Series B Biological Sciences* 266: 1623–1628.

LENGAGNE, T., LAUGA, J. & JOUVENTIN, P. 1997. A method of independent time and frequency decomposition of bioacoustic signals—inter-individual recognition in four species of penguins. *Comptes Rendus de l Academie des Sciences Serie III Sciences de la Vie Life Sciences* 320: 885–891.

LISHMAN, G. S. 1985a. The comparative breeding biology of Adelie and Chinstrap Penguins *Pygoscelis adeliae* and *Pygoscelis antarctica* at Signy Island, South Orkney Islands. *Ibis* 127: 84–99.

LISHMAN, G. S. 1985b. The food and feeding ecology of Adelie Penguins (*Pygoscelis adeliae*) and Chinstrap Penguins (*Pygoscelis antarctica*) at Signy Island, South Orkney Islands. *Journal of Zoology, London Series A* 205: 245–263.

LIVEZEY, B. C. 1989. Morphometric patterns in recent and fossil penguins (Aves, Sphenisciformes). *Journal of Zoology, London* 219: 269–307.

LOEB, V., SIEGEL, V., HOLM-HANSEN, O., HEWITT, R., FRASER, W., TRIVELPIECE, W. & TRIVELPIECE, S. 1997. Effects of sea-ice extent and krill or salp dominance on the Antarctic food web. *Nature* 387: 897–900.

LORMÉE, H., JOUVENTIN, P., CHASTEL, O. & MAUGET, R. 1999. Endocrine correlates of parental care in an Antarctic winter breeding seabird, the Emperor Penguin, *Aptenodytes forsteri*. *Hormones and Behavior* 35: 9–17.

LUNDBERG, V. U. & BANNASCH, R. 1983. Beobachtungen und analysen zum futterwettlauf bei pinguinen (Observations and analysis of the feeding chase among penguins). *Zool. Jb. Physio* 87: 391–404.

MADDISON, W. P. 1997. Gene trees in species trees. *Systematic Biology* 46: 523.

MADDISON, W. P., DONOGHUE, M. J. & MADDISON, D. R. 1985. Outgroup analysis and parsimony. *Systematic Zoology* 33: 83–103.

MAGRATH, R. D. 1989. Hatching asynchrony and reproductive success in the blackbird. *Nature* 339: 536–538.

MAGRATH, R. D. 1990. Hatching asynchrony in altricial birds. *Biological Reviews of the Cambridge Philosophical Society* 65: 587–622.

MANGEL, M. & SWITZER, P. V. 1998. A model at the level of the foraging trip for the indirect effects of krill (*Euphausia superba*) fisheries on krill predators. *Ecological Modelling* 105: 235–256.

MARCHANT, S. & HIGGINS, P. J. 1990. *Pygoscelis adeliae* Adelie Penguins. In *Handbook of Australian, New Zealand and Antarctic Birds* (Ed. by Marchant, S. and Higgins, P. J.), pp. 158–173. Oxford University Press, Melbourne.

MASSARO, M., DARBY, J., DAVIS, L. S., EDGE, K.-A. & HAZEL, M. J. 2002. Investigation of interacting effects of female age, laying dates and egg size in Yellow-eyed Penguins (*Megadyptes antipodes*). *Auk* 119: 1137–1141.

MASSARO, M., DAVIS, L. S. & DARRY, J. in press Carotenoid-derived ornaments reflect parental quality in male and female yellow-eyed penguins (*Megadyptes, antipedes*) *Behavioural Ecology and Sociobiology*.

MATTERN, T. 2001. *Foraging strategies and breeding success in the Little Penguin,* Eudyptula minor*: a comparative study between different habitats.* MSc thesis, University of Otago, Dunedin, New Zealand.

MAUGET, R., GARCIA, V. & JOUVENTIN, P. 1995. Endocrine basis of the reproductive pattern of the Gentoo Penguin (*Pygoscelis papua*): winter breeding and extended laying period in northern populations. *General and Comparative Endocrinology* 98: 177–184.

MAUGET, R., JOUVENTIN, P., LACROIX, A. & ISHII, S. 1994. Plasma LH and steroid hormones in King Penguin (*Aptenodytes patagonicus*) during the onset of the breeding cycle. *General and Comparative Endocrinology* 93: 36–43.

MCKAY, R., LALAS, C., MCKAY, D. & MCCONKEY, S. 1999. Nest-site selection by Yellow-eyed Penguins *Megadyptes antipodes* on grazed farmland. *Marine Ornithology* 27: 29–35.

MCLEAN, I. G. 2000. Breeding Success, brood reduction, and the timing of breeding in the Fiordland Crested Penguin (*Eudyptes pachyrhynchus*). *Notornis* 47: 55–58.

MCLEAN, I. G., KAYES, S. D., MURIE, J. O., DAVIS, L. S. & LAMBERT, D. M. 2000. Genetic monogamy mirrors social monogamy in the Fiordland Crested Penguin. *New Zealand Journal of Zoology* 27: 311–316.

MCLEAN, I. G. & RUSS, R. B. 1991. The Fiordland Crested Penguin survey, Stage I: Doubtful to Milford Sounds. *Notornis* 38: 183–190.

MCLEAN, I. G., STUDHOLME, B. J. S. & RUSS, R. B. 1993. The Fiordland Crested Penguin Survey, Stage III: Breaksea Island, Chalky and Preservation Inlets. *Notornis* 40: 85–94.

MCNAB, B. K. 1994. Energy conservation and the evolution of flightlessness in birds. *American Naturalist* 144: 628–642.

MCQUEEN, S. M., DAVIS, L. S. & YOUNG, G. 1998. The reproductive endocrinology of Fiordland Crested Penguins (*Eudyptes pachyrhynchus*). *Emu* 98: 127–131.

MCQUEEN, S. M., DAVIS, L. S. & YOUNG, G. 1999. Sex steroid and corticosterone levels of Adélie Penguins (*Pygoscelis adeliae*) during courtship and incubation. *General and Comparative Endocrinology* 114: 11–18.

MEAD, P. S. & MORTON, M. L. 1985. Hatching asynchrony in the Mountain White-crowned Sparrow (*Zonotrichia leucophrys oriantha*): a selected or incidental trait? *Auk* 102: 781–792.

MEATHREL, C. E. & KLOMP, N. I. 1990. Predation of Little Penguin eggs by King's skinks on Penguin Island, Western Australia. *Corella* 14: 129–130.

MEIJER, T. & DRENT, R. 1999. Re-examination of the capital and income dichotomy in breeding birds. *Ibis* 141: 399–414.

MEREDITH, M. A. M. & SIN, F. Y. T. 1988a. Morphometrical analysis of four populations of the Little Blue Penguin, *Eudyptula minor*. *Journal of Natural History* 22: 801–809.

MEREDITH, M. A. M. & SIN, F. Y. T. 1988b. Genetic variation of four populations of the Little Blue Penguin, *Eudyptula minor*. *Heredity* 60: 69–76.

MICOL, T. & JOUVENTIN, P. 2001. Long-term population trends in seven Antarctic seabirds at Pointe Geologie (Terre Adelie)—human impact compared with environmental change. *Polar Biology* 24: 175–185.

MILLER, G. D. & DAVIS, L. S. 1993. Foraging flexibility of Adelie Penguins *Pygoscelis adeliae*: consequences for an indicator species. *Biological Conservation* 63: 223–230.

MOCK, D. W. & SCHWAGMEYER, P. L. 1990. The peak load reduction hypothesis for avian hatching asynchrony. *Evolutionary Ecoogy* 4: 249–260.

MOCZYDLOWSKI, E. 1989. Protection of eggs and chicks against flooding as a part of nesting strategy of pygoscelid penguins at King George Island, South Shetlands. *Polish Polar Research* 10: 163–181.

MØLLER, A. P. 1988. Female choice selects for male sexual tail ornaments in the monogamous swallow. *Nature* 332: 640–642.

MOLLER, H., KEEDWELL, R., RATZ, H. & BRUCE, L. 1998. Lagomorph abundance around Yellow-eyed Penguin (*Megadyptes antipodes*) colonies, South Island, New Zealand. *New Zealand Journal of Ecology* 22: 65–70.

MONOD, J. L., ARNAUD, P. M. & ARNOUX, A. 1992. The level of pollution of Kerguelen Islands biota by organochlorine compounds during the seventies. *Marine Pollution Bulletin* 24: 626–629.

MOORE, G. J., ROBERTSON, G. & WIENERKE, B. 1998. Food requirements of breeding King Penguins at Heard Island and potential overlap with commercial fisheries. *Polar Biology* 20: 293–302.

MOORE, P. J. 1992. Breeding biology of the Yellow-eyed Penguin *Megadyptes antipodes* on Campbell Island. *Emu* 92: 157–162.

MOORE, P. J. 1999. Foraging range of the Yellow-eyed Penguin *Megadyptes antipodes*. *Marine Ornithology* 27: 49–58.

MOORE, P. J. & MOFFAT, R. D. 1992. Predation of Yellow-eyed Penguin by Hooker's Sealion. *Notornis* 39: 68–69.

MOORS, P. J. & MERTON, D. V. 1984. First records for New Zealand of Moseley's Rockhopper Penguin (*Eudyptes chrysocome moseleyi*). *Notornis* 31: 262–265.

MORENO, J., AMAT, J. A., SANZ, J. J. & CARRASCAL, L. M. 1998. Determinants of feeding chases in the Chinstrap penguin *Pygoscelis antarctica*. *Emu* 98: 192–196.

MORENO, J., BARBOSA, A., POTTI, J. & MERINO, S. 1997. The effects of hatching date and parental quality on chick growth and creching age in the Chinstrap penguin (*Pygoscelis antarctica*): a field experiment. *Auk* 114: 47–54.

MORENO, J., CARRASCAL, L. M. & SANZ, J. J. 1996. Parent-offspring interactions and feeding chases in the Chinstrap Penguin *Pygoscelis antartica*. *Bird Behaviour* 11: 31–34.

MORENO, J., CARRASCAL, L. M., SANZ, J. J., AMAT, J. A. & CUERVO, J. J. 1994. Hatching asynchrony, sibling hierarchies and brood reduction in the Chinstrap Penguin *Pygoscelis antarctica*. *Polar Biology* 14: 21–30.

MULLER-SCHWARZE, D. & MULLER-SCHWARZE, C. 1973. Differential predation by South Polar Skuas in an Adelie Penguin rookery. *Condor* 75: 127–131.

MURIE, J. O., DAVIS, L. S. & MCLEAN, I. G. 1991. Identifying the sex of Fiordland Crested Penguins by morphometric characters. *Notornis* 38: 233–238.

MURPHY, E. J., WATKINS, J. L., REID, K., TRATHAN, P. N., EVERSON, I., CROXALL, J. P., PRIDDLE, J., BRANDON, M. A., BRIERLEY, A. S. & HOFMANN, E. 1998. Interannual variability of the South Georgia marine ecosystem: biological and physical sources of variation in the abundance of krill. *Fisheries Oceanography* 7: 381–390.

MURPHY, M. E., KING, J. R., TARUSCIO, T. G. & GEUPEL, G. R. 1990. Amino acid composition of feather barbs and rachises in three species of Pygoscelid Penguins: nutritional implications. *Condor* 92: 913–921.

NAPIER, R. B. 1968. Erect-crested and Rockhopper Penguins interbreeding in the Falkland Islands. *British Antarctic Survey Bulletin* 16: 71–72.

NIMON, A. J., SCHROTER, R. C. & STONEHOUSE, B. 1995. Heart rate of disturbed penguins. *Nature* 374: 415.

NORBERG, R. A. 1981. Optimal flight speed in birds when feeding young. *Journal of Animal Ecology* 50: 473–477.

NORDIN, K. E. 1988. Vocalization of the Yellow-eyed Penguin. *Cormorant* 16: 132.

NORHEIM, G. 1987. Levels and interactions of heavy metals in seabirds from Svalbard and the Antarctic. *Environmental Pollution* 47: 83–94.

NORMAN, F. I., CULLEN, J. M. & DANN, P. 1992. Little penguins *Eudyptula minor* in Victoria: past, present and future. *Emu* 91: 402–408.

NUMATA, M. 2000. *Nest attendance patterns of Little Penguins (*Eudyptula minor*): conflicts between breeding and foraging*. MSc thesis, University of Otago, Dunedin, New Zealand.

NUMATA, M., DAVIS, L. S. & RENNER, M. 2000. Prolonged foraging trips and egg desertion in Little Penguins (*Eudyptula minor*). *New Zealand Journal of Zoology* 27: 277–289.

NUNN, G. B. & STANLEY, S. E. 1998. Body size effects and rates of cytochrome b evolution in tube-nosed seabirds. *Mol. Biol. Evol.* 15: 1360–1371.

O'HARA, R. J. 1989. An estimate of the phylogeny of the living penguins (Aves: Spheniscidae). *American Zoologist* 29: 11A.

OELKE, V. H. 1975. Breeding behaviour and success in a colony of Adelie Penguins *Pygoscelis adeliae* at Cape Crozier, Antarctica. In *The Biology of Penguina* (Ed. by Stonehouse, B.), pp. 363–395. Macmillan, London.

OLSSON, O. 1997. Clutch abandonment: a state-dependent decision in King Penguins. *Journal of Avian Biology* 28: 264–267.

OLSSON, O. 1998. Divorce in King Penguins: asynchrony, expensive fat storing and ideal free mate choice. *Oikos* 83: 574–581.

OLSSON, O. & NORTH, A. W. 1997. Diet of the King Penguin *Aptenodytes patagonicus* during three summers at South Georgia. *Ibis* 139: 504–512.

PAREDES, R. & ZAVALAGA, C. B. 1998. Overview of the effects of El Nino 1997–1998 on Humboldt Penguins and other seabirds at Punta San Juan, Peru. *Penguin Conservation* 11: 5–7.

PAREDES, R. & ZAVALAGA, C. B. 2001. Nesting sites and nest types as important factors for the conservation of Humboldt Penguins (*Sphensicus humboldti*). *Biological Conservation* 100: 199–205.

PAREDES, R., ZAVALAGA, C. B. & BONESS, D. J. 2002. Patterns of egg laying and breeding success in Humboldt Penguins (*Spheniscus humboldti*) at Punta San Juan, Peru. *Auk* 119: 244–250.

PATERSON, A. M., GRAY, R. D. & WALLIS, G. P. 1996. Behavioural evolution in penguins: phylogenetic implications, homology and character evolution. *Systematic Biology.* <?>

PATERSON, A. M., WALLIS, G. P. & GRAY, R. D. 1995. Penguins, petrels, and parsimony: does cladistic analysis of behavior reflect seabird phylogeny? *Evolution* 49: 974–989.

PATERSON, A. M., WALLIS, G. P., WALLIS, L. J. & GRAY, R. D. 2000. Seabird and louse coevolution: complex histories revealed by 12S rRNA sequences and reconciliation analyses. *Systematic Biology* 49: 383–399.

PEACOCK, L., PAULIN, M. & DARBY, J. 2000. Investigations into climate influence on population dynamics of Yellow-eyed Penguins *Megadyptes antipodes*. *New Zealand Journal of Zoology* 27: 317–325.

PENNEY, R. L. 1968. Territorial and social behavior in the Adelie Penguin. In *Antarctic Bird Studies* (Ed. by Austin Jr, O. L.), pp. 83–131. American Geophysical Union, Washington, D.C.

PENNEY, R. L. & LOWRY, G. 1967. Leopard Seal predation of Adelie Penguins. *Ecology* 48: 878–882.

PERRIMAN, L., HOUSTON, D., STEEN, H. & JOHANNESEN, E. 2000. Climatic fluctuation effects on breeding of Blue Penguins (*Eudyptula minor*). *New Zealand Journal of Zoology* 27: 261–267.

PERRIMAN, L. & STEEN, H. 2000. Blue penguin (*Eudyptula minor*) nest distribution and breeding success on Otago Peninsula, 1992 to 1998. *New Zealand Journal of Zoology* 27: 269–275.

PIATKOWSKI, U. & PUTZ, K. 1994. Squid diet of Emperor Penguins (*Aptenodytes forsteri*) in the eastern Weddell Sea, Antarctica during late summer. *Antarctic Science* 6: 241–247.

PLOETZ, J., Weidel, H. and Bersch, M. 1991. Winter aggregations of marine mammals and birds in the north-eastern Weddell Sea (Antarctica) pack ice. *Polar Biology* 11: 305–310.

PREVOST, J. 1961. *Ecologie du manchot Empereur.* Hermann, Paris.

PREVOST, J. & VILTER, V. 1963. Histologie de la sécrétion oesophagienne de Manchot Empereur. In *Proceedings of the Thirteenth International Ornithological Congress* (Ed. by Sibley, G. C.), pp. 1085–1094. American Ornithological Union, Baton Rouge, Louisiana.

PROFFITT, F. M. & McLEAN, I. G. 1990. Recognition of parents' calls by chicks of the Snares Crested Penguin. *Bird Behaviour* 9: 103–113.

PUDDICOMBE, R. A. & JOHNSTONE, G. W. 1988. The breeding season diet of Adelie Penguins at Vestfold Hills, East Antarctica. *Hydrobiologia* 165: 239–253.

PUTZ, K., INGHAM, R. J. & SMITH, J. G. 2000. Satellite tracking of the winter migration of Magellanic Penguins *Spheniscus magellanicus* breeding in the Falkland Islands. *Ibis* 142: 614–622.

PUTZ, K., INGHAM, R. J. & SMITH, J. G. 2002. Foraging movements of Magellanic Penguins *Spheniscus magellanicus* during the breeding season in the Falkland Islands. *Aquatic Conservation: marine and Freshwater Ecosystems* 12: 75–87.

PUTZ, K., ROPERT COUDERT, Y., CHARRASSIN, J. B. & WILSON, R. P. 1999. Foraging areas of King Penguins *Aptenodytes patagonicus* breeding at Possession Island, southern Indian Ocean. *Marine Ornithology* 27: 77–84.

QUAMMEN, D. 1997. *The Song of the Dodo—island biogeography in an age of extinctions.* Touchstone Simon and Schuster, New York.

RACLOT, T., GROSCOLAS, R. & CHEREL, Y. 1998. Fatty acid evidence for the importance of myctophid fishes in the diet of King Penguins, *Aptenodytes patagonicus*. *Marine Biology* 132: 523–533.

RADL, A. & CULIK, B. M. 1999. Foraging behaviour and reproductive success in Magellanic Penguins (*Spheniscus magellanicus*): a comparative study of two colonies in southern Chile. *Marine Biology* 133: 381–393.

RAHN, H. & AR, A. 1974. The avian egg incubation time, water loss and nest humidity. *Condor* 76: 147–152.

RAIKOW, R. J., BICANOVSKY, L. & BLEDSOE, A. 1988. Forelimb joint mobility and the evolution of wing-propelled diving in birds. *Auk* 105: 446–451.

RANDALL, R. M. & RANDALL, B. M. 1990. Cetaceans as predators of Jackass Penguins *Spheniscus demersus*: deductions based on behaviour. *Marine Ornithology* 18: 9–12.

RATZ, H. 1997. *Ecology, identification and control of introduced mammalian predators of Yellow-eyed Penguins* (Megadyptes antipodes*)*. PhD thesis, University of Otago, Dunedin, New Zealand.

RATZ, H. 2000. Movements by stoats (*Mustela erminea*) and ferrets (*M. furo*) through rank grass of Yellow-eyed Penguin (*Megadyptes antipodes*) breeding areas. *New Zealand Journal of Zoology* 27: 57–69.

RATZ, H. & MURPHY, B. 1999. Effects of habitat and introduced mammalian predators on the breeding success of Yellow-eyed Penguins *Megadyptes antipodes*, South Island, New Zealand. *Pacific Conservation Biology* 5: 16–27.

RATZ, H. & THOMPSON, C. 1999. Who is watching whom? Checks for impacts of tourists on Yellow-eyed Penguins *Megadyptes antipodes*. *Marine Ornithology* 27: 205–210.

REID, B. E. 1965. The Adelie Penguin (*Pygoscelis adeliae*) egg. *New Zealand Journal of Science* 8: 503–514.

REID, B. E. & BAILEY, C. 1966. The value of the yolk reserve in Adelie Penguin chicks. *Records of the Dominion Museum.* 5: 185–193.

REID, K. 1995. Oiled penguins observed at Bird Island, South Georgia. *Marine Ornithology* 23: 53–57.

REID, W. V. & BOERSMA, P. D. 1990. Parental quality and selection on egg size in the Magellanic Penguin. *Evolution* 44: 1780–1786.

REILLY, P. N. & CULLEN, J. M. 1981. The Little Penguin *Eudyptula minor* in Victoria, II. Breeding. *Emu* 81: 1–19.

RENNER, M. 1998. *Survival of Little Penguin chicks*. MSc thesis, University of Otago, Dunedin, New Zealand.

RENNER, M. & DAVIS, L. S. 1999. Sexing Little Penguins *Eudyptula minor* from Cook Strait, New Zealand using discriminant function analysis. *Emu* 99: 74–79.

RENNER, M. & DAVIS, L. S. 2001. Survival analysis of Little Penguin *Eudyptula minor* chicks on Motuara Island, New Zealand. *Ibis* 143: 369–379.

RENNER, M., VALENCIA, J., DAVIS, L. S., SAEZ, D. & CIFUENTES, O. 1998. Sexing of adult Gentoo Penguins in Antarctica using morphometrics. *Colonial Waterbirds* 21: 444–449.

RICHDALE, L. E. 1951. *Sexual behaviour in penguins*. Kansas University, Lawrence, Kansas.

RICHDALE, L. E. 1957. *A population study of penguins*. Clarendon Press, Oxford.

RIDOUX, V. & OFFREDO, C. 1989. The diets of five summer breeding seabirds in Adelie Land, Antarctica. *Polar Biology* 9: 137–145.

Robertson, G. 1986. Population size and breeding success of the Gentoo Penguin, *Pygoscelis papua*, at Macquarie Island. *Australian Wildlife Research* 13: 583–587.

ROBERTSON, G., KENT, S. & SEDDON, J. 1994a. Effects of the water-offloading technique on Adelie Penguins. *Journal of Field Ornithology* 65: 376–380.

ROBERTSON, G., WILLIAMS, R., GREEN, K. & ROBERTSON, L. 1994b. Diet composition of Emperor Penguin chicks *Aptenodytes forsteri* at two Mawson Coast colonies, Antarctica. *Ibis* 136: 19–31.

ROBISSON, P., AUBIN, T. & BREMOND, J.-C. 1993. Individuality in the voice of the Emperor Penguin *Aptenodytes forsteri*: adaptation to a noisy environment. *Ethology* 94: 279–290.

ROBISSON, P., AUBIN, T. & BREMOND, J. C. 1989. Individual recognition in the Emperor Penguin (*Aptenodytes forsteri*): respective parts of the temporal pattern and the sound structure of the courtship song. *C. R. Hebd. Seances Acad. Sci. Iii, Paris* 309: 383–388.

ROGERS, T. & BRYDEN, M. M. 1995. Predation of Adelie Penguins (*Pygoscelis adeliae*) by Leopard Seals (*Hydrurga leptonyx*) in Prydz Bay, Antarctica. *Canadian Journal of Zoology* 73: 1001–1004.

ROUNSEVELL, D. E. 1982. Growth rate and recovery of a King Penguin, *Aptenodytes patagonicus*, population after exploitation. *Australian Wildlife Research* 9: 519–525.

ROUNSEVELL, D. E. & BROTHERS, N. P. 1984. The status and conservation of seabirds at Macquarie Island. In *No 2, ICBP Seabird Conservation Symposium, 1982: Status and conservation of the world's seabirds* (Ed. by Croxall, J. P., Evans, P. G. H. and Schreiber, R. W.), pp. 587–592. International Council for Bird Preservation. ICBP Technical Publication., Cambridge.

ROWLEY, I. 1983. Re-mating in birds. In *Mate Choice* (Ed. by Bateson, P.), pp. 331–360. Cambridge University Press, Cambridge.

RYAN, P. G. & BOIX-HINZEN, C. 1998. Tuna longline fisheries off Southern Africa: the need to limit seabird bycaatch. *South African Journal of Science* 94: 179–182.

RYAN, P. G. & COOPER, J. 1991. Rockhopper Penguins and other marine life threatened by driftnet fisheries at Tristan da Cunha. *Oryx* 25: 76–79.

SADLEIR, R. M. F. & LAY, K. M. 1990. Foraging movements of Adelie Penguins (*Pygoscelis adeliae*) in McMurdo Sound. In *Penguin Biology* (Ed. by Davis, L. S. and Darby, J. T.), pp. 157–180. Academic Press, San Diego, California.

SCHWARTZ, M. K., BONESS, D. J., SCHAEFF, C. M., MAJLUF, P. & PERRY, E. A. 1999. Female-solicited extrapair matings in Humboldt Penguins fail to produce extrapair fertilizations. *Behavioural Ecology* 10: 242–250.

SCHWEIGMAN, P. & DARBY, J. T. 1997. Predation of Yellow-eyed Penguins (*Megadyptes antipodes*) on mainland New Zealand by Hooker's Sealion (*Phocarctos hookeri*). *Notornis* 44: 265–266.

SCOLARO, J. A. 1984. Timing of nest relief during incubation and guard stage period of chicks in Magellanic Penguin (*Spheniscus magellanicus*) (Aves: Spheniscidae). *Historia Natural* 4: 281–284.

SCOLARO, J. A. 1987. A model life table for Magellanic Penguins (*Spheniscus magellanicus*) at Punta Tombo, Argentina. *Journal of Field Ornithology* 58: 432–441.

SCOLARO, J. A., HALL, M. A. & XIMENEZ, I. M. 1983. The Magellanic Penguin (*Spheniscus magellanicus*): sexing adults by discriminant analysis of morphometric characters. *Auk* 100: 221–224.

SEDDON, P. J. 1989. Patterns of nest relief during incubation, and incubation period variability in the Yellow-eyed Penguin (*Megadyptes antipodes*). *New Zealand Journal of Zoology* 16: 393–400.

SEDDON, P. J. & DARBY, J. T. 1990. Activity budget for breeding Yellow-eyed Penguins. *New Zealand Journal of Zoology* 17: 527–532.

SEDDON, P. J. & DAVIS, L. S. 1989. Nest-site selection by Yellow-eyed Penguins. *Condor* 91: 653–659.

SEDDON, P. J. & VAN HEEZIK, Y. 1990. Diving depths of the Yellow-eyed Penguin, *Megadyptes antipodes*. *Emu* 90: 53–57.

SEDDON, P. J. & VAN HEEZIK, Y. 1991a. Effects of hatching order, sibling asymmetries, and nest site on survival analysis of Jackass Penguin chicks. *Auk* 108: 548–555.

SEDDON, P. J. & VAN HEEZIK, Y. 1991b. Hatching asynchrony and brood reduction in the Jackass Penguin: an experimental study. *Animal Behaviour* 42: 347–356.

SEDDON, P. J. & VAN HEEZIK, Y. 1991c. Patterns of nest relief during incubation by jackass penguins *Spheniscus demersus*. *Ostrich* 62: 82–83.

SEDDON, P. J. & VAN HEEZIK, Y. 1993a. Chick creching and intraspecific aggression in the Jackass Penguin. *Journal of Field Ornithology* 64: 90–95.

SEDDON, P. J. & VAN HEEZIK, Y. M. 1993b. Parent-offspring recognition in the Jackass Penguin. *Journal of Field Ornithology* 64: 27–31.

SEN GUPTA, R., SARKAR, A. & KUREISHEY, T. W. 1996. PCBs and organochlorine pesticides in krill, birds and water from Antartica. *Deep-Sea Research Part II-Topical Studies in Oceanography* 43: 119–126.

SHANNON, L. J. & CRAWFORD, R. J. M. 1999. Management of the African Penguin *Spheniscus demersus*—insights from modelling. *Marine Ornithology* 27: 119–128.

SHUFORD, W. D. & SPEAR, L. B. 1988. Surveys of breeding Chinstrap Penguins in the South Shetland Islands, Antarctica. *British Antarctic Survey Bulletin* 81: 19–30.

SIBLEY, C. G. & AHLQUIST, J. E. 1990. *Phylogeny and classification of birds. A study in molecular evolution*. Yale University Press, New Haven.

SIBLEY, C. G., AHLQUIST, J. E. & MONROE Jr, B. L. 1988. A classification of the living birds of the world based on DNA-DNA hybridization studies. *Auk* 105: 409–423.

SIBLEY, C. G., MONROE, B. L. J. C. G. S. & MONROE, B. L. J. 1990. *Distribution and taxonomy of birds of the world*. Yale University Press, New Haven.

SIEGEL-CAUSEY, D. 1997. Phylogeny of the Pelacaniformes: molecular systematics of a privative group. In *Avian molecular evolution and systematics* (Ed. by Mindell, D. P.), pp. 159–171. Academic Press, San Diego, California.

SIEGFRIED, W. R., FROST, P. G. H., KINAHAN, J. B. & COOPER, J. 1975. Social behaviour of Jackass Penguins at sea. *Zoologica Africana* 10: 87–100.

SIMEONE, A., BERNAL, M. & MEZA, J. 1999. Incidental mortality of Humboldt Penguins *Spheniscus humboldti* in gill nets, central Chile. *Marine Ornithology* 27: 157–161.

SIMPSON, G. G. 1946. Fossil penguins. *Bulletin of the American Museum of Natural History* 87: 1–99.

SIMPSON, G. G. 1975. Fossil Penguins. In *The Biology of Penguins* (Ed. by Stonehouse, B.), pp. 19–41. Macmillan, London.

SIMPSON, G. G. 1976. *Penguins. Past and present, here and there*. Yale University, New Haven and London.

SLADEN, W. J. L. 1958. The Pygoscelid Penguins. I. Methods of study. II. The Adélie Penguin. *Scientific Reports of Falkland Island Dependency Survey* 17: 97pp.

SPEEDIE, C. 1992. An Erect-crested Penguin in the southern Indian Ocean. *Notornis* 39: 58–60.

SPEIRS, E. A. H. & DAVIS, L. S. 1991. Discrimination by Adelie Penguins (*Pygoscelis adeliae*), between the Loud Mutual calls of mates, neighbours and strangers. *Animal Behaviour* 41: 937–944.

SPURR, E. B. 1975a. Behavior of the Adelie Penguin chick. *Condor* 77: 272–280.

SPURR, E. B. 1975b. Breeding of the Adelie penguin (*Pygoscelis adeliae*) at Cape Bird. *Ibis* 117: 324–338.

SPURR, E. B. 1977. Adaptive significance of the reoccupation period of the Adelie Penguin. *Adaptations within Antarctic Biosystem: Proceedings of the third SCAR Symposium of Antarctic Biology*: 605–618.

ST. CLAIR, C. C. 1990. *Mechanisms of brood reduction in Fiordland Crested Penguins* (Eudyptes pachyrhynchus). MSc thesis, University of Canterbury, Christchurch, New Zealand.

ST. CLAIR, C. C. 1992. Incubation behaviour, brood patch formation and obligate brood reduction in Fiordland Crested Penguins. *Behavioural Ecology and Sociobiology* 31: 409–416.

ST. CLAIR, C. C., McLEAN, I. G., MURIE, J. O., PHILLIPSON, S. M. & STUDHOLME, B. J. S. 1999. Fidelity to nest site and mate in Fiordland Crested Penguins *Eudyptes pachyrhynchus*. *Marine Ornithology* 27: 37–41.

ST. CLAIR, C. C. & ST. CLAIR, R. C. 1992. Weka predation on eggs and chicks of Fiordland Crested Penguins. *Notornis* 39: 60–63.

ST. CLAIR, C. C., WAAS, J. R., ST. CLAIR, R. C. & BOAG, P. T. 1995. Unfit mothers? Maternal infanticide in Royal Penguins. *Animal Behaviour* 50: 1177–1185.

STAHEL, C. & GALES, R. 1987. *Little Penguin. Fairy Penguins in Australia.* New South Wales University Press, Kensington, Australia.

STENNING, M. J. 1996. Hatching asynchrony, brood reduction and other rapidly reproducing hypotheses. *Trends in Ecology and Evolution* 11: 243–246.

STOKES, D. L. & BOERSMA, P. D. 1999. Where breeding Magellanic Penguins *Spheniscus magellanicus* forage: satellite telemetry results and their implications for penguin conservation. *Marine Ornithology* 27: 59–65.

STOKES, D. L., BOERSMA, P. D. & DAVIS, L. S. 1998. Satellite tracking of Magellanic Penguin migration. *Condor* 100: 376–381.

STOLESON, S. H. & BEISSINGER, S. R. 1995. Hatching asynchrony and the onset of incubation in birds, revisited. When is the critical period? In *Current Ornithology* (Ed. by Power, D. M.), pp. 191–271. Plenum Press, New York.

STONEHOUSE, B. 1953. The Emperor Penguin *Aptenodytes forsteri* Gray. 1. Breeding behaviour and development. *Scientific Reports of Falkland Island Dependency Survey* 6: 1–33.

STONEHOUSE, B. 1960. The King Penguin *Aptenodytes patagonica* of South Georgia 1. Breeding behaviour and development. *Falkland Islands Dependency Survey Scientific Report* 23: 1–81.

STONEHOUSE, B. 1963. Observations on Adelie Penguin (*Pygoscelis adeliae*) at Cape Royds, Antarctica. *Proceedings of the 13th International Ornithological Congress, Ithaca, 1962* 13: 766–779.

STONEHOUSE, B. 1967. The general biology and thermal balances of penguins. *Advances in Ecological Research* 4: 131–196.

STONEHOUSE, B. 1969. Environmental temperatures of Tertiary penguins. *Science* 163: 673–675.

STONEHOUSE, B. 1970a. Geographic variation in Gentoo Penguins *Pygoscelis papua*. *Ibis* 112: 52–57.

STONEHOUSE, B. 1970b. Adaptation in polar and subpolar penguins (*Spheniscidae*). In *Antarctic Ecology*. (Ed. by Holdgate, M. W.), pp. 526–541. London and New York, Academic Press.

STONEHOUSE, B. 1975. Introduction: the Spheniscidae. In *The Biology of Penguins* (Ed. by Stonehouse, B.), pp. 1–16. Macmillan, London.

SZEFER, P., PEMPKOWIAK, J., SKWARZEC, B., BOJANOWSKI, R. & HOLM, E. 1993. Concentration of selected metals in penguins and other representative fauna of Antarctica. *The Science of the Total Environment* 138: 281–288.

TAYLOR, R. H. 1962. The Adelie Penguin *Pygoscelis adeliae* at Cape Royds. *Ibis* 104: 176–204.

TAYLOR, R. H. & WILSON, P. R. 1990. Recent increase and southern expansion of Adelie Penguin populations in the Ross Sea, Antarctica, related to climate warming. *New Zealand Journal of Ecology* 14: 25–29.

TENNYSON, A. J. D. & MISKELLY, C. M. 1989. "Dark-faced" Rockhopper Penguins at the Snares Islands. *Notornis* 36: 183–189.

THOMAS, T. & BRETAGNOLLE, V. 1988. Non-breeding birds of Point Geologie Archipelago, Adelie Land, Antarctica. *Emu* 88: 104–106.

THOMPSON, D. H. 1981. Feeding chases in the Adelie Penguin. *Antarctic Research Series* 30: 105–122.

THOMPSON, D. H. & EMLEN, J. T. 1968. Parent-chick individual recognition in the Adelie Penguin. *Antarctic Journal of the United States* 3: 132.

THOMPSON, K. R. 1993. Variation in Magellanic Penguin *Spheniscus magellanicus* diet in the Falkland Islands. *Marine Ornithology* 21: 57–67.

TODD, F. S. 1988. Weddell Seal preys on Chinstrap Penguin. *Condor* 90: 249–250.

TRIVELPIECE, S. G., TRIVELPIECE, W. Z. & VOLKMAN, N. J. 1985. Plumage characteristics of juvenile Pygoscelid penguins. *Ibis* 127: 378–380.

TRIVELPIECE, W. Z. & TRIVELPIECE, S. G. 1990. Courtship period of Adélie, Gentoo and Chinstrap Penguins. In *Penguin Biology* (Ed. by Davis, L. S. and Darby, J. T.), pp. 113–127. Academic Press, San Diego, California.

TRIVELPIECE, W. Z., TRIVELPIECE, S. G., GEUPEL, G. R., KJELMYR, R. & VOLKMAN, N. J. 1990. Adélie and Chinstrap Penguins: their potential as monitors ot the Southern Ocean marine ecosystem. In *Ecological Change and Conservation* (Ed. by Kerry, K. R. and Hempel, G.), pp. 191–202. Springer-Verlag, Berlin and Heidelberg.

TRIVELPIECE, W. Z., TRIVELPIECE, S. G. & VOLKMAN, N. J. 1987. Ecological segregation of Adelie, Gentoo, and Chinstrap Penguins at King George Island, Antarctica. *Ecology* 68: 351–361.

TRIVELPIECE, W. Z., TRIVELPIECE, S. G., VOLKMAN, N. J. & WARE, S. H. 1983. Breeding and feeding ecologies of Pygoscelid penguins. *Antarctic Journal of the United States* 18: 209–210.

TRIVELPIECE, W. Z. & VOLKMAN, N. J. 1982. Feeding strategies of sympatric South Polar *Catharacta maccormicki* and Brown Skuas *C. lonnbergi. Ibis* 124: 50–54.

TRIVERS, R. 1985. *Social evolution.* Benjamin/Cummings, Menlo Park.

TRIVERS, R. L. 1972. Parental investment and sexual selection. In *Sexual Selection and the Descent of Man 1871–1971* (Ed. by Campbell, B.), pp. 136–179. Aldine, Chicago.

ULBRICHT, J. & ZIPPEL, D. 1994. Delayed laying and prolonged fasting in Adelie Penguins *Pygoscelis adeliae. Polar Biology* 14: 215–217.

UNDERHILL, L. G., BARTLETT, P. A., BAUMANN, L., CRAWFORD, R. J. M., DYER, B. M., GILDENHUYS, A., NEL, D. C., OATLEY, T. B., THORNTON, M., UPFOLD, L., WILLIAMS, A. J., WHITTINGTON, P. A. & WOLFAARDT, A. C. 1999. Mortality and survival of African Penguins *Spheniscus demersus* involved in the Apollo Sea oil spill: an evaluation of rehabilitation efforts. *Ibis* 141: 29–37.

VALLE, C. A., CRUZ, F., CRUZ, J. B., MERLEN, G. & COULTER, M. C. 1987. The impact of the 1982–1983 El Niño-Southern Oscillation on seabirds in the Galapagos Islands, Ecuador. *J. Geophys. Res. C Oceans* 92: 14437–444.

VAN HEEZIK, Y. M. 1988. *Growth and diet of the yellow-eye penguin,* Megadyptes antipodes. PhD thesis, University of Otago, Dunedin, New Zealand.

VAN HEEZIK, Y. 1989. Diet of the Fiordland Crested Penguin during the post-guard phase of chick growth. *Notornis* 36: 151–156.

VAN HEEZIK, Y. 1990a. Diets of Yellow-eyed, Fiordland Crested, and Little Blue Penguins breeding sympatrically on Codfish Island, New Zealand. *New Zealand Journal of Zoology* 17: 543–548.

VAN HEEZIK, Y. 1990b. Seasonal, geographical, and age-related variations in the diet of the Yellow-eyed Penguin (*Megadyptes antipodes*). *New Zealand Journal of Zoology* 17: 201–212.

VAN HEEZIK, Y. & DAVIS, L. S. 1990. Effects of food variability on growth rates, fledgling sizes and reproductive success in the Yellow-eyed Penguin *Megadyptes antipodes. Ibis* 132: 354–365.

VAN HEEZIK, Y. & SEDDON, P. 1989. Stomach sampling in the Yellow-eyed Penguin: erosion of otoliths and squid beaks. *Journal of Field Ornithology* 60: 451–458.

VAN HEEZIK, Y. & SEDDON, P. J. 1990. Effect of human disturbance on beach groups of Jackass Penguins. *South African Journal of Wildlife Research* 20: 89–93.

VAN HEEZIK, Y. M. & SEDDON, P. J. 1991. Influence of hatching order and brood size on growth in jackass penguins. *South African Journal of Zoology* 26: 199–203.

VAN HEEZIK, Y. M. & SEDDON, P. J. 1996. Scramble feeding in Jackass Penguins—within-brood food distribution and the maintenance of sibling asymmetries. *Animal Behaviour* 51: 1383–1390.

VIÑUELA, J. 1997. Adaptation vs. constraint—intraclutch egg-mass variation in birds. *Journal of Animal Ecology* 66: 781–792.

VIÑUELA, J., MORENO, J., CARRASCAL, L. M., SANZ, J. J., AMAT, J. A., FERRER, M., BELLIURE, J. & CUERVO, J. J. 1996. The effect of hatching date on parental care, chick growth, and chick mortality in the Chinstrap Penguin *Pygoscelis antarctica*. *Journal of Zoology, London* 240: 51–58.

VOLKMAN, N. J. & TRIVELPIECE, W. Z. 1981. Nest-site selection among Adelie, Chinstrap and Gentoo Penguins in mixed species rookeries. *Wilson Bulletin* 93: 243–248.

WAAS, J. R. 1990. Intraspecific variation in social repertoires from cave-dwelling and burrow-dwelling Little Blue Penguins. *Behaviour* 115: 63–99.

WAAS, J. R. 1995. Social stimulation and reproductive schedules: does the acoustic environment influence the egg-laying schedule in penguin colonies? In *The Penguins: Ecology and Management* (Ed. by Dann, P., Norman, I. and Reilly, P.), pp. 111–137. Surrey Beatty & Sons, Chipping Norton, NSW, Australia.

WANWIMOLRUK, S., ZHANG, H., COVILLE, P. F., SAVILLE, D. J. & DAVIS, L. S. 1999. In vitro hepatic metabolism of CYP3A-mediated drug, quinine, in Adelie Penguins. *Comparative Biochemistry And Physiology Part C* 124: 301–307.

WARHAM, J. 1974. The Fiordland Crested Penguin *Eudyptes pachyrhynchus*. *Ibis* 116: 1–27.

WARHAM, J. 1975. The Crested Penguins. In *The Biology of Penguins* (Ed. by Stonehouse, B.), pp. 189–269. MacMillan, London.

WAUGH, S. M., TROUP, T., FILIPPI, D. P. & WEIMERSKIRCH, H. 2002. Foraging zones in southern Royal Albatross. *Condor* 104: 662–667.

WEAVERS, B. W. 1992. Seasonal foraging ranges and travels at sea of Little Penguins *Eudyptula minor*, determined by radio tracking. *Emu* 91: 302–317.

WEILER, J. L. & HOELZER, G. A. 1997. Escaping from the Felsenstein zone by detecting long branches in phylogenetic data. *Molecular Phylogenetics and Evolution* 8: 375–384.

WEIMERSKIRCH, H., SALAMOLARD, M., SARRAZIN, F. & JOUVENTIN, P. 1993. Foraging strategy of Wandering Albatross through the breeding season: a study using satellite telemetry. *Auk* 110: 325–342.

WEIMERSKIRCH, H., STAHL, J. C. & JOUVENTIN, P. 1992. The breeding biology and population dynamics of King Penguins *Aptenodytes patagonica* on the Crozet Islands. *Ibis* 134: 107–117.

WHITEHEAD, M. D., JOHNSTONE, G. W. & BURTON, H. R. 1988. The food, over seven breeding seasons, of the Adélie Penguin in Prydz Bay, Antarctica. *Cormorant* 16: 136.

WIENECKE, B. C. 1993. *The Size and Breeding Patterns of Little Penguins* Eudyptula minor *in Australia: a comparative study*. PhD thesis, Murdoch University, Perth, Australia.

WIENECKE, B. C., LAWLESS, R., RODARY, D., BOST, C. A., THOMSON, R., PAULY, T., ROBERTSON, G., KERRY, K. R. & LEMAHO, Y. 2000. Adelie Penguin foraging behaviour and krill abundance along the Wilkes and Adelie Land coasts, Antarctica. *Deep-Sea Research Part II-Topical Studies in Oceanography* 47: 2573–2587.

WIENECKE, B. C. & ROBERTSON, G. 1997. Foraging space of emperor penguins *Aptenodytes forsteri* in antarctic shelf waters in winter. *Marine Ecology Progress Series* 159: 249–263.

WIENECKE, B. C. & ROBERTSON, G. 2000. Variability of foraging behaviour of King Penguins at Macquarie Island. 4th International penguin Conference, Coquimbo, Chile.

WIENECKE, B. C., WOOLLER, R. D. & KLOMP, N. I. 1995. The ecology and management of Little Penguins on Penguin Island, Western Australia. In *The Penguins: Ecology and Management* (Ed. by Dann, P., Norman, I. and Reilly, P.), pp. 440–467. Surrey Beatty & Sons, Chipping Norton, NSW, Australia.

WILLIAMS, A. J. 1981. Why do penguins have long laying intervals? *Ibis* 123: 202–204.

WILLIAMS, A. J. 1984. The status and conservation of seabirds on some islands in the African sector of the southern ocean. In *No 2, ICBP Seabird Conservation Symposium, 1982: Status and conservation of the world's seabirds* (Ed. by Croxall, J. P., Evans, P. G. H. and Schreiber, R. W.), pp. 627–635. International Council for Bird Preservation. ICBP Technical Publication., Cambridge.

WILLIAMS, A. J., DYER, B. M., RANDALL, R. M. & KOMEN, J. 1990. Killer whales *Orcinus orca* and seabirds: "play", predation and association. *Marine Ornithology* 18: 1–2.

WILLIAMS, A. J., SIEGFRIED, W. R. & COOPER, J. 1982. Egg composition and hatchling precocity in seabirds. *Ibis* 124: 456–470.

WILLIAMS, T. D. 1988. Plumage characteristics of juvenile and adult Gentoo Penguins *Pygoscelis papua*. *Ibis* 130: 565–566.

WILLIAMS, T. D. 1990. Growth and survival in Macaroni Penguin, *Eudyptes chrysolophus*, A- and B- chicks: do females maximise investment in the large B-egg? *Oikos* 59: 349–354.

WILLIAMS, T. D. 1992. Reproductive endocrinology of Macaroni (*Eudyptes chrysolophus*) and Gentoo (*Pygoscelis papua*) Penguins: I Seasonal changes in plasma levels of gonadal steroids and LH in breeding adults. *General and Comparative Endocrinology* 85: 230–240.

WILLIAMS, T. D. 1995. *The Penguins: Spheniscidae*. Oxford University Press, Oxford.

WILLIAMS, T. D. & CROXALL, J. P. 1991a. Annual variation in breeding biology of Macaroni Penguins, *Eudyptes chrysolophus*, at Bird Island, South Georgia. *Journal of Zoology, London* 223: 189–202.

WILLIAMS, T. D. & CROXALL, J. P. 1991b. Chick growth and survival in Gentoo Penguins *Pygoscelis papua*: effect of hatching asynchrony and variation in food supply. *Polar Biology* 11: 197–202.

WILLIAMS, T. D., GHEBREMESKEL, K., WILLIAMS, G. & CRAWFORD, M. A. 1992. Breeding and moulting fasts in Macaroni Penguins: do birds exhaust their fat reserves? *Comparative Biochemical Physiology A* 103: 783–785.

WILLIAMS, T. D. & RODWELL, S. 1992. Annual variation in return rate, mate and nest-site fidelity in breeding Gentoo and Macaroni Penguins. *Condor* 94: 636–645.

WILSON, G. J. 1979. Oiled penguins in Antarctica. *New Zealand Antarctic Record* 2: 3.

WILSON, K.-J., TAYLOR, R. H. & BARTON, K. J. 1990. The impact of man on Adelie Penguins at Cape Hallett, Antarctica. In *Antarctic Ecosystems. Ecological Change and Conservation* (Ed. by Kerry, K. R. and Hempel, G.), pp. 183–190. Springer-Verlag, Berlin Heidelberg.

WILSON, R. P. 1984. An improved stomach pump for penguins and other seabirds. *Journal of Field Ornithology* 55: 109–112.

WILSON, R. P. 1985a. The Jackass Penguin (*Spheniscus demersus*) as a pelagic predator. *Marine Ecology Progress Series* 25: 219–227.

WILSON, R. P. 1985b. Seasonality in diet and breeding success of the Jackass Penguin *Spheniscus demersus*. *Journal fur Ornithologie* 126: 53–62.

WILSON, R. P. 1991. The behaviour of diving birds. In *Acta XX Congressus Internationalis Ornithologici* (Ed. by Bell, B. D., Cossee, R. O., Flux, J. E. C., Heather, B. D., Hitchmough, R. A., Robertson, C. J. R. and Williams, M. J.), pp. 1853–1867. New Zealand Ornithological Congress Trust Board, Wellington, New Zealand.

WILSON, R. P. 1995. Foraging Ecology. In *The Penguins: Spheniscidae* (Ed. by Williams, T. D.), pp. 81–106. Oxford University Press, Oxford, New York.

WILSON, R. P. 2001. Beyond rings on birds for determination of movements: wither the archival tag? *Ardea* 89: 231–240.

WILSON, R. P., ADELUNG, D. & LATORRE, L. 1998. Radiative heat loss in Gentoo Penguin (*Pygoscelis papua*) adults and chicks and the importance of warm feet. *Physiological Zoology* 71: 524–533.

WILSON, R. P., CULIK, B., DANFELD, R. & ADELUNG, D. 1991. People in Antarctica—how much do Adelie Penguins *Pygoscelis adeliae* care? *Polar Biology* 11: 363–370.

WILSON, R. P. & GREMILLET, D. 1996. Body temperatures of free-living African Penguins (*Spheniscus demersus*) and Bank Cormorants (*Phalacrocorax neglectus*). *Journal of Experimental Biology* 199: 2215–2223.

WILSON, R. P., SCOLARO, J. A., PETERS, G., LAURENTI, S., KIERSPEL, M., GALLELLI, H. & UPTON, J. 1995. Foraging areas of Magellanic Penguins *Spheniscus magellanicus* breeding at San Lorenzo, Argentina, during the incubation period. *Marine Ecology Progress Series* 129: 1–6.

WILSON, R. P. & WILSON, M.-P. T. 1990. Foraging ecology of breeding *Spheniscus* penguins. In *Penguin Biology* (Ed. by Davis, L. S. and Darby, J. T.), pp. 181–206. Academic Press, San Diego, California.

WILSON, R. P. & WILSON, M.-P. T. 1995. The foraging behaviour of the African Penguin *Spheniscus demersus*. In *The Penguins: Ecology and Management* (Ed. by Dann, P., Norman, I. and Reilly, P.), pp. 244–265. Surrey Beatty & Sons, Chipping Norton, NSW, Australia.

WOEHLER, E. J. 1995. Bill morphology of Royal and Macaroni Penguins and geographic variation within Eudyptid penguins. In *The Penguins: Ecology and Management* (Ed. by Dann, P., Norman, I. and Reilly, P.), pp. 319–330. Surrey Beatty & Sons, Chipping Norton, NSW, Australia.

WOEHLER, E. J., PENNEY, R. L., CREET, S. M. & BURTON, H. R. 1994. Impacts of human visitors on breeding success and long-term population trends in Adelie Penguins at Casey, Antarctica. *Polar Biology* 14: 269–274.

YEATES, G. W. 1975. Microclimate, climate and breeding success in Antarctic penguins. In *The Biology of Penguins* (Ed. by Stonehouse, B.), pp. 397–409. MacMillan, London.

YODA, K., SATO, K., NIIZUMA, Y., KURITA, M., BOST, C. A., LE MAHO, Y. & NAITO, Y. 1999. Precise monitoring of porpoising behaviour of Adelie Penguins determined using acceleration data loggers. *Journal of Experimental Biology* 202: 3121–3126.

YORIO, P. & BOERSMA, P. D. 1992. The effects of human disturbance on Magellanic Penguin *Spheniscus magellanicus* behaviour and breeding success. *Bird Conservation International* 2: 161–173.

YORIO, P. & BOERSMA, P. D. 1994a. Causes of nest desertion during incubation in the Magellanic Penguin (*Spheniscus magellanicus*). *Condor* 96: 1076–1083.

YORIO, P. & BOERSMA, P. D. 1994b. Consequences of nest desertion and inattendance for Magellanic Penguin hatching success. *Auk* 111: 215–218.

YOUNG, E. C. 1963. Feeding habits of the South Polar Skua. *Ibis* 105: 301–318.

YOUNG, E. C. 1994. *Skua and Penguin: predator and prey*. Cambridge University Press, Auckland, New Zealand.

ZUSI, R. L. 1975. An interpretation of skull structure in penguins. In *Biology of Penguins* (Ed. by Stonehouse, B.), pp. 59–z84. Macmillan, London.

# Index